LEARNING & TEACHING
WITH TECHNOLOGY

LEARNING & TEACHING WITH TECHNOLOGY

principles and practices

Edited by **Som Naidu**

RoutledgeFalmer
Taylor & Francis Group

LONDON AND NEW YORK

First published in Great Britain and the United States in hardback in 2003 by Kogan Page
First published in Great Britain and the United States in paperback in 2004 by
RoutledgeFalmer, 2 Park Square, Milton Park, Oxon OX14 4RN
270 Madison Avenue, New York, NY 10016

RoutledgeFalmer is an imprint of the Taylor & Francis Group

© Individual contributors, 2003

ISBN 0 7494 3776 6 (hardback)
ISBN 0 4153 4610 X (paperback)

British Library Cataloguing in Publication Data

A CIP record for this book is available from the British Library.

Library of Congress Cataloging in Publication Data

Learning and teaching with technology : principles and practices /
edited by Som Naidu.
    p. cm. -- (Open and distance learning series)
Includes bibliographical references and index.
 ISBN 0-7494-3776-6 (hardback)
 ISBN 0-4153-4610-X (paperback)
 1. Telecommunication in higher education. 2. Education,
Higher--Effect of technological innovations on. 3. Learning, Psychology
of. I. Naidu, Som, 1952- II. Series.
 LB2342.75 .L43 2003
 378.1'33--dc21

                                                          2002152260

Typeset by JS Typesetting Ltd, Wellingborough, Northants
Printed and bound in Great Britain by Biddles Ltd, King's Lynn

Contents

Part V. Providing feedback

Notes on contributors

John Baird is from the Faculty of Education at the University of Melbourne. His research interests are in the use of interactive, video-based multimedia to stimulate teacher learning using metacognition, guided reflection, and situated cognition. *Address:* Faculty of Education, University of Melbourne, Parkville, 3010, Australia. E-mail: j.baird@edfac.unimelb.edu.au.

John Baro is from NASA Classroom of the Future Program, Wheeling Jesuit University, USA. He develops multimedia instructional material for elementary through high school math, science, and social studies curriculum. *Address:* NASA Classroom of the Future Program, Center for Educational Technologies, Wheeling Jesuit University, USA. E-mail: jabaro@cet.edu.

Pål Davidsen is from the Department of Information Science, University of Bergen, Norway. He will be acting as president (effective 2003) of the System Dynamics Society. His current areas of research include System Dynamics (SD) and SD-based Interactive Learning Environments (ILEs). *Address:* Department of Information Science, University of Bergen, Norway. E-mail: davidsen@ifi.uib.no.

Robert Debski is from the Horwood Language Center at the University of Melbourne, where he coordinates and teaches courses, supervises postgraduate students, and conducts research in computer-assisted language learning (CALL). His research is currently focused on the methodology and directions of inquiry in CALL, reading and writing hypertext by second language students, and the significance of technology for the maintenance of indigenous and community languages. *Address:* Horwood Language Centre, University of Melbourne, E-mail: r.debski@hlc.unimelb.edu.au.

Helena Dedic is from the Department of Physics, Vanier College, Canada. Her current research interests include: physics education, mathematics education, computer-mediated learning, and the effectiveness of simulations in post-secondary mathematics and science education. *Address:* Vanier College, 821 Avenue Ste-Croix, St-Laurent, Canada. E-mail: dedich@vaniercollege.qc.ca.

Kristine Elliott is from the Faculty of Medicine, Dentistry & Health Sciences, the University of Melbourne, Australia. Her extensive involvement in the conceptualization and development of triggers for medical problems, reflects a research focus on the use and design of visual media for educational purposes. *Address:* Faculty IT Unit, University of Melbourne, Australia. E-mail: kaelli@unimelb. edu.au.

Susan Elliott is from the Faculty of Medicine, Dentistry & Health Sciences, the University of Melbourne, Australia. Sue has overall responsibility for the transformation of the medical curriculum into a problem-based learning curriculum. *Address:* Faculty Education Unit, University of Melbourne, Australia. E-mail: s.elliott@unimelb.edu.au.

Stuart Evans is from the Department of Social Work, University of Melbourne, Australia. He has extensive practice and educational experience, particularly in relation to the use of technology in the teaching of interpersonal practice skills. *Address:* Department of Social Work, University of Melbourne, Australia, 3010. E-mail: swe@unimelb.edu.au.

Yakut Gazi is from the College of Education at Texas A&M University. Her research interests are in the construction of identity in online environments, computer-mediated communication, and Web-based instruction. *Address:* Texas A&M University, 703 Harrington Tower, College Station, TX 77843-4225, USA. E-mail: yakut@tamu.edu.

Peter Goodyear is from the Centre for Studies in Advanced Learning Technology, Lancaster University, UK. Peter's current research focuses on understanding the design of complex learning environments, teaching with the aid of new technology and technology-supported continuing professional development, seen as the collaborative construction of 'working knowledge'. *Address:* Centre for Studies in Advanced Learning Technology, Lancaster University, Lancaster LA1 4YL, UK. E-mail: p.goodyear@lancaster.ac.uk.

Cathy Gunn is Educational Technology Program Leader at the Center for Professional Development, University of Auckland. Her current research interests in educational technology include quality assurance, staff development, gender issues and organizational change management. *Address:* Center for Professional Development, University of Auckland, Private Bag 92019, Auckland, New Zealand. E-mail: ca.gunn@auckland.ac.nz.

Barbara de la Harpe is from the Faculty of Education, Languages and Community Services, RMIT University. Her research focus is on student learning and creating powerful learning environments that support learning, writing and generic skill development and assessment online. *Address:* Faculty of Education, Language and Community Services, RMIT University, Building 220, Bundoora Campus, Plenty Road, Bundoora, PO Box 71, Bundoora, Victoria 3083, Australia. E-mail: barbara.delaharpe@rmit.edu.au.

Peter Harris is from the Faculty of Medicine, Dentistry & Health Sciences, the University of Melbourne, Australia. He has been responsible for the development of a series of innovative interactive multimedia tutorials in physiology and is also active in experimental research in physiology and hypertension and in the development of digital imaging systems for microscopy. *Address:* Faculty IT Unit, the University of Melbourne, Australia. E-mail: pjharris@unimelb.edu.au.

Andrew Higgins is from the Flexible Learning Section of The Higher Education Development Center, University of Otago. *Address:* 75 Union Place, PO Box 56, Dunedin, New Zealand. E-mail: andrew.higgins@stonebow.otago.ac.nz.

Annamarie Jagose teaches in the English Department with Cultural Studies at the University of Melbourne. She combines her interests in computer-assisted learning with research in contemporary culture, media and everyday life. *Address:* English with Cultural Studies, the University of Melbourne. E-mail: arjagose@unimelb.edu.au.

Chris Jones is from the Centre for Studies in Advanced Learning Technology, Lancaster University, UK. Chris is interested in the connections between technology and social life and his recent research focused on understanding the roles and experiences of students and tutors in networked learning environments. Chris is also interested in the politics of networked learning understood as both the formal politics expressed by government in policy initiatives and the micro politics involved in day-to-day interactions. *Address:* Centre for Studies in Advanced Learning Technology (CSALT), Department of Educational Research, Lancaster University, Lancaster LA1 4YL, UK. E-mail: c.r.jones@lancaster.ac.uk.

Carol Johnston is from the Faculty of Economics and Commerce at the University of Melbourne. Her research interests are in the areas of online assessment and feedback. *Address:* Teaching and Learning Unit, Faculty of Economics and Commerce, the University of Melbourne, Parkville, Victoria 3010, Australia. E-mail: cgj@unimelb.edu.au.

Gregor Kennedy is from the Faculty of Medicine, Dentistry & Health Sciences, the University of Melbourne, Australia. His particular interest is in educational technology research and evaluation. His research interests include students' problem-based and self-directed learning and the role motivation plays in students' learning processes. *Address:* Biomedical Multimedia Unit, The University of Melbourne, Australia. E-mail: gek@unimelb.edu.au.

Mike Keppell is from the Faculty of Medicine, Dentistry & Health Sciences, the University of Melbourne, Australia. Mike's expertise lies in his ability to combine the operational and development tasks of educational software with the academic study of curriculum, instructional design and evaluation. Specifically he focuses on processes involved in optimizing the instructional designer-subject matter expert interaction. *Address:* Biomedical Multimedia Unit, the University of Melbourne. E-mail: mkeppell@unimelb.edu.au.

Kinshuk is from the Information Systems Department at Massey University, New Zealand. His research interests include learning technologies, distance learning and adaptive interfaces, with particular focus on Web-based learning systems. *Address:* Information Systems Department, Massey University, Private Bag 11-222, Palmerston North, New Zealand. E-mail: kinshuk@massey.ac.nz.

Yiping Lou is from the Department of Educational Leadership, Research, and Counseling at Louisiana State University, United States. Her current research interests include small group and individual learning with technology, technology-mediated learning processes, feedback design and interactive distance learning. *Address:* Department of Educational Leadership, Research, and Counseling at Louisiana State University, 111 Peabody Hall, Baton Rouge, LA 70803, USA. E-mail: ylou@lsu.edu.

Catherine McLoughlin is from the School of Education at the Australian Catholic University in Canberra Australia. Her background combines instructional technology, curriculum design and staff development in higher education. Catherine has published and researched a range of issues surrounding the use and evaluation of informational and communications technologies to support learning. *Address:* Australian Catholic University, PO Box 256, Dickson, ACT 2602, Australia. E-mail: c.mcloughlin@signadou.acu.edu.au.

Marcelo Milrad is from the School of Mathematics and Systems Engineering, at Växjö University in Sweden. He is also responsible for the Center for Learning Technologies (CLT), a multidisciplinary research center at Växjö University. His current research interests include the design of learning environments to support learning about complex domains, collaborative discovery learning and the development of mobile and wireless applications to support collaborative learning. *Address:* Växjö University, SE-351 95 Växjö, Sweden. E-mail: marcelo.milrad@ msi.vxu.se.

Christopher Morgan is from the Faculty of Rural Management of the University of Sydney located at the Orange campus. He has a particular research interest in making effective use of information and communications technology for supporting students at a distance. A focus of his research is approaches to the use of technology to influence educational participation and persistence. *Address:* Faculty of Rural Management, the University of Sydney, P.O. Box 883 Orange, NSW 2800, Australia. E-mail: cmorgan@orange.usyd.edu.au.

Karen Murphy is from the Educational Technology Program, College of Education, Texas A&M University. She earned her doctoral degree at the University of Washington in Educational Curriculum and Instruction with a focus on distance learning. Her research interests are learning collaboratively in online environments, design of online instruction for constructivist learning environments, and socio-cultural context of learning at a distance. *Address:* Texas A&M University, 703 Harrington Tower, College Station, TX 77843-4225, USA. E-mail: kmurphy@tamu.edu.

Ashok Patel is from De Montfort University, Leicester, United Kingdom. His research interests include Human Cognition, Intelligent Tutoring Systems and Human Computer Interaction. *Address:* CAL Research and Software Engineering Centre, Bosworth House, De Montfort University, The Gateway, Leicester LE1 9BH, UK. E-mail: apatel.aqua@btinternet.com.

Alex Radloff is from the Faculty of Life Sciences, RMIT University, Australia. Her research focus is on the development of self-regulation of student learning, academic and generic skills and their learning and assessment online. *Address:* Faculty of Life Sciences, RMIT University, Bundoora Campus, PO Box 71, Bundoora, Victoria 3083, Australia. E-mail: alex.radloff@rmit.edu.au.

Steven Rosenfield is from the Department of Mathematics, Vanier College, St-Laurent, Canada. His current research interests include mathematics education, physics education, computer-mediated learning, and the effectiveness of simulations in post-secondary mathematics and science education. *Address:* Department of Mathematics, Vanier College, 821 Avenue Ste-Croix, St-Laurent, Canada. E-mail: rosenfis@vaniercollege.qc.ca.

Laurie Ruberg is from NASA Classroom of the Future Program, Center for Educational Technologies, Wheeling Jesuit University, USA. She designs and develops curriculum elements for multimedia instructional products and establishes collaborations with research and development organizations. *Address:* NASA Classroom of the Future Program, Center for Educational Technologies, Wheeling Jesuit University, USA. E-mail: lruberg@cet.edu.

David Russell is from the Graduate School of Business, De Montfort University, Leicester, United Kingdom. His research interests include Environmental Accounting and ICT based systems, and pedagogic aspects of Teaching & Learning systems. *Address:* Graduate School of Business, Bede Island Building, De Montfort University, The Gateway, Leicester LE1 9BH, UK. E-mail: drussell@dmu.ac.uk.

Rod Sims is from the Educational Design and Research group at Deakin University, Australia. He has worked in the broad field of computers and education for the past twenty years and his research interests are in the different ways in which learners interact with content in the context of computer-based learning environments. *Address:* Learning Services, Deakin University (Waterfront Campus), Geelong, Victoria 3217, Australia. E-mail: rsims@deakin.edu.au.

Peter Smith is from the Faculty of Education at Deakin University in Australia. His current research foci are the use of computer-mediated learning in the provision of distance education to postgraduate students; and the use of technology to mediate the delivery of flexible learning programs in industry. *Address:* Faculty of Education, Deakin University, Victoria, Australia. E-mail: pjbs@deakin.edu.au.

Michael Spector is from the Instructional Design, Development and Evaluation Program, Syracuse University, USA. He is also the executive vice president and treasurer of the International Board of Standards for Training, Performance and Instruction. His current research interests include: Intelligent support for instructional design and development, cost-effective use of technology in online teaching, learning in and about complex systems, system dynamics based learning environments, technology integration in learning and working environments. *Address:* Department Instructional Design, Development and Evaluation. Syracuse University, USA, E-mail: Spector@syr.edu.

Elizabeth Stacey is from the Faculty of Education at Deakin University in Australia. Her current research focus is the development of collaborative learning through computer-mediated communication among undergraduate and post-graduate distance education students. *Address:* Faculty of Education, Deakin University, Victoria 3217, Australia. E-mail: estacey@deakin.edu.au.

Phillip Swain is from the Department of Social Work, the University of Melbourne, Australia. His principal teaching focus is the legal content of social work practice. *Address:* Department of Social Work, the University of Melbourne, Australia, 3010. E-mail: paswain@unimelb.edu.au.

Karen Swan is from the Department of Educational Theory and Practice at the University of Albany, where she is also the Director of the Learning Technologies Laboratory and the Summer Technology Institute. Her current research interests focus on interactivity and presence in asynchronous Web-based course environments and their effects on learning. *Address:* 114A, SUNY, Albany, NY 12222, USA. E-mail: KSwan@uamail.albany.edu.

Lee Wallace teaches in the Women's Studies Program at the University of Auckland and has research interests in computer-assisted learning, film theory and cultural studies. *Address:* Women's Studies Program, University of Auckland, Private Bag 92019, Auckland, New Zealand. E-mail: l.wallace@auckland.ac.nz.

Series editor's foreword

Those of us involved in teaching and training are facing unprecedented challenges – challenges that are both self-imposed and posed by governments and funding agencies. We are being asked, not unreasonably, to continually monitor the academic quality and teaching effectiveness of our courses, identifying and disseminating good practice, making learning more *learner focused*, fostering lifelong learning and independent learning – and to do this more efficiently. In this context the contribution to be made by information and communication technologies (ICT) is evident – as Tony Bates realized several years ago in his book, *Technology, Open and Distance Education:* 'Those countries that harness the power of the new communication and information technologies will be the powerhouses of the twenty first century' (Routledge, 1995, p 249).

Certainly, within the UK the decision to increase the proportion of 18–30-year-olds who benefit from higher education, from about 33 per cent in 2001 to 50 per cent in 2010, represents a formidable challenge. The increase in the number of learners on our courses and in our institutions will be equivalent to the creation of another 75 universities, to be achieved without a corresponding increase in funding. It is an education environment in which the characteristics of the population of learners with which we have become familiar will change; it is an environment in which the skills learners need will also change. The student body will become more heterogeneous as we attract learners from previously under-represented groups who do not have the traditional entry qualifications – but different experience and expertise. It will include increasing numbers of mature-age learners, learners who wish to study part time or flexibly and who not only have high expectations – since many will be funding themselves – but who will be demanding. It will be a student body that will need to be IT literate if it is to benefit from the opportunities available. In such a changing education and training environment it will not be possible to simply scale up previous provision – we will have to teach differently. It is a challenge currently being faced by colleagues in the USA and Southern Africa, Europe, the Far East and Australasia as they invest in their country's main asset – its people – and draw upon the potential of ICT.

This edited collection by Som Naidu makes a significant contribution to meeting the challenge facing us. Som has not only assembled an international team with considerable experience, but has succeeded in focusing their energy and expertise on the core learning and teaching issues that confront those who are attempting to address this challenge (ie, subject matter representation, activation of learning, supporting interaction and socialization, assessing learning outcomes and providing feedback).

I am sure, like me, you will find the discussion on the principles and practices in many of the chapters reassuring – others will challenge our current thinking and practice. Without doubt the ideas and findings will contribute to the ongoing debate about learning, teaching and technology; it can only benefit our teaching and our students' learning.

Fred Lockwood
Manchester, June 2002

Acknowledgements

Several people have contributed to the successful completion of this book project. My thanks are due foremost to all the authors of the chapters in this book for their commitment to excellence and rigor in the reporting of their work. It has been a pleasure working with you all. A large part of the credit goes to Professor Fred Lockwood, the Series Editor, for his initial impetus and encouragement to embark on such a project, and then for the pivotal support that he continued to provide throughout the project. I am very grateful to Dr Angela Bridgland, Director of the Department of Teaching, Learning and Research Support at the University of Melbourne for supporting this project and allowing me the time to work on it. Thanks are due also to Kogan Page, for undertaking the publication of this work and seeing it through its publication process.

Thank you all.

Som Naidu
Melbourne, August 2002

Introduction

The use of information and communications technology (ICT) in education is transforming learning and teaching practices in significant ways. For instance, the integration of computer-mediated communication with multimedia courseware, electronic libraries and databases has led to the emergence of a whole new kind of educational experience, namely e-learning or networked learning (Rosenberg, 2001; Steeples and Jones, 2002). Affordances and opportunities offered by ICT are also causing educators and educational providers to rethink and reengineer the nature of their educational practices (Gibson, 1977; Turvey, 1992). A significant product of this reengineering includes a shift in the roles of teachers from being 'providers and deliverers of subject matter content' to becoming 'moderators and facilitators of learning' within student-centred models of learning and teaching. Some of these models of learning and teaching include 'computer-supported collaborative learning' (Koschmann, 1996; McConnell, 2000), 'computer-supported problem based learning' (Koschmann *et al,* 1996), and 'distributed problem based learning' (Koschmann, 2002).

These models of learning and teaching are closely associated with a growing interest among educators and educational technologists in the capabilities of ICT for leveraging the learning and teaching transaction. Educators are enthusiastic about how they can use ICT to improve their teaching activities, which include the engagement of students with subject matter content, activation of learning, assessment of learning outcomes and provision of feedback to their students. Educational technology researchers are inquisitive about the influences of ICT on the achievement of content-specific as well as generic learning outcomes and the processes of learning, including students' approaches to study, their motivation for learning and engagement with the subject matter content.

This book is an attempt to address that interest and enthusiasm of educators and educational technologists. It is neither a book about information and communications tools and technologies nor a book full of case study reports of educational technology applications. It is a book about the core processes of the learning and teaching transaction, specifically addressing how ICT can be used to leverage these core processes to achieve rich and productive learning environments. The contributions in this book are organized around the core processes of learning and teaching namely:

● subject matter representation;
● activation of learning and engagement of students with that subject matter content;
● encouragement of socialization and interaction between and among students;
● assessment of learning outcomes; and
● provision of feedback to students.

Together, these contributions demonstrate how the opportunities that ICT affords can be used creatively to leverage the entire learning and teaching transaction, and individually they show how these opportunities can be used to leverage particular activities in the learning and teaching transaction.

The contributions in this book will be of interest to educators and courseware developers in all sectors of education and training who are either using or planning on integrating ICT into their teaching activities. However, due to the selection of material in the book, it will be of particular use to teachers in the higher education sector who have an interest in the opportunities afforded by ICT for leveraging the learning and teaching transaction.

Part I of the book focuses attention on *subject matter content representation*. Every learning and teaching transaction incorporates a defined body of content, which may be in the form of a set of facts, principles, procedures, skills or attitudes in which a group of targeted learners are expected to demonstrate competency. Quite often this body of subject matter content is organized according to themes or by topics. While this is an expedient and at times a useful way of organizing the selected body of subject matter, constructivist thinkers argue that this approach is not the only way, and certainly not a very meaningful way of representing content (Cognition and Technology Group at Vanderbilt, 1990, 1993; Schank, 1997; Schank and Cleary, 1995). They suggest that focusing attention on the facts, principles or procedures runs the risk of rote learning and learning for short-term gains such as passing impending examinations. There have been long standing and very strong arguments put forth in favour of building and orchestrating learning environments that immerse learners in authentic learning experiences where facts, principles and procedures are embedded in activities, and engagement in this experience leads to the development of desirable competencies (Brown *et al*, 1989; Dewey, 1933, 1938; Piaget, 1952). These learning experiences are designed not so much to instruct as to provide the contexts wherein understanding and insight can be uniquely cultivated. They serve as 'micro worlds and incubators for knowledge' within which learners are able to deal with complex concepts in tangible and concrete ways (Papert, 1993, p 120), and where subject matter knowledge is allowed to evolve through the processes of exploring, inquiring, and constructing representations and/or artefacts (Hannafin and Land, 1997).

The four chapters in this part articulate key principles in the representation of subject matter content with the help of notable experiences with ICT. In the first chapter, Milrad, Spector and Davidsen develop a very powerful and convincing argument for the use of a theoretically grounded instructional design framework they call 'model-facilitated learning', which incorporates the use of modelling tools, construction kits and system dynamics simulations to provide multiple representations to help students develop an understanding of problem scenarios that are complex and dynamic. The concept of model-facilitated learning comprises a significant advancement to instructional design practice as it adds to the corpus of existing knowledge on perspectives on instructional design such as 'learning by designing' (Kolodner *et al*, 1998), case-based reasoning (Schank and Cleary, 1995), problem-based learning (Barrows and Tamblyn, 1980), and role-play simulation (Naidu *et al*, 2000). The approach distinguishes 'learning by modelling' from 'learning using models'.

In Chapter 2 Goodyear and Jones draw on the formative evaluation of a major learning technology development programme to illustrate the value of uncovering implicit, informal theories about learning, and also about educational change that can be found embedded in the work of courseware development teams. Ruberg and Baro show how such a team comprising curriculum developers, instructional designers, software engineers, scientists, researchers and practising teachers set about to employ graphical, interactive simulations to model problem solving and promote scientific inquiry. Capping the topic of subject matter content representation, Kinshuk and Patel also propose something along those lines, which they call the 'multiple representation' approach and which articulates a set of guidelines for presenting domain knowledge by guiding the process of multimedia objects selection, navigational objects selection and integration of multimedia objects to suit different learner needs.

Part II in the book focuses attention on *activation of learning* and engagement of students with the subject matter content. This involves selective use of learning strategies to advance learning and enhance learning capability. Technology-enhanced student-centred learning environments do not necessarily lead to learning efficiency or effectiveness. Indeed for some learners such open-ended learning environments can be quite daunting, posing a real threat to their success and motivation to learn. While creating opportunities for learning, these open-ended learning environments also create demands on learners for new skills in managing complex information and higher order cognitive processes. Being successful in such learning environments requires learners to possess the ability to organize, evaluate and monitor the progress of their learning. Not all learners possess these skills, and have to be taught how to take advantage of the opportunities that technology-enhanced and open-ended learning environments afford (see Jonassen, 1988; Weinstein and Mayer, 1986).

The four chapters in this part focus attention on creative uses of ICT in influencing learning by engaging students with the subject matter. In the first chapter on this subject, Baird shows how video captures of teachers and children engaged in live and authentic classroom activities can be employed to scaffold learning in professional teacher education. In the following chapter, Keppell, Elliott, Kennedy, Elliot and Harris describe a similar strategy that uses multimedia-based authentic patient encounters to engage medical students in a problem-based learning curriculum. These simulated patient encounters are called 'medical triggers' and they involve the use of photographs, shockwave movies and Quick-Time video clips to produce powerful learning materials. In the next chapter Wallace, Jagose and Gunn describe powerful applications of animation along with photographs, shockwave movies and QuickTime video clips to engage students in the study of new and evolving subject matter domains such as Cultural Studies. Rounding off this part, the final chapter by Evans and Swain shows how simulated case encounters of authentic practice situations can be cleverly used to address the challenges posed in the study of practice-based subject matter such as Social Work, which requires the integration of theoretical knowledge, practice wisdom and organizational contexts.

Part III in the book focuses attention on *supporting interaction* and *socialization* between and among students. There is evidence that social climate and the influence of peers is positively correlated with a range of learning outcomes (see Slavin, 1990; 1994). However, unstructured social contact and communication alone are not enough. Formal mechanisms such as cooperative and collaborative learning practices have to be integrated into the teaching and learning transaction to benefit student learning in any significant way. The four chapters in this part focus attention on how ICT is used to integrate such processes into educational practice and how these practices are influencing teachers' approaches to teaching and students' approaches to learning. In the first chapter Debski explores how computer-mediated communications technology can support the role of project-based work and social interaction in second language learning. The critical ingredient is the careful orchestration and moderation of that social interaction, because interaction alone, with or without technology, is not going to be sufficient. In the following chapter, Swan shows how social presence can be engendered in asynchronous computer-mediated conferencing, which can be rather alienating in the absence of vocal and non-verbal interactions. Swan raises issues surrounding the development of feelings of presence and notions of immediacy, and suggests categories of verbal immediacy behaviours to account for the development of presence in the absence of vocal and non-verbal interactions in asynchronous online discussions.

The importance of structure in computer-supported collaborative learning opportunities is also taken up by Smith and Stacey in the following chapter. They describe their experiences in relation to student participation, style of contributions, and the relationship between socialization processes and knowledge construction within the context of two computer-mediated communication structures, which make a different set of demands on participants and provide differing collaborative learning opportunities. In the final chapter on supporting interaction and socialization, Murphy and Gazi discuss how collaboration and community building can be supported in a computer-mediated collaborative learning environment with scenario-based role-play designs that can also support multiple role representation for participants (ie, students-as-facilitators and students-as-participants) within the technology infrastructure.

Part IV focuses attention on *assessing learning outcomes,* as learning and learner performance have to be appropriately assessed. A wide range of strategies may be applied as part of this process, and the choice of strategy will vary according to the intended learning outcomes and the learning tasks that have been prescribed. Assessing learning outcomes is concerned with determining whether or not learners have acquired the desired type or level of capability, and whether learners have benefited from the educational experience (ie, if they have achieved the intended learning outcomes, and if their performance has changed in any way). A measure of learning outcomes requires learners to complete tasks that demonstrate the extent to which they have achieved the standards specified in the learning outcomes. In order to ascertain the most realistic and valid assessment of performance, these tasks have to be as authentic as possible, or similar to on-the-job conditions. Methods of assessment can be classified as either criterion- or norm-referenced (Grondlund, 1985). A criterion-referenced measure is targeted at the criteria specified in the learning outcome. Criterion-referenced measures require learners to demonstrate presence of learned capabilities at specific criterion levels. A norm-referenced measure on the other hand, compares a learner's performance with that of other learners in the cohort.

The four chapters in this part focus attention on how ICT affordances can be used to leverage approaches to the assessment of learning outcomes. In the first chapter McLoughlin suggests that traditional models of assessment do not readily transfer to the online learning environment, as they are often 'one-shot' quantitative measures of student performance. She suggests that newer models of authentic forms of online assessment are needed to utilize the rich communicative resources of ICT and offer expanded opportunities for assessing learning outcomes. In this chapter she discusses design guidelines for how creative uses of ICT can help extend the range of assessment strategies. Some of these strategies include digital portfolios, team-based assessment and online problem-solving tasks for self and peer assessment.

In the following chapter Radloff and de la Harpe reiterate similar sentiments in suggesting that conventional assessment practices need to be adapted to include both content and process learning outcomes in order to enhance student learning online. They suggest that opportunities afforded by ICT are able to expand the focus of conventional assessment practices and support the assessment of motivational, affective and metacognitive aspects of learning. The challenge for course developers is to be able to apply sound principles of designing assessment strategies to expand this focus. The following two chapters show how this goal might be achieved. In her chapter, Johnston shows how online assessment strategies can be used to influence a deeper approach to learning among students that is most likely to achieve the desired outcomes of the various stakeholders in higher education.

In the following chapter, Patel, Kinshuk and Russell show how formative computer-based assessment has been used in the 'Byzantium' intelligent tutoring system to achieve far transfer of knowledge. Byzantium was produced by a consortium of six universities under the Teaching and Learning Technology Program (TLTP) of the UK Higher Education Funding Councils.

Part V in the book focuses attention on *providing feedback* to students. Any learning and teaching transaction that views learning as a process of mutual influence between learners and their instructional resources must involve feedback, for without it any meaningful mutual influence is impossible. From a review of research on the effects of feedback more generally, Kulhavy (1977) described four conditions of feedback:

1. Feedback is most potent when it corrects errors.
2. The error-correcting action of feedback is more effective when it follows a response about which the student felt relatively certain.
3. The effectiveness of feedback is enhanced if it is delivered after the learner has made a response
4. Feedback is more effective when its availability in advance of learner response is controlled.

Furthermore, as suggested by Kulhavy, feedback is also distinguishable according to its content, which is identifiable by:

- *load* (ie, the amount of information given in the feedback from simple correct-incorrect responses to fuller explanations);
- *form* (ie, the structural similarity between information in the feedback compared to that in the instructional presentation); and
- *type* of information (ie, whether the feedback restated information from the original task, referred to information given elsewhere in the instruction, or provided new information).

Feedback may differ according to its intention, which refers to whether it was intentional and designed specifically to inform learners about the quality and accuracy of their responses, or if it happened to be an incidental consequence of the instructional environment. Intentional feedback can be delivered in a variety of ways: via direct interpersonal communication between instructor and learners, and/or through mediated forms such as with innovative use of ICT. Intentional feedback is highly specific and directly related to the performance of the task (Bangert-Drowns *et al*, 1991). Feedback also differs according to its target. Some feedback may be primarily designed to influence affective learning outcomes such as interest and motivation. Other forms of feedback are designed to influence the achievement of specific subject matter knowledge. Most commonly though, feedback is targeted at indicating how learners are performing specified tasks and whether they are correctly applying the learned principles and procedures (Schimmel, 1983).

The three chapters in this part of the book focus attention on how these fundamental principles of feedback can be leveraged with clever use of ICT. In the first chapter Lou, Dedic and Rosenfield posit that effective feedback requires careful design and orchestration. Based on their experience in science and social science classes, these authors discuss a model of effective feedback, which they argue can be used to support student learning in computer-mediated learning environments. Their model portrays learners and teachers as actors who provide and receive feedback in interlocking loops during learning activities. In the following chapter Sims argues that successful and effective feedback is brought about by focusing on principles of good communication, the specific roles of learners and teachers, the interactions between people and content, and the impact of cognitive, social, and teaching presence. Furthermore, he suggests that appropriate implementation of these factors will enable informative, timely and individual feedback for the learner that will support consistent communication, engagement with content, and meaningful construction of knowledge. In the third and final chapter, Morgan draws attention to the problems of providing feedback to learners where geographical isolation or other circumstances diminish the potential for learners to receive formative feedback from their instructors or their peers in a timely fashion. He argues that effective feedback strategies lie at the core of educational success for such students, that these strategies are fundamental to a rich educational experience, and their absence will negatively influence course completion rates. He reviews several such strategies to overcome this disadvantage and form bridges with and among students in such difficult circumstances, with astute use of ICT.

We hope that you find the contributions in this volume inspiring and useful. Your reflections on this material and reactions to the ideas presented here will be most welcome. Please direct all such correspondence to the editor of the book at s.naidu@unimelb.edu.au.

References

Bangert-Drowns, R L, Kulik, C-L C, Kulik, J A and Morgan, M T (1991) The instructional effects of feedback in test-like events, *Review of Educational Research,* **61,** pp 213–8

Barrows, H S and Tamblyn, R (1980) *Problem-based Learning: An approach to medical education,* Springer, New York

Brown, J S, Collins, A and Duguid, P (1989) Situated cognition and the culture of learning, *Educational Researcher,* **18** (1), pp 32–42

Cognition and Technology Group at Vanderbuilt (1990) Anchored instruction and its relationship to situated cognition, *Educational Researcher,* **19** (6), pp 2–10

Cognition and Technology Group at Vanderbuilt (1993) Designing learning environments that support thinking, in *Designing Environments for Constructivist Learning,* eds T M Duffy, J Lowyck and D H Jonassen, pp 9–36, Springer-Verlag, New York

Dewey, J (1933) *How We Think: A restatement of the relation of reflective thinking to the educative process,* Heath, Boston MA

Gibson, J J (1977) The theory of affordances, in *Perceiving, Acting, and Knowing: Toward an ecological psychology,* eds R Shaw and J Bransford, Lawrence Erlbaum, Hillsdale, NJ

Grondlund, N E (1985) *Measurement and Evaluation in Teaching,* 5th edn, Macmillan, New York

Hannafin, M J and Land, S M (1997) The foundations and assumptions of technology-enhanced student-centred learning environments, *Instructional Science,* **25,** pp 167–202

Jonassen, D H (1988) Integrating learning strategies into courseware to facilitate deeper processing, in *Instructional Designs for Microcomputer Courseware,* ed D H Jonassen, pp 151–81, Lawrence Erlbaum, Hillsdale, NJ

Kolodner, J L, Crismond, D, Gray, J, Holbrook, J and Puntambekar, S (1998) Learning by design: from theory to practice, in *Proceedings of the International Conference of the Learning Sciences 1998,* eds A S Bruckman, M Guzdial, J L Kolodner and A Ram, pp 16–22, Association for the Advancement of Computing in Education, Charlottesville, VA

Koschmann, T (ed) (1996) *CSCL: Theory and practice of an emerging paradigm,* Lawrence Erlbaum, Mawah, NJ

Koschmann, T (2002) Introduction to special issue on studying collaboration in distributed problem based learning environments, *Distance Education,* **23** (1), pp 5–9

Koschmann, T, Kelson, A C, Feltovich, P J and Barrows, H S (1996) Computer-supported problem-based learning: a principled approach to the use of computers in collaborative learning, in *CSCL: Theory and practice of an emerging paradigm,* ed T Koschmann, pp 83–124, Lawrence Erlbaum, Mawah, NJ

Kulhavy, R W (1977) Feedback in written instruction, *Review of Educational Research,* **47,** pp 211–32

McConnell, D (2000) *Implementing Computer Supported Cooperative Learning,* Kogan Page, London

Naidu, S, Ip, A and Linser, R (2000) Dynamic goal-based role-play simulation on the Web: a case study, *Educational Technology and Society: Journal of International Forum of Educational Technology and Society and IEEE Learning Technology Task Force* http://ifets.ieee.org/periodical/vol_3_2000/b05.html Special Issue on 'Online Collaborative Learning Environments' (Guest Editor: Roger Hartley), *Educational Technology and Society,* **3** (3), 2000 http://ifets.ieee.org/periodical/vol_3_2000/v_3_2000.html

Papert, S (1993) *Mindstorms,* 2nd edn, Basic Books, New York

Piaget, J (1952) *The Origins of Intelligence in Children,* International University Press, New York

Rosenberg, M J (2001) *E-Learning: Strategies for delivering knowledge in the digital age,* McGraw-Hill, New York

Schank, R C (1997) *Virtual Learning: A revolutionary approach to building a highly skilled workforce,* McGraw-Hill, New York

Schank, R C and Cleary, C (1995) *Engines for Education,* Lawrence Erlbaum, Hillsdale, NJ

Schimmel, B J (1983) A meta-analysis of feedback to learners in computerized and programmed instruction, Paper presented at the annual meeting of the American Educational Research Association, April, Montreal (ERIC document Reproduction Service No 233 708)

Slavin, R E (1990) *Cooperative Learning: Theory, research and practice*, Prentice-Hall, Englewood Cliffs, NJ

Slavin, R E (1994) Student teams-achievement divisions, in *Handbook of Cooperative Learning,* ed S Sharan, pp 3–19, Greenwood Press, Westport, CT

Steeples, C and Jones, J (2002) *Networked Learning: Perspectives and issues,* Springer-Verlag, London

Turvey, M T (1992) Affordances and prospective control: an outline of ontology, *Ecological Psychology,* **4,** pp 173–87

Weinstein, C E and Mayer, R E (1986) The teaching of learning strategies, in *Handbook of Research on Teaching,* ed M Wittrock, pp 315–27, Macmillan, New York

Part I

Content representation

Chapter 1

Model facilitated learning

Marcelo Milrad, Michael Spector and Pål Davidsen

Introduction

Technology changes what we do and what we can do. People change on account of technology. Technology in support of learning and instruction is no different. Instructional technology changes what teachers and learners do and can do. This is especially true when the Internet and distributed technologies are taken into consideration. Learning research has also evolved and increased our understanding of how people learn different things in different situations. There has been a trend to apply emerging instructional technologies to support learning and instruction in ever more challenging and complex domains (Spector and Anderson, 2000). Such a trend is quite natural. Once it is understood how to use technology to support mastery of simple skills, it makes good sense to explore more advanced uses of technology. We support this trend and believe, along with many others, that technology can be effectively used in distributed learning environments to support learning in and about complex systems, which is the focus of the discussion in this chapter (Spector and Anderson, 2000).

Modelling and simulation tools are gaining importance as a means to explore, comprehend, learn and communicate complex ideas, especially in distributed learning and work environments (Maier and Größler, 2000). Students are building and using simulations in both guided discovery and expository learning environments (Alessi, 2000). Of particular interest is whether and when one learns by building simulations or by interacting with existing simulations (Spector, 2000). To explore this interest, we provide a framework for the integration of modelling and simulations deployable in collaborative tele-learning environments. We focus on a particular modelling and simulation approach called 'system dynamics' (Forrester, 1985).

The system dynamics community has focused primarily on learning by creating simulation models, although some researchers are becoming more sophisticated in recognizing a variety of different learning situations and requirements (Alessi, 2000; Gibbons, 2001; Spector, 2000). The system dynamics community believes in the value of using system dynamics to improve understanding of complex, dynamic systems (Davidsen, 1996; Forrester, 1985; Sterman, 1994). This general commitment allows for both learning with models and learning by modelling.

The ability to model complex systems requires being able to define a model and use it to understand some complex phenomena – to make connections between and among parts and to analyse the model's ability to represent relevant aspects of the perceived world (Jackson *et al, 2000*). In the construction of models using systems dynamics tools, learners engage in cognitive and social processes that appear to promote understanding. However, it seems unreasonable to conclude that deep understanding in a complex domain always requires one to become an expert system dynamics modeller (Spector, 2000).

Considerable research has documented a variety of difficulties with learning concepts relevant to understanding complex systems in a variety of disciplines (Dörner, 1996; Kozma, 2000). For example, many people have difficulty with the following:

● understanding the effects of non-linear relationships over time;
● keeping the entire system in mind when trying to resolve an apparently localized problem;
● appreciating the full range of control and influence possible within a complex system; and
● generalizing lessons learnt from a particular problem context to a different problem situation.

How can learners acquire and maintain deep understanding about difficult-to-understand subject matter? How can modelling and simulation in complex domains be best used to facilitate learning? Understanding complex system behaviour involves the ability to provide causal and structural explanations as well as the ability to anticipate and explain changes in underlying causes and structures. This kind of understanding is not acquired easily nor is it likely to be acquired from observations of either real or simulated behaviour (Dörner, 1996). However, an appropriate methodology linked with collaborative and distributed technologies can significantly enhance such learning.

Our motivating concern is to help learners manage complexity in ways that contribute to improved learning and deep understanding. To achieve this goal, learning theory (socio-constructivism), methodology (system dynamics) and technology (collaborative tele-learning) should be suitably integrated (Spector and

Anderson, 2000). We call this integration Model Facilitated Learning (MFL) (Spector and Davidsen, 2000).

A theoretically grounded framework

Our understanding of the developmental, cognitive, and social dimensions of learning improved in the last half of the 20th century. Research inspired by Vygotsky and others suggests that recognizing the need for learners to engage peers in dialogue concerning challenging new concepts and to work in collaboration with colleagues on difficult tasks produces desirable and persisting improvements in understanding (Jonassen *et al*, 2000; Rouwette *et al*, 2000; Spector *et al*, 1999; Wells, 1999). Distributed technologies (eg, networked learning communities) are well suited to support such collaboration.

Learning in complex and ill-structured domains places significant cognitive demands on learners, as appropriately recognized by the medical community. Feltovich *et al* (1996) note that one of the difficulties involves the misunderstanding of situations in which there are multiple, co-occurring processes or dimensions of interaction. In these kinds of situations, learners often confine their understanding to one or a small number of the operative dimensions rather than the many that are pertinent (see also Dörner, 1996). Technology that depicts dynamic interactions can be of particular help in this area. The learning perspective we find most appropriate is based on notions derived from situated and problem-based learning (Lave and Wenger, 1990), especially as informed by cognitive flexibility theory (Spiro *et al*, 1988). Instructional design methods and principles consistent with this learning perspective can be derived from elaboration theory (Reigeluth and Stein, 1983) and from cognitive apprenticeship (Collins *et al*, 1989). MFL is derived from these learning and instructional theories. That these theories are reasonably well established but not embraced by the system dynamics learning community is somewhat disturbing.

Situated learning (Lave and Wenger, 1990) is a general theory of knowledge acquisition based on the notion that learning (stable, persisting changes in knowledge, skills and behaviour) occurs in the context of activities that typically involve a problem, others, and a culture. This perspective is based on observations indicating that learners gradually move from newcomer status (operating on the periphery of a community of practitioners) to more advanced status (operating at the centre of the community of practitioners). As learners become more advanced in a domain, they typically become more engaged with the central and challenging problems that occupy a particular group of practitioners.

Cognitive Flexibility Theory (CFT) (Spiro *et al*, 1988) shares with situated and problem-based learning the view that learning is context dependent, with the associated need to provide multiple representations and varied examples so as to promote generalization and abstraction processes. Feltovich *et al* (1996) argue that CFT and related approaches can help learners develop skills for thinking and learning about complex subject matter. Multiple representations naturally emerge in collaborative and group work. When learners are distributed in various settings and circumstances, it is essential to support multiple representations; CFT suggests this is important even for individual learners. Moreover, learning should be supported with a variety of problems and cases, which is especially important in distributed learning environments. However, people seem to prefer single and simple models. These restricted perspectives may be detrimental to learning (Feltovich *et al*, 1996; Kozma, 2000). As knowledge is used and represented in many ways it becomes more meaningful and more powerful. Towards this end, CFT advocates multiple types of models, multiple representations, alternative conceptualizations, varying levels of representational granularity, and so on. Additionally, CFT places particular emphasis on the importance of learner-constructed and learner-modifiable representations.

MFL, as a realization of CFT through system dynamics and distributed technology, provides learners with the opportunity and challenge to become model builders, to exchange and discuss models with peers, and to experiment with models to test hypotheses and explore alternative explanations for various phenomena. We believe that such modelling activities are often appropriate activity for advanced learners, but model building is not always required in order to understand some aspects of a complex and dynamic system. Moreover, we believe that other activities, including interacting with existing models and simulations, are often appropriate precursors to model building activities. MFL advocates a sequence of learning activities that begins with some kind of concrete operation, manipulating tangible objects in order to solve specific problems (Milrad *et al*, 2000). As these operations are mastered, learners can then progress to more abstract representations and solve increasingly complex problems. A set of principles to guide a MFL elaboration sequence is:

1. Situate the learning experience. Provide an opening scenario or a concrete case to familiarize learners with the complexity of the domain and with typical problems encountered in that domain.
2. Present problems and challenges of increasing complexity related to the opening scenario. For instance, suppose the initial situation involves managing a production plant. A problem sequence might be to determine existing inventory, predict future orders and provide a plan for maintaining a stable inventory. As participants gain expertise, other aspects of the enterprise can be brought into consideration, such as the effect of overtime on workers as they try to keep up with orders or the effect of backlogged orders on future orders and so on.
3. Involve learners in responding to a set of increasingly complex inquiries about the problem situation. For example, suppose that the sales force has predicted a seasonal increase in orders. A number of inquiries about the effect on existing inventories can be constructed and used to stimulate individual and small group discussion and experimentation in order to provide answers about predicted system behaviour.

4. Challenge learners to develop decision-making rules and guidelines for a variety of anticipated situations. In this case, a great deal of experimentation with models and simulations is appropriate. As the challenges increase in complexity, it is at this stage of learning that it is appropriate to provide opportunities for learners to modify models or create new models.

To summarize, we accept the notion that complex concepts are best learnt in context – a problem setting in which the learner must apply and use the relevant concepts and knowledge to solve meaningful problems. Such learning should improve both retention (by providing a relevant context) and transfer (by providing multiple representations). The principle of graduated complexity (Spector and Davidsen, 2000) is used to guide the design of learning sequences. In addition, the notion of socially-situated learning experiences threads throughout such a sequence. Such learning principles suggest that the coupling of system dynamics with collaborative and distributed technologies has strong potential. Next we examine the role of models in learning.

The potentials of models in learning

In this section we illustrate how models can be used to represent complex subject matter. It is worth emphasizing that the steps in a graduated complexity model should not be considered fixed or rigid. The model we advocate recognizes individual and group differences and supports the notion of iterative development of learning, understanding and expertise.

Learning with models and learning by modelling are discussed separately here, but in a learning or problem-solving environment it is conceivable that both might be involved (albeit for different purposes and in different ways). In MFL, there are three stages of learner development with associated instructional approaches (Spector and Davidsen, 2000):

1. *problem-orientation* (problem confronting and problem solving), in which learners are presented with typical problem situations and asked to solve relatively simple problems;
2. *inquiry-exploration* (hypothesis formulation and experimentation), in which learners are challenged to explore a complex domain and asked to identify and elaborate causal relationships and dominant underlying structures; and
3. *policy-development* (decision-making rule and global system elaboration), in which learners are immersed in the full complex system and asked to develop rules and heuristics to guide decision making in order to create stability or avoid undesirable situations.

The stages and principles of MFL correspond with major components of van Merriënboer's (1997) 4C/ID model and Dreyfus and Dreyfus (1986) (see Table 1.1).

Table 1.1 *MFL, learning development and related models*

Major Activity	MFL	4C/ID	Dreyfus and Dreyfus, 1986
Introduction to the domain	Problem-orientation and learning with models	Whole task introduction and prerequisite knowledge	Absolute beginner
Familiarization with the situation/ system	Problem-orientation and learning with models	Part- or whole-task practice with prerequisite and supportive knowledge	Apprentice
Identification of causal relationships	From problem-orientation to inquiry-exploration	Part-task practice and algorithmic methods	Competent performer
Elaboration of causal relationships	Inquiry-exploration with learning with models and by modelling	Whole-task practice and heuristic methods	Competent and proficient performer
Reflection on the whole situation or system	From inquiry-exploration to policy-development with learning with models and by modelling	Heuristic methods	Competent and proficient performer
Understanding and solving new problems	Policy-development and learning by modelling	Whole-task practice and heuristic methods	Proficient performer

Interestingly, the methods in the 4C/ID model are primarily focused on an analysis of the subject domain whereas Dreyfus and Dreyfus focus primarily on the learner. Naturally, both are important considerations for an instructional designer.

The principle of graduated complexity in MFL suggests a sequence of learner challenges:

1. Challenge learners to characterize the standard behaviour of the complex system (how the system behaves over time with an indication of how components are interrelated).
2. Challenge learners to identify key variables and points of leverage with respect to a desired outcome.

3. Challenge learners to identify and explain the causes for observed system behaviour, especially in terms of key influence factors that might be subject to control and manipulation.
4. Challenge learners to reflect on the dynamic aspects of the system in the context of decision and policy guides to achieve desired outcomes.
5. Challenge learners to encapsulate learning in terms of a rationale for system structure, decision-making guidelines, and an elaborated strategy for policy formulation.
6. Challenge learners to diversify and generalize to new problem situations. (To assess deep understanding one might ask learners to create a dynamic model relevant to an apparently new problem situation that is likely to have an underlying structure similar to a problem situation already resolved by the learner.)

Throughout the various stages learners are challenged to start meaningful discussions with peers about problems, models and proposed solutions, all of which are well supported by available Web-based technologies. Such discussions help learners reflect about the subject matter and encourage peer-peer learning and group collaboration.

Next we shall provide examples. We follow Alessi (2000) in distinguishing learning with models from learning by modelling. We believe that learning with models is generally well suited for the earlier learning stages that often involve simple procedural tasks and simpler conceptual foundations (similar to algorithmic-based learning in 4C/ID), whereas learning by modelling is generally better suited to more advanced stages of development targeted at causal understanding and mastery of complex procedures not amenable to formulaic or standard solution (similar to heuristic-based learning in 4C/ID).

MFL emphasizes socially-situated learning processes. A suggestion of how to support collaboration with modelling tools in a discovery setting has been made by van Joolingen (2000). In the construction of models using systems dynamics tools, learners engage in cognitive and social processes that promote collaborative knowledge building. Rouwette et al (2000) argue that a collaborative approach to model and policy design is effective for learning and understanding. In these cases, we see theory, methodology and technology all coming together.

Learning with models

Model facilitated learning advocates learning with models as an instructional approach to introduce learners to a new domain or problem situation and to promote learning simpler procedures and associated concepts. Causal loop diagrams (also called causal influence diagrams) are quite good at providing a representation of an entire system. Such diagrams can be used to support an elaboration of a problem scenario, knowledge elicitation and assessment of understanding (Davidsen et al, 1999).

A meaningful learning activity consistent with MFL is to present learners with a problem scenario and ask them to construct an annotated causal loop diagram. Such an activity serves to centre thinking around meaningful problems and is typically effective in facilitating small group collaboration. This activity can also be used to assess progress of learning and predict how well a learner will perform in future complex situations (Christensen *et al*, 2000). Here is a sample scenario that we have used in our research:

> The Kaibab Plateau is situated on the north side of the Grand Canyon in Arizona in the USA and consists of some 727,000 acres. Prior to 1907 the deer herd there numbered about 4,000. In 1907, a law was passed banning all hunting of deer from the area. By 1918 the deer population increased tenfold, and by 1924 the herd had reached 100,000. Then it started to decrease and by 1936 to 1940 it was around 10,000. The deer feed on grass. Their natural predators in the region are primarily cougars (mountain lions).

Causal loop diagrams can be used to represent the problem situation and help facilitate problem solving. A simple problem might be to indicate how a hunting policy affects the deer population over time. A more complex problem is to develop a hunting policy that achieves a particular goal over a sustained period of time. Causal loop diagrams can also be used to initially determine how people think about a complex domain in comparison with domain experts and then for assessment of progress through a sequence of learning activities.

For example, learners discuss how an increase in deer created by a restrictive hunting policy might lead to competition for a limited source of food (grass) and eventually result in overgrazing and elimination of that source of food. This could then lead to starvation of a significant portion of the deer population in spite of well-intentioned attempts to help deer thrive. It is useful in the early stages of learning development to challenge learners to identify what they believe to be the most influential factor, perturb the system with a slight change and then predict the outcome. This technique is especially effective when the outcome is counter-intuitive as this begins to instil in learners an appreciation of the complexity of the situation, generates much discussion, and initiates a search for an explanation. Such cognitive dissonance can promote learning. In the terminology of MFL, learner-recognized and learner-generated knowledge gaps in the problem-orientation stage provide an effective stepping stone for the inquiry-exploration stage of learner development.

Interaction with a simulation is useful in determining if predicted outcomes occur. If historical data exist, then those data are relevant as well. In short, the inquiry-exploration stage is well supported with learner interactions with simulation models. This type of learning has a reasonably well-developed history within the system dynamics educational community in the form of 'management flight simulators' (Sterman, 1988). There exist popular simulations to support such interactions, such as SimCity and related simulation models (Alessi, 2000). Typically these simulations are run in cycles. After each cycle, small groups of learners are asked to indicate the current state of the system, provided an opportunity to change a few key factors and asked to predict what the state of the system will be at the end of the next cycle. Spector and Davidsen (1997) report that this black–box approach has certain advantages and disadvantages. The advantages are that peer-peer discussion and collaboration are effectively supported. Indeed, most of the learning appears to occur in the small group discussions and not in direct interaction with the simulation model. This type of activity is suitable for networked learning environments where learners can collaborate in this discussion process, and it is consistent with evidence presented by van Joolingen (2000) that discovery behaviour displayed by learners may improve under the influence of collaboration.

The disadvantage is that without access to the underlying simulation model, learners are unable to develop deep causal understanding of a complex system. As learners become more proficient in using the simulation, they require access to the underlying simulation model in order to advance their understanding (Davidsen and Spector, 1997; Spector and Davidsen, 1997).

Learning by modelling

As learners gain confidence in a complex system, it is appropriate and productive to provide opportunities to modify existing simulation models and to create alternative representations. There are two principles that provide a foundation for making the transition from learning with models to learning by modelling. First, learners need to appreciate that there exist connections between underlying system structure and observed outcomes (system behaviour). There are a number of ways to support this transition requirement. Including multiple representations (eg, causal loop diagrams, stock and flow diagrams and behavioural diagrams) appears to be an effective technique based on the earlier discussion of cognitive flexibility theory (Spiro *et al*, 1988); see Figure 1.1.

The second principle that lays the foundation for learning by modelling is a direct application of graduated complexity. The notion is that the learner should first establish the ability to fill in parts of an existing model in a way that is consistent with observed system behaviour. This principle is closely linked with the previous principle and contributes to the learner's understanding of structure (cause) and behaviour (effect). Davidsen (1996) suggests that linking structure to behaviour and creating structures to account for behaviour are important building blocks of deep understanding. In a more general sense, hypothesizing about potential causal relationships and then testing those hypotheses is important to building up understanding in a complex domain.

An interesting technique used by Davidsen (1996) to facilitate progress in the policy-development stage is to start with what might be characterized as simpler complex system behaviour and ask learners to create models that account for system behaviour. Learners are then given a goal (eg, stabilize the deer population in the Kaibab Plateau) and asked to develop a decision-making guideline to achieve that goal. The policy is then tested in an arbitrarily wide variety of situations that

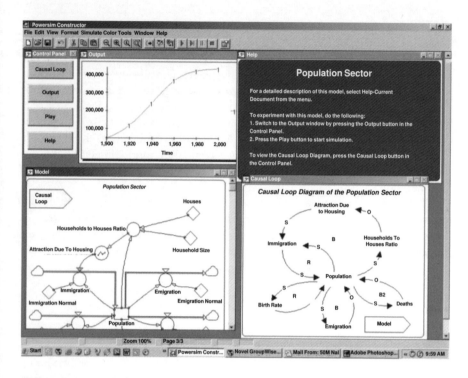

Figure 1.1   *Multiple representations*

might conceivably arise with regard to such a system (eg, drought conditions, diseases among the predator population, etc). Learners are asked to reflect on their understanding of the situation along the way.

Moreover, the process of constructing such simulation models requires a person to do all of the kinds of activities typically associated with experts: representing causal relationships, formulating hypotheses about those relationships, creating experimental settings to test hypotheses, identifying key leverage points and influence factors in a system, developing policies to guide decision making with regard to those factors subject to human control, and so on. These in fact represent patterns of expert behaviour that are generally desirable to engender in advanced learners.

Learning by modelling and learning with models

In this particular section we will illustrate how these two approaches can be combined for the design of meaningful learning activities to support complex learning. An example used in our research consists of giving learners the opportunity to understand the behaviour and underlying structure of a complex problem in an ecological system (Ford, 1999). Learners should also be able to understand the dynamics of the decision-making process with regard to a complex system; in this case it is in the domain of water quality.

To learn about acid rain, learners build and test a dynamic model or portions of a model. Relevant situated learning takes place as learners build a device with sensors and a software tool for collecting and analysing data, and then hypothesize about relationships and test those hypotheses. Learners have access to a number of interactive tools supporting different aspects of complex learning, including a modelling tool, a construction and programmable kit and a simulation environment, all of which are open for student use and manipulation. The specific tools provided to learners are Model Builder, the LEGO-DACTA Robotics System, the ROBOLAB programming language, and Powersim. Following the design principles of MFL, learners are challenged to solve a variety of complex problems (see Table 1.2) according to the three stages of learner development: 1) problem-orientation; 2) inquiry-exploration; and 3) policy-development.

Table 1.2   *Computational media to support learning about complex domains*

Task/Complex thinking component	Cognitive/Social skills	Learning tools and strategies	Computational-support
Which are the factors that influence the PH level of a lake?	*Identifying main ideas* *Inferring* *Hypothesizing* *Reflection*	*Mental Models* *Concept Mapping* *Modeling*	*Inspiration* *Model Builder*
Problem-Orientation		**Problem–Based Learning**	
Putting the problem in a context. Build a device that can monitor the PH and the temperature of the lake.	*Planning* *Determining criteria* *Concretizing* *Inventing a product* *Group discussion* *Collaboration*	*Construction* *Manipulation* *Visualization* *Situated Learning* *Constructionism*	*Lego Robotics* *Robolab* *Software*
Inquiry-Exploration		**Inquiry–Based Learning**	
Giving the problem, a time perspective and a new context. What will happen with the fish population of the lake in 5 years from now?	*Hypothesis formulation* *Identifying causal relationships* *Inferring* *Synthesis*	*Casual Loops* *Model building* *Simulation*	*Powersim* *Web Based Simulations*
Policy-Development	*Predicting* *Group discussion*	**Decision–Based Learning**	

Figure 1.2 shows results obtained while learners used the system dynamics simulation to explore the impact of acid rain on the fish population of the lake during a five-year period.

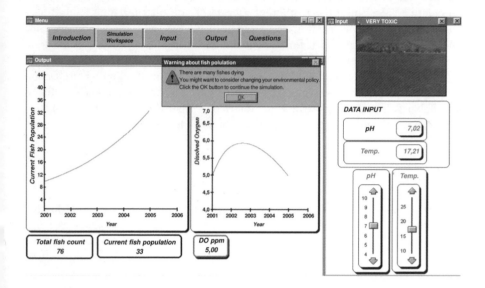

Figure 1.2   *Using system dynamics simulation*

In this particular example, we see theory, methodology and technology all coming together. Preliminary results suggest that the MFL approach is effective in the sense that this learning environment engages learners in solving complex problems through collaborative knowledge building and through interactive modelling, design and construction of system dynamics simulations (Milrad, 2001).

Conclusions

We conclude with a few comments about evaluating MFL and recommendations for future development and exploration. MFL should be held to established instructional design principles. Merrill (2001) provides a set of first principles for instruction:

1.   *Principle of Problem Centeredness:* Learning is effective when learners are engaged in solving real-world problems.
2.   *Principle of Learner Activation:* Learning is effective when existing learner knowledge is activated as a foundation for new knowledge and skills.
3.   *Principle of Demonstration:* Learning is effective when desired knowledge applications and skills are demonstrated for learners.

4. *Principle of Application:* Learning is effective when learners are required to apply new knowledge and skills.
5. *Principle of Integration:* Learning is effective when new knowledge and skills are integrated into the learner's world.

Does MFL satisfy these principles? The MFL problem-orientation stage satisfies Merrill's principle of problem centeredness, and the inquiry-exploration stage satisfies Merrill's principle of application. We accept all of Merrill's principles and believe that MFL provides an appropriate guide for application of these principles in complex domains using models and simulations.

Our work suggests that the following deserve further exploration:

- support for representing multiple perspectives of complex, dynamic problems;
- technology support for learning as a shared, collaborative activity, particularly in the context of bridging multiple perspectives in distributed settings;
- simulation and model-centred support in terms of interactions, collaborations and reflections 'around the simulation' and 'beyond the simulation'.

References

Alessi, S (2000) Building versus using simulations, in *Integrated and Holistic Perspectives on Learning, Instruction and Technology: Understanding complexity,* eds J M Spector and T M Anderson, pp 175–96, Kluwer, Dordrecht

Christensen, D L, Spector, J M, Sioutine, A and McCormack, D (2000) Evaluating the impact of system dynamics based learning environments: preliminary study. Paper presented at the 18th International Conference of the System Dynamics Society, August, Bergen, Norway

Collins, A, Brown, J S and Newman, S E (1989) Cognitive apprenticeship: teaching the crafts of reading, writing, and mathematics, in *Knowing, Learning, and Instruction: Essays in honor of Robert Glaser,* ed L B Resnick, pp 453–94, Lawrence Erlbaum, Hillsdale, NJ

Davidsen, P I (1996) Educational features of the system dynamics approach to modelling and simulation, *Journal of Structural Learning,* **12** (4), pp 269–90

Davidsen, P I and Spector, J M (1997) Cognitive complexity in system dynamics based learning environments, in *Systems Dynamics Proceedings: Systems approach to learning and education in the 21st century,* eds Y Barlas, V G Diker and S Polat, Vol. 2, pp 757–60, Bogaziçi University, Istanbul

Davidsen, P I, Spector, J M and Milrad, M (1999) Learning in and about simple systems, in *Proceedings of the 17th International Conference of the Systems Dynamics Society and 5th Australian and New Zealand Systems Conference,* eds R Y Cavana, J A Vennix, E Rouwette, M Stevenson-Wright and J Cavendish, Webrights, Wellington, NZ

Dörner, D (1996) *The Logic of Failure: Why things go wrong and what we can do to make them right,* trans R Kimber and R Kimber, Holt, New York

Dreyfus, H L and Dreyfus, S E (1986) *Mind Over Machine: The power of human intuition and expertise in the era of the computer,* Macmillan, New York

Feltovich, P, Spiro, R, Coulson, R and Feltovich, J (1996) Collaboration with and among minds: mastering complexity, individually and in groups, in *CSCL: Theory and practice of an emerging paradigm,* ed T Koschman, pp 25–44, Lawrence Erlbaum, Mahwah, NJ

Ford, A (1999) *Modelling the Environment: An introduction to system dynamics modelling of environmental systems,* Island Press, Washington, DC

Forrester, J (1985) The 'model' versus a modelling 'process', *System Dynamics Review,* **1** (1), pp 133–4

Gibbons, A S (2001) Model-centered instruction, *Journal of Structural Learning,* **14–15,** pp 511–40

Jackson, S, Krajcik, J and Soloway, E (2000) Model-IT: a design retrospective, in *Innovations in Science and Mathematics Education: Advanced designs for technologies of learning,* eds M J Jacobson and R B Kozma, pp 77–115, Lawrence Erlbaum, Mahwah, NJ

Jonassen, D H, Hernandez-Serrano, J and Choi, I (2000) Integrating constructivism and learning technologies, in *Integrated and Holistic Perspectives on Learning, Instruction and Technology: Understanding complexity,* eds J M Spector and T M Anderson, pp 103–28, Kluwer, Dordrecht

Kozma, R B (2000) The use of multiple representations and the social construction of understanding in chemistry, in *Innovations in Science and Mathematics Education: Advanced designs for technologies of learning,* eds M J Jacobson and R B Kozma, pp 11–46, Lawrence Erlbaum, Mahwah, NJ

Lave, J and Wenger, E (1990) *Situated Learning: Legitimate peripheral participation,* Cambridge University Press, Cambridge

Maier, F and Größler, A (2000) What are we talking about? A taxonomy of computer simulations to support learning, *System Dynamics Review,* **16** (2), pp 135–48

Merrill, M D (2001) First principles of instruction, *Journal of Structural Learning,* **14–15,** pp 459–68

Milrad, M (2001) Supporting collaborative knowledge building through interactive modelling, design and construction. Paper presented at the 2nd Nordic Baltic Conference on Activity Theory and Sociocultural Research, September, Ronneby, Sweden

Milrad, M, Spector, J M and Davidsen, P I (2000) Building and using simulation-based environments for learning about complex domains, in *MSET/2000 Conference Proceedings,* ed R Robson, pp 304–8, Association for the Advancement of Computing in Education (AACE), Charlottesville, VA

Reigeluth, C M and Stein, F S (1983) The elaboration theory of instruction, in *Instructional-design Theories and Models: An overview of their current status,* ed C M Reigeluth, pp 335–82, Lawrence Erlbaum, Mahwah, NJ

Rouwette, E A J A, Vennix, J A M and Thijssen, C M (2000) Group model building: a decision room approach, *Simulation and Gaming,* **31** (3), pp 359–79

Spector, J M (2000) System dynamics and interactive learning environments: lessons learnt and implications for the future, *Simulation and Gaming*, **31** (4), pp 528–35

Spector, J M and Anderson, T M (eds) (2000) *Integrated and Holistic Perspectives on Learning, Instruction and Technology: Understanding complexity*, Kluwer, Dordrecht

Spector, J M and Davidsen, P I (1997) Creating engaging courseware using systems dynamics, *Computers in Human Behaviour*, **13** (2), pp 127–56

Spector, J M and Davidsen, P I (2000) Designing technology enhanced learning environments, in *Instructional and Cognitive Impacts of Web-based Education*, ed B Abbey, Idea Group, Hershey, PA

Spector, J M, Guriby, F, Wasson, B and Lindström, B (1999) Theoretical foundations for the design of collaborative distance learning. Paper presented at the 8th European Conference for Research on Learning and Instruction, August, Göteborg, Sweden

Spiro, R J, Coulson, R L, Feltovich, P J and Anderson, D (1988) Cognitive flexibility theory: advanced knowledge acquisition in ill-structured domains, in *Proceedings of the 10th Annual Conference of the Cognitive Science Society*, ed V Patel, pp 375–83, Lawrence Erlbaum, Mahwah, NJ

Sterman, J D (1988) *People Express Management Flight Simulator*, Sloan School of Management, Cambridge, MA

Sterman, J (1994) Learning in and about complex systems, *Systems Dynamics Review*, **10** (2–3), pp 291–330

van Joolingen, W R (2000) Designing for collaborative discovery learning, in *Intelligent tutoring systems*, eds G Gauthier, C Frasson and K VanLehn, Springer, Berlin

van Merriënboer, J J G (1997) *Training Complex Cognitive Skills: A four-component instructional design model for technical training*, Educational Technology Publications, Englewood Cliffs, NJ

Wells, G (1999) *Dialogic Inquiry: Toward a sociocultural practice and theory of education*, Cambridge University Press, Cambridge

Chapter 2

Implicit theories of learning and change: their role in the development of e-learning environments for higher education

Peter Goodyear and Chris Jones

Introduction

This chapter addresses the twin issues of *content* and *educational design*. Neither term can be read unproblematically. In this chapter, we take 'content' to mean electronic information resources, which students may (or may not) use in their work as learners. By 'educational design' we mean the set of processes entailed in planning the creation of good learning tasks, good learning resources and the conditions in which convivial learning communities may grow and prosper.

This perspective on design places learning, not content, at the centre of the educational design problem space. It stresses the importance of the learner's *activity* – primarily their mental activity – in determining the success of a learning episode. It also asserts the importance of the social and physical setting as key influences on learning and its outcomes. To a greater or lesser extent, learning is socially situated and recognition of this fact has drawn many towards the idea of supporting learning activity within a community of learners (eg, Scardamalia and Bereiter, 1994). Learning is also *physically* situated. Technology of various kinds – books, notepaper, a laptop, the Web – can have a strong influence on how learning and its associated cognitive activity take place, to the extent that many are persuaded that it makes sense to think of cognition being distributed across people and the artefacts around them (eg, Salomon, 1993). This invests the quality of the 'learnplace' with considerable importance (Bliss *et al,* 1999; Ford *et al,* 1996). While the quality of the learners' activity, the support they obtain from a learning community and the nature of the resources available to them in their learnplace are the three sets of factors most influential in determining the success of learning, as educational designers we rarely have direct access to them. As we have argued in detail elsewhere, designers cannot (and probably should not) control the learner's activity, create learning communities or aim to specify in exhaustive detail the tools and resources available in their learnplace (Goodyear, 2000). Rather, a more indirect approach is needed – one in which design focuses attention on specifying productive learning tasks, creating the organizational conditions for convivial learning and stocking the wider learning environment with tools and resources that the learners can customize and reconfigure to furnish their own personal learnplace (cf Crook, 2001).

Where does content sit in this schema? On a broad view, it is distributed. It can be found in the cognitions and utterances of peers. It emerges and is transformed in the activity of the learner. But given the focus of this chapter and this section of the book, we shall locate content in the space-place area of our schema. That is, we shall treat content in terms of its reification in texts, tools and other artefacts. We return to this in a moment.

Terry Mayes (eg, Mayes and Neilson, 1996) has developed a three-phase model of students' use of technology in higher education that invokes a cycle of conceptualization, construction and critique. These phases are best supported by what he calls primary, secondary and tertiary courseware. Tertiary courseware is created by interactions among learners and teachers (discourse; critique). Secondary courseware is customized by teachers to support the knowledge-construction activities of their students. Primary courseware is created by teams of teachers and/or professional courseware producers and is intended for use by students of many different institutions, for the initial 'conceptualization' kinds of learning activity.

We can map these three kinds of courseware onto the space-place area of the design schema. Think of 'space' as denoting an abstract and/or public field, where common goods can be located. In contrast, place is concrete, personal and local. Primary, secondary and tertiary courseware relate to space and place through processes of transformation and relocation. Primary and secondary courseware reside in the common/public space. Among the tasks we set students are ones that encourage them to interact with primary and secondary courseware, and in so doing to construct both internal and external personal representations of knowledge. (By internal representations we mean various cognitive/knowledge structures – mental models, propositions, etc. By external representations we mean such things as personal notes, diagrams, etc.) Other tasks we set students encourage them to create texts and other shareable representations of knowledge, and to move these – when ready – from private to public. For example, in electronic seminars we encourage students to create electronic texts and, when ready, to post these in their seminar group's online discussion area. These processes of transformation and relocation underpin the creation of what Mayes calls tertiary courseware.

In this chapter our main focus is on primary courseware, but we are especially concerned about how the people designing and producing it conceive of its integration with learning activity. Within the UK there have been four major initiatives aimed at creating such primary resources – NDPCAL (the National Development Programme for Computer Assisted Learning, in the 1970s), CTI (the Computers in Teaching Initiative, in the 1980s), TLTP (the Teaching and Learning Technology Programme, in the 1990s) and DNER (the Distributed National Electronic Resource, now). The products of TLTP and their impact upon UK higher education were the focus of substantial evaluation studies. A significant conclusion from these studies was that, in general, insufficient attention was paid to pedagogy, design and the integration of courseware into the mainstream curriculum. The implicit pedagogical beliefs of the courseware production teams became embedded in the courseware and this, among other things, restricted take-up of the courseware by teachers whose pedagogical beliefs and practices were not compatible with those of the courseware producers.

DNER is taking a different tack. Like TLTP it is intent on producing and/or improving access to primary resources but it is doing so with what appears to be a much more open sense of possible pedagogical usage. Part of our job as the people responsible for the formative evaluation of DNER is to try to surface the implicit theories of learning and change that are informing, and are embedded in, the work of the DNER project teams. Both the process and the outcome of our work casts further light on important issues concerning students' use of primary courseware, especially in relation to presentational (teachers' view) and conceptualization (learners' view) activities.

This chapter draws on the pedagogical evaluation of the DNER. More specifically, it focuses on the work of some 35 projects, each of which is concerned with contributing new digital information resources for learning and teaching. This chapter presents an analysis of the 'implicit theories of learning and change' that are embedded in the day-to-day work of the projects. We take an implicit theory of learning to be an unarticulated set of assumptions about how learning occurs (and, by extension, about how learning resources can best support learning). Such assumptions can be a powerful influence on the nature of the learning resources created by a project team. Similarly, an implicit theory of change is an unarticulated set of assumptions about how the creation of new learning resources is expected to change educational practice. Among these assumptions, we can find expectations about the ways in which teachers in higher education will seek to connect electronic information resources with the rest of the e-learning environment, and beliefs about how discrete information resources can be turned into reusable learning objects through appropriate tagging with meta-data, for example.

Implicit theories of learning and change

In this section we report the outcomes of an analysis of brief project descriptions produced by key members of the project teams. These project descriptions were elicited as part of a 'History of the future' exercise, in which projects were asked to focus on their intended core achievements. After this, we present some further evidence to triangulate with our initial set of findings – this time drawn from the projects' published descriptions of themselves. Finally, we illustrate some of the difficulties projects have in linking their activities to definable pedagogical benefits, using the mechanism of 'project logic maps' to do so.

Main study

The study context

The DNER is:

> a managed environment for accessing quality assured information resources on the Internet which are available from many sources. These resources include scholarly journals, monographs, textbooks, abstracts, manuscripts, maps, music scores, still images, geospatial images and other kinds of vector and numeric data, as well as moving picture and sound collections. (DNER, 2001)

It is funded by the JISC – the Joint Information Systems Committee of the four UK funding councils for higher education, with an investment to date of over £30 million. The DNER is aimed at users in tertiary education in the UK, not just for learning and teaching but also for research and scholarship. However, the study reported in this chapter involved staff from some 35 projects that were funded under a single call for proposals aimed at enhancing the *educational* use of DNER. The original proposal formulated by JISC for additional government funding captures some of the core intention:

> Although this data has been primarily used for research purposes, it is beginning to find a use in learning and teaching. However, this work has been slow and some additional funding would enable the JISC services to be used in totally different ways than originally envisaged. There is a strong require-ment to improve the interaction between the people who are involved in the development of new learning environments and the national information systems and services being developed by the JISC. It is therefore proposed that an initiative be funded to integrate learning environments with the wider information landscape aimed at increasing the use of on-line electronic information and research datasets in the learning and teaching process. (JISC, 1999, para 8)

Among the criteria to be used in selecting bids for funding was 'impact on the learning and teaching environment in UK HE' (JISC, 1999, para 97).

Method

Our main data were collected during a two-day meeting of representatives of the project teams in London in June 2001. All the project personnel were gathered together in a single room and were asked to engage in a version of a 'History of the future' exercise. One of the authors introduced this exercise by a) displaying a large PowerPoint slide whose text is reproduced below, and b) by asking the participants to spend 10 minutes drafting a response, without conferring. It was emphasized that the responses should be anonymous, that only the authors and a secretarial assistant would see the responses and that we would make no comments about the work of individual projects. The participants hand wrote their responses on paper and at the end of 10 minutes all the responses were collected by the authors. After this, the authors made a presentation about the use of 'History of the future' exercises and project logic mapping exercises in helping bring to the surface what might otherwise be implicit assumptions, beliefs, goals and causal attributions. The subsequent discussion session suggested that at least those participants who spoke saw the point of the exercise and regarded it as worthwhile. We saw no reason to assume that the participants had done anything other than treat the exercise seriously.

The text shown on the slide (after Nash *et al*, 2000) was:

> To facilitate this process for complex projects, we propose that the project staff write a history of the future. Imagine that your intervention project is completed and that it succeeded in all of its goals. You are to appear tomorrow at a press conference to explain what you have accomplished. Write a press release for distributing at this meeting, explaining in a few paragraphs what it is that you have accomplished, who is benefiting from this, why it's important (that is, what problem it solves and why this problem needed to be solved), and what it was that you did that led to or caused this success.

The responses of the participants were typed into a single word-processor document file by a secretarial assistant at Lancaster. An identification number was added to each response and a page break inserted between responses. The secretarial assistant, as far as possible, reproduced any layout features used in the originals; paragraphs were preserved, etc.

Data

The data file contained 69 responses. The average length of response was 107 words. Inspection of the responses revealed none that was obviously flippant or facetious and reinforced the view that participants had engaged in the exercise with a reasonable degree of seriousness. It may be useful to give a flavour of the responses at this point. Here are two examples, which we have modified very slightly to make it impossible to identify the projects concerned. (Passages we have changed for this purpose are marked with square brackets. Passages where we have expanded acronyms are marked with round brackets.)

Response 40

What it has accomplished – Has made accessible 1,000 text or 3000 images of a collection of museum objects and archives from a museum collection. Made by outstanding [artists. . .]

Will benefit – students of [various craft and design areas] and applied arts in higher and further education.

It's overcome – Problem faced by museums – objects have to be stored away for their protection. Only x% seen at any one time – now several thousands of such collections can be seen and used as a learning resource for many students.

Response 48

The service has succeeded in making a positive impact with all the relevant subject communities within F(urther) E(ducation), H(igher) E(ducation).

The service is perceived to be

– a useful 'first stop' or 'trawl' for general information
– a 'spring board' to more detailed sources
– a 'signpost' or evolving map for the community to help them find their way around the subjects.

Students within further education are introduced to sources they do not know existed. Users within HE are supported in their project and research work.

Bridges have been built with the relevant professional bodies and the service has acted as a successful 'networker' – bringing together different strands of the overall community that studies these subjects.

Analysis

Our first analysis of the data took the form of a classification of the responses into categories, based upon the ways in which projects referred to what students would do with the electronic resources that were being created and/or set in place for them. Our principal distinction was based upon the idea of 'access'. That is, we started by dividing the responses into a) those that only talked about making new or better resources accessible to students or about improving their access to such resources, and b) those which, in some way, went 'beyond access'. Table 2.1 summarizes the results.

Table 2.1 *First level summary of the classification of responses*

Responses that:	%
Say anything that goes 'beyond access'	42
Refer to anything that might be recognizable as a description of learning activity	20
Talk about providing accompanying teaching and learning materials	25
Talk about working with teachers	7
Refer to anything that might be recognizable as a description of learning activity *and* talk about providing accompanying teaching and learning materials *and* talk about working with teachers	3

Less than half of the responses said anything that went 'beyond access'. That is, the majority of the project staff restricted their comments to the description of project outcomes that were concerned with improving students' access to electronic information resources and/or enriching such resources. The nature of this category becomes clearer if we turn to what else they might have said. For example, there are good reasons to believe that simply making resources available to students will have no impact on the quality of their learning. Students in higher education will need a reason to use such resources, and to use them well. When resource use is integrated with learning tasks prescribed or suggested by teachers then there is a greater probability that students will use them. If the outcomes of the students' work on such tasks are assessed and the assessment counts towards the students' degree results, then there is an even higher probability that they will make use of the resources concerned. If the assessment criteria can distinguish between outcomes that are the consequence of poor, satisfactory and excellent use of such resources, then there is an increased probability that students will not just use the resources but use them well. So what might project team staff be expected to say that goes 'beyond access'?

Table 2.1 reveals three such categories of response. Some of the responses *did* talk about ways in which students might use electronic information resources in their learning. That is, they gave some kind of description of possible learning activities. But only 20 per cent of the responses fall into this category. In 80 per cent of the cases, there was no description of intended or envisaged student learning activity. Another way of 'going beyond access' would be if project staff mentioned that their goals included providing learner and/or teacher support materials to help with the integration of an electronic information resource into the curriculum; 25 per cent of the responses did this. The third and final category that goes 'beyond access' includes all of those projects that mentioned that they had been working with teachers in developing their electronic information resources; 7 per cent of the responses mentioned they had been working with teachers (or intended to do so).This figure may well under-report the proportion of projects that had worked, or were planning to work, with teachers.The reason is that the 'History of the future' exercise causes respondents to start with project goals and move on to project methods. Inspection of the projects' published descriptions of themselves (see below) reveals that more of them mention working with teachers.The point to emphasize here is that for 93 per cent of the project staff, working with teachers (eg to make sure the resources being produced would be usable in real learning and teaching situations) was not a sufficiently salient issue to figure in their responses to this exercise.

The final point to be made with the aid of Table 2.1 is that the intersection of these three sets of responses that go 'beyond access' is very small indeed. Only 3 per cent of the responses fall into this category.This equates to just two of the 69 respondents and probably represents the work of just one of the projects.

Analysis of the published descriptions of the projects

The previous analysis draws on data collected directly from staff of the projects in response to a particular stimulus.Their responses were produced under tight time constraints and were anonymous. We decided that it would be valuable to triangulate the outcomes from our analysis of these responses with an analysis of some of the core assumptions contained within the projects' published descriptions of themselves.The dataset here consists of a set of A4 publicity sheets – one for each project – produced by the projects themselves, but working to a template provided by the programme coordinators.These sheets are used individually by the projects but are also used as a set for publicity and dissemination purposes at the programme level.Table 2.2 reports the outcomes of our analysis of these published project self-descriptions.

Looking at this table, we can see that only two of the projects provide more than a rudimentary account of how students' learning will improve through use of project outcomes; these are in categories 5 and 6 in Table 2.2. Perhaps we (the authors) are accustomed to seeing educational technology project rationales rooted in an explicit account of student learning and/or drawing directly on theories about how students learn and how their interaction with electronic resources can be expected to improve aspects of their learning.We should not assume that projects funded under an initiative concerned with making electronic information resources more useful to learning and teaching in UK tertiary education will necessarily be motivated to construct or publish a pedagogical rationale. Instead, we merely observe a) that very few of these projects have done so, and b) that the lack of an explicit pedagogical rationale may make it harder for projects to convey the potential educational value of their work, which may in turn make it harder for others (especially teachers in HE) to recognize, evaluate, take up and integrate the project outcomes into their own work as educators.

If we move above the bold line marking off categories 5 and 6, we find a number of contrasting and usually implicit assumptions apparently motivating the work of numbers of projects. Some project descriptions indicate a clear commitment to

Table 2.2 *(Usually) implicit assumptions about pedagogical purpose*

Key assumption(s) embedded in the project rationales	Number of projects fitting this category (projects can appear in more than one category)
1. There exists a set of material objects (such as artefacts in a museum or documents in a public records office) which, if rendered into a digitized form, would be accessed and used by learners, to their educational advantage	9
2. There exists (or will exist) a set of digitized resources which, if used more frequently or more widely, would be of educational benefit to learners. The main barriers to greater use are:	
– teachers do not know they exist or find it hard to locate them	3
– access to the resources is complicated; seamless or simpler access methods are needed	3
– access to the resources alone, by students, will not be as beneficial as access that is mediated through carefully crafted educational packages and/or contextualizing material or courses	3
– access by students requires special skills	2
– teachers need to be shown or advised about how to incorporate them into their teaching	10
3. In general, students' use of DNER-type resources will be constrained by the complexities of access	1
4. Our basic (scientific?) understanding of new media (etc) in HE needs improving if we are to make good design/ pedagogical decisions	5
5. Students get a deeper understanding of economic theory and processes (etc) through use of models or simulations	1
6. Students of minority languages need good access to the target language, to a broad range of other learning resources and to a critical mass of fellow students	1

research (category 4: five projects). The underlying claim here is that so little is known about the educational use of new media that development work needs to have a strong research component to it. None of these projects is funded as a research project. Rather, they have been funded to engage in development activity into which they have built a research component.

Categories 1 and 2 differ in the following way. Category 1 represents projects that are concerned with the digitization of existing material resources. In contrast, our category 2 projects are concerned with making existing electronic information resources easier to use within teaching and learning practices in UK tertiary education. The main perceived barriers to easier and/or wider and/or more productive usage give us the five main sub-categories in category 2. They vary from a belief that teachers find existing resources hard to locate (or are ignorant of their existence) to the provision of advice about ways of using the resources. Ten of the projects fall into this last sub-category.

Around one-third of the projects, according to their published descriptions, are committed to producing learning and teaching materials. This compares with the figure of 25 per cent of responses reported in Table 2.1. This difference of just one or two projects can probably be accounted for in terms of the relative salience of producing learning and teaching materials, compared with other project goals, and the effect of the time constraints in the 'History of the future' exercise in causing respondents to restrict themselves to what they perceived as the most important outcomes of their work.

The internal logic of projects

The data discussed thus far tell us something about the 'outcomes of interest' of the projects and about their methods, including something about their assumptions concerning how their activities may connect with improvements in teaching and learning. A useful tool for exploring this further is the 'project logic map' (McClauglin and Jordan, 1998; Nash *et al*, 2000). Figure 2.1 gives an example of an internal logic map for projects in this area.

The logic map is read as follows. At the right-hand side we see the main 'outcome(s) of interest'. These are the main kinds of things that are meant to emerge in the 'History of the future' exercise. They capture what the project is meant to achieve – what difference it will make in the world. On the left-hand side are the project team's initial resources – what they have to hand in embarking on the project. In between are the entities that the team needs to create or otherwise set in place in executing its work. The arrows linking the main entities encapsulate the team's sense (its implicit theory) of causation. For example, placing a link between 'well-designed learning tasks' and 'constructive alignment of tasks and assessment' implies that it is not enough to design good tasks: they must also be aligned with course assessment requirements. Team members' beliefs about the nature of this link can be probed through discussion, for example to reveal beliefs that what students in UK higher education choose to do is in part a satisficing response to the course assessment demands placed upon them (Biggs, 1999).

The logic map has been divided into two parts. The lower part (below the thick horizontal line) is absent from many of the projects in the set with which we are concerned – whether one creates a logic map from their published documentation or begins to sketch one from the data in the 'History of the future' exercise. The upper part is present in most projects. The goal of improved student achievement

Project logic

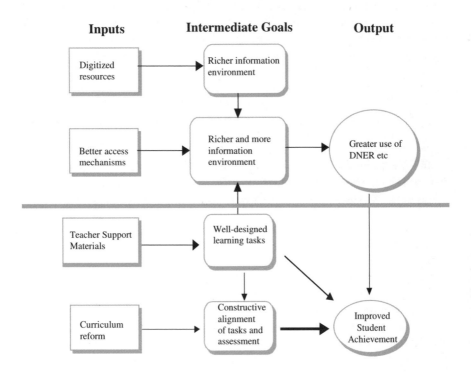

Inputs **Intermediate Goals** **Output**

Figure 2.1 *Project logic map*

is at least implicit in most projects, though causal links with project inputs and goals are absent or not apparent.

Part of our task in providing the formative pedagogical evaluation of the DNER is to help project teams articulate and then enrich their project logic maps. Part of the intention is to help them move towards methods of making content available that stand a good chance of allowing integration with students' learning activity. Though the maps provide a useful resource for internal discussion, their main value lies in their capacity for supporting action. Assessing this capacity is an important task for the next stage of our work.

Implications for the development of e-learning environments for higher education

What can this specific evaluation experience tell us that may be useful in a more general consideration of e-learning in higher education?

First, we would argue that research of this kind helps to fill in some of the details that are glossed over in arguments about 'technology-led' and 'pedagogically-led' development projects. In the case of DNER, many of the projects are driven by beliefs about the value of improved access to electronic content. Access is primarily conceived in technical terms: it is addressed in terms of 'cross-searching', 'fusion services' and 'interoperability', for example. Access is not linked, conceptually, with pedagogically-informed beliefs about students' learning activities. There is no clear view of how learning activity and information resource (content) are meant to relate. Such a lacuna is startling to people brought up in a tradition of instructional systems design (ISD), where definition of learning goals and learning activities would precede and inform selection of content. In the absence of an ISD perspective, content is conjured up on the assumption that *somehow* it may prove useful. The design and development of complex e-learning environments, especially in areas like higher education where some degree of autonomous learning is valued, can no longer depend wholly on the ISD tradition. But neither can it rely solely on vague intuitions about the potential utility of content. Rather, those developing primary courseware need to structure their work by taking the kind of holistic or ecological approach to design implied in the discussion above (see also Goodyear, 2000).

Second, formative evaluation work of this kind underlines the value of causing development teams to articulate, confront, critique and improve the assumptions embodied in their activity – especially with respect to their beliefs about learning and educational change. Project staff, especially if they come from more technical areas, rarely have a sharp and robust set of conceptual tools for thinking about and discussing learning. Vernacular constructs about learning are not adequate for the job.

Finally – though there may be other lessons to share – we would want to argue that *programmatic* funding of the development of technological support for learning needs to be informed by the best of what is known about 'good learning'. The staff of individual projects cannot be blamed for silence or ambivalence with respect to learning if the programme within which their work is commissioned and managed is similarly silent or ambivalent. Given the uncertain and contested status of much educational knowledge, this necessitates some risk-taking, courage and personal commitment. Nevertheless a programme of development work which starts with a manifesto about good learning (and how it may be supported by good technology) stands a better chance than one in which such fundamental beliefs remain tacit and unexamined.

Acknowledgement

We gratefully acknowledge the financial support of JISC in carrying out the evaluation work on which this chapter is based. It should not be assumed that JISC, its committees or its staff share the views we have put forward here, nor that they are shared by other members of the DNER evaluation team.

References

Biggs, J (1999) *Teaching for Quality Learning at University: What the student does,* Open University Press, Buckingham

Bliss, J, Saljo, R and Light, P (eds) (1999) *Learning Sites: Social and technological resources for learning,* Elsevier, Oxford

Crook, C (2001) The campus experience of networked learning, in *Networked Learning: Perspectives and issues,* eds C Steeples and C Jones, pp 293–308, Springer, London

DNER (2001) JISC Distributed National Electronic Resource. Accessed 11 December 2001, from www.jisc.ac.uk/dner

Ford, P, Goodyear, P, Heseltine, R, Lewis, R, Darby, J, Graves, J, Sartorius, P, Harwood, D and King, T (1996) *Managing Change in Higher Education: A learning environment architecture,* Open University Press, Buckingham

Goodyear, P (2000) Environments for lifelong learning: ergonomics, architecture and educational design, in *Integrated and Holistic Perspectives on Learning, Instruction and Technology: Understanding complexity,* eds J M Spector and T Anderson, pp 1–18, Kluwer Academic, Dordrecht

JISC (1999) Developing the DNER for Learning and Teaching, JISC Circular 5/99. Accessed 11 December 2001, from http://wwwjiscacuk/pub99/c05_99html

Mayes, T and Neilson, I (1996) Learning from other people's dialogues: questions about computer-based answers, in *Innovative Learning with Innovative Technology,* eds B Collis and G Davies, North Holland, Amsterdam

McClauglin, J and Jordan, G (1998) Logic models: a tool for telling your program's performance story. Accessed 5 June 2001, from http://wwwpmnnet/education/Logichtm

Nash, J, Plugge, L and Eurelings, A (2000) Defining and evaluating CSCL projects: managing towards evaluation. Paper presented at the European Conference on Computer Supported Collaborative Learning (ECSCL 2000), Maastricht, Netherlands

Salomon, G (ed) (1993) *Distributed Cognitions: Psychological and educational considerations,* Cambridge University Press, Cambridge

Scardamalia, M and Bereiter, C (1994) Computer support for knowledge building communities, *Journal of the Learning Sciences,* **3** (3), pp 265–83

Chapter 3

Designing graphical, interactive simulations to model scientific problem solving

Laurie Ruberg and John Baro

Introduction

How do scientists solve problems? How does their thinking differ from that of non-scientists facing a problem? By using ideas as generative models for interpreting observations and events, scientists and other experts see meaningful patterns in problems regardless of the subject matter (Bransford *et al,* 2000). Besides being a body of epistemological ideas and facts, science is a way of perceiving and interpreting experiences and natural phenomena. Thus, learning the process of scientific problem solving has value to all and applies to any field. A goal in the USA and in many other countries is to educate all citizens to achieve a scientifically literate society (National Research Council, 1996).

In this chapter we examine how graphical, interactive simulations in a strategically designed learning environment can be used to model scientific problem solving and promote scientific inquiry. To achieve these goals, a set of design principles was applied. They combined components of problem-based learning pedagogy, cognitive psychology research, and empirical evidence from media research. The design strategy began with a compelling problem that allowed students to take diverse positions and then moved students into a rich, graphical, computer-based learning environment for a series of guided, interactive experiences.

This chapter uses specific examples from a multimedia program called BioBLAST®. It offers a six-week high school biology curriculum. A select group of teacher-leaders, practising scientists and a curriculum development team collaborated on the design and development of this program. In the examples provided, students were given complex problem-solving experiences within a learning environment that gradually progresses from simple to more complex cognitive processing and interactions. Each interactive event was designed to move students forward with advanced simulation activities offering increasingly more open inquiry experiences. The chapter concludes with a set of design principles to apply to the development of future computer-based simulations.

Theoretical background

With the goal of promoting scientific inquiry, the design team viewed learners as 'model-builders' and provided them with tools they could use to create models of an idealized world that could be inspected, evaluated, reflected upon and publicly discussed. This approach to simulation design included a three-step process. First, identify a suitable problem. Second, present the problem-solving task in a way that learners can handle the content and cognitive processing and can effectively mediate their emerging solutions. Third, present the problem, tools and resources in a way that promotes questioning, discussion, analysis and reflection on core scientific principles. This section provides a summary of the theoretical framework that guided each of these three steps.

Problem-based learning

Having a compelling problem-solving framework that stimulates student interest allows students to see where they are headed and why. It also encourages them to take diverse perspectives on critical issues. The need to begin with problems that are real and meaningful to students is evident across educational research theories (Germann et al, 1996; Hofer and Pintrich, 1997; Kuhn, 1997). Learning is a goal-oriented activity. Students need a compelling problem to solve.

The problem posed in the instructional system in this research is how to design a biologically based life support system that could support humans in space for long periods of time without resupply. The National Aeronautics and Space Administration (NASA) was actively researching this problem when this program was created. Because of the problem's complex nature, many diverse solutions could be proposed.

Both teachers and students need to know that the problem scenario and simulation models were based on data from authentic research studies. As Brown *et al* (1989) suggest, the problem posed must be applied in an authentic context. Kuhn (1997) reinforces this point when she suggests that students should have a chance to experience the *big picture* through different media and interactive events that frame the problem in a dramatic, narrative and engaging context. The teacher who introduces the simulation can also draw on relevant news items or classroom events to set up the problem's framework.

Designing cognitive guideposts

Ideas are carriers of meaning (Bransford *et al*, 2000). In this context all inquiry processes, interactions, and activities are designed to reinforce the underlying theme: the interrelatedness of all living things. The challenge for science education designers is to create model-building tools that allow students to think with critical components and discuss physical attributes with their peers. The design strategy was to develop instructional events organized around core concepts, or big ideas, to model how experts organize information and solve problems. The level of complexity of the models was designed to suit learner level of knowledge and skill. In the examples cited, the simulation experiences explicitly reinforce the concept that photosynthesis and respiration are reciprocal processes. Students create models of living systems that they then systematically interact with, test and analyse using simulation tools.

Studies comparing cognitive strategies of experts with novices (Bransford *et al*, 2000) were used to design the sequence of interactive simulation experiences. Experts' abilities to reason and solve problems depend on well-organized knowledge that affects what they notice and how they represent problems, whereas novices' knowledge is much less organized around key ideas and is more fragmentary in structure. Experts recognize meaningful patterns of information across all domains. Pattern recognition is an important strategy for helping students develop competence and confidence in problem solving. The exercises designed to model effective use of the simulators were designed to reinforce observation of patterns and relationships. Recognition of these patterns provides triggering conditions for accessing knowledge relevant to any problem.

The simulation activities were designed to support the shift in focus from generalities to in-depth analysis and testing of core components of the problem. Student activities were structured so that students would use three component simulations to produce relevant data that would later be integrated and applied to developing a testable solution to the overall problem. A primary goal was to provide a strong core theme that unites a variety of disciplines, including mathematics, technology education, chemistry, psychology and sociology with the biological sciences. The content taxonomy had to consider not only the fundamental biological principles to be addressed, but also related principles and knowledge from other disciplines that were required for problem-solving tasks. Therefore, the presentation of inquiry experiences for students had to consider what level of knowledge of core concepts students should be expected to know and could be expected to learn from the experiences presented to them in this software (Matthews, 2000).

Scientific reasoning and inquiry

Analysing the common features between student and scientific problem solving can help researchers and instructional designers understand where students need help in making the transition from ordinary response to application of scientific inquiry. Professional scientists conduct their research by building and testing models (Penner, 2001). Among practising scientists, model building and testing are essential to the development of theory. Scientists use theoretical models of processes and concepts they are investigating to organize their observations and frame their interpretations of what they have tested and observed. According to Germann *et al* (1996) as well as Jacobson *et al* (1996), explicit, incremental development of the science process skills of formulating hypotheses and identifying variables when linked with model examples might facilitate student success in teaching inquiry skills, such as the ability to design science experiments.

Tools such as computer simulations that allow scientists to represent and test their understanding of natural phenomena are also useful. They engage students in using models to construct and test their conceptual understanding. As Park and Hannafin (1993) suggest, a learning environment designed to support scientific reasoning and inquiry integrates student learning experiences and interactive activities in a way that allows learners to control their experiences and movement within the computer interface. In the long run, inquiry instruction will result in students who are reflective, self-regulating investigators. They will be able to defend their questions, procedures and conclusions and will see inquiry as a way of knowing the world (National Research Council, 1996). To achieve this goal, students need opportunities to do their own background research, interpret information and share their opinions with others as part of the inquiry process.

The instructional context was designed to begin and end with students working in cooperative teams outside the software interface. By giving users access to view, export and examine the simulation data as well as graphical and numeric description of data relationships, the simulations are much more than conceptual models that demonstrate reciprocal relationships among plants, humans and recycling systems. With access to the underlying data and dynamic calculation model, students can inspect, question, discuss, critique and redefine the underlying model through their own design ideas, test runs and data analysis.

Examples of successful simulation designs

This section uses specific examples from simulations that were designed based on the principles in the previous section. The examples are part of a multimedia program called BioBLAST®. It integrates the three-tiered design process into the development of a learning environment for high school biology students. The final software reflects the socially-mediated interpretation of what was an appropriate problem to pose, cognitive support to interject, and level of reasoning to require. Figure 3.1 shows screenshots of the virtual reality interface (A), background

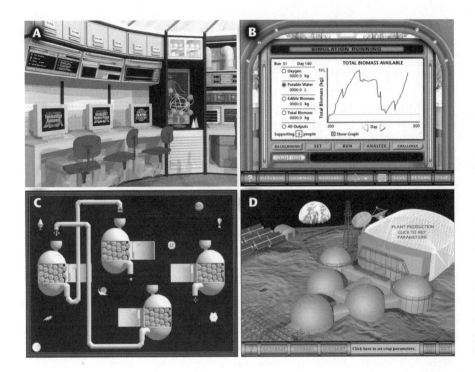

Figure 3.1   *These screens illustrate the BioBLAST interface*

Note: Panel A is part of the virtual reality lunar base interface. Panel B is an output screen showing data during a Plant Production Simulator run. Panel C is from the introductory arcade-style game. Panel D is the main interface of the BaBS Simulator.

research simulators (B), introductory game (C), and culminating integrated modelling system (D).

Examples of problem-based learning

The BioBLAST approach to problem-based learning starts with an authentic, compelling problem for students to solve. Students are placed in a virtual lunar base and must design a bioregenerative life support system that will keep their crew of six alive for three years without resupply. The context is authentic because at the time BioBLAST was developed, researchers were trying to solve that very problem. The lunar base design is realistic, based on current and projected future technologies. The simulations are also as realistic as possible, based on data from a number of current research projects at NASA centres. To make the data useful in a classroom setting, the system was simplified somewhat. An attractive, easy-to-use graphical interface was implemented.

Before students begin the computer-based portion of BioBLAST, they complete a number of discussions or thought problems. These jump-start the exploration by asking students to consider issues such as: How much food and water will they require? How much room will they need to live comfortably? How far away is the Moon, and what would it cost to get there? These activities familiarize students with the overarching problem and the kinds of questions they will address. The opening activities encourage group discussions of qualitative components of the overall problem. The open-ended explorations and journal writing activities encourage students to consider diverse approaches to the problem and to be aware of the breadth of issues and need for collaboration and sharing of ideas regarding possible solutions.

The first computer-based activities focus on orientation, both to the problem scenario and to the software. The launch sequence places students on a virtual ship to the Moon, where they receive the first formal statement of their mission objective. Through a series of videos and introductory readings, students learn their goal and the means to achieve it. Also included in this sequence is an arcade-style video game that introduces a number of important concepts relevant to living in and balancing a closed system. They also take a guided tour of the virtual lunar base.

Examples of designing cognitive guideposts

BioBLAST follows a whole-to-part-to-whole approach to problem-based learning. Students initially learn their ultimate goal, the design of a bioregenerative life support system. During orientation, they explore concepts necessary to accomplish this goal, such as the interrelatedness of all living things and, in particular, the reciprocal relationship between photosynthesis and respiration. During the research phase, the problem is broken down into components. Through simulation and laboratory experiments students test and analyse specific aspects of the system, such as the relationship between plant growth and atmospheric carbon dioxide level. In the mission phase, they integrate the results they obtained in their research to design a complete life support system. In the reporting phase they share their results, using PowerPoint® slides that include supporting data tables and graphs.

Initial prototypes of the program did not include the three component simulations. From an early 'proof of concept' for the software, students moved from the introduction to the overall problem to a structured presentation with accompanying exercises that introduced the problem-solving process. The structured exercises guided students through identifying, gathering and collecting the data they would need to create their model solution. The quantitative data collected from the exercises would then be used as simulation settings to be tested in the model-building simulator called BaBS.

The BaBS simulator is considered the 'capstone' event for the whole program. It is the primary source from which students evaluate the success of their design. Once the proof of concept for this simulator was tested and refined into a working prototype, the design team turned its focus back to creating the three component simulations. These simulations had to be carefully designed so that students could use what they learnt from the hands-on lab activities as well as their prior knowledge of photosynthesis and respiration to reason about the new problem context. This design approach was guided by the constructivist view of learning as a process of knowledge refinement and reorganization, not replacement (Schoenfeld, 1992).

The three component simulations are used primarily during the research phase. Guided activities introduce students to the simulations and the experimental procedures they model. These activities outline a number of experimental manipulations. The guided experiments provide students with a theoretical model and empirical data upon which to base future investigations. Students observe patterns and relationships they could use as the basis for more experiments. Additional exploration in the simulations is encouraged by providing a large number of simulation parameters beyond those outlined in the guided activities that could be set. Figure 3.2 provides a screen shot from one of the component simulators. It allows students to focus on one aspect of the conceptual model and one part of the biological life support processes – in this case, biomass production.

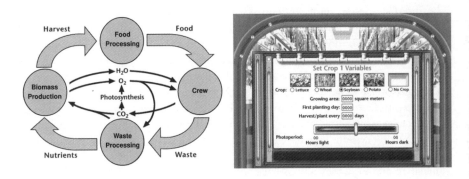

Figure 3.2   *This input screen from the Plant Production Simulator shows several parameters that affect plant growth*

The sequence of simulation exercises was designed to give students repeated practice using the simulators to complete problem-solving tasks. In these exercises students were required to look for patterns, relationships and underlying models they could use to explain the results of their test runs. At first, students interacted with the simulators via guided instructional exercises. Later, students used the simulators on their own to assess the outcomes of their hypothetical designs. This permitted students to focus on a particular part of the system without concern for the large number of interactions inherent in the complete system.

The BaBS simulator combines the components into a full-scale system. By the time students start the BaBS simulation, they are expected to have had experience with the component simulators and to be familiar with the concepts illustrated.

Students must be able to apply the data and strategies they've already acquired to set up a complete bioregenerative life support system. The BaBS simulation is more open-ended than the component simulations. Unlike the component simulations, no step-by-step guidelines are provided. Instead, students start with a descriptive overview of the six categories of input parameters that can be set (crew, crops, resource recycling, storage items, energy systems and food processing mechanisms).

The students' goal – design and test a model for a bioregenerative life support system that will keep a crew of six alive for at least three years without resupply – has thousands of possible solutions. In effect, students are generating their own unique data set each time they run the simulation, rather than relying on 'canned' data that are always the same. Further, each unsuccessful run requires an analysis of the output in order to modify the system parameters to reduce or eliminate previous problems in future designs. Simulation results can be exported to spreadsheet-format files for further data analysis and graphing with an application such as Excel™.

Examples of scientific reasoning and inquiry

The interface design starts students with a simple, arcade-style interactive game. They move to hypotheses-based, structured, simulator-based investigations and then to a model-building simulator that requires them to fit their ideas into an authentically designed, physically limited prototype system. Throughout this sequence, students have access to additional software tools, Internet-based resources and hands-on lab experiences. The 'research journal', a resource integrated into the software interface (shown in Figure 3.3) includes assignments that ask the students to reflect on what they have done and to visually conceptualize the relationships between living systems they have explored. From the virtual launch to return home, students have access to virtual mentors, library resources, a glossary and a research journal. In addition, they always have access to the simulators, which lets them test alternative model settings or compare output between the BaBS modelling system and component system settings.

The goal was to design software tools, interface design techniques and resources to give students repeated and diverse opportunities for guided practice with scientific inquiry experiences. The introductory experiences with the software allow students to interact with diverse media resources so that they experience the *big picture* of the overarching problem. Once students complete the research and mission phases, they use the resources and tools provided by the software interface to export data, graphics, observations and background research material. They then construct their final reports. In these they reflect on the models they designed and compile the results of the testing of their designs. They can export all their simulation settings and results from the research journal or directly from the simulators. The simulation set-up and results files can be imported into Excel™ or another spreadsheet program for review, analysis and graphing for presentation in the final report.

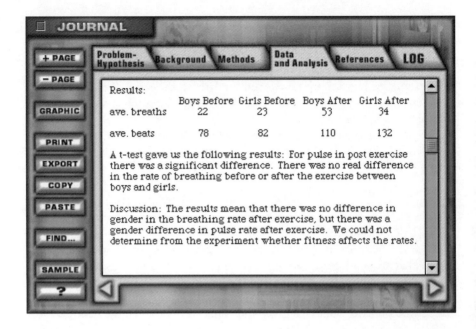

Figure 3.3 *The online research journal is a tool students use to guide and record their progress*

Refinements to design based on field testing

Refinement to problem-based learning

Teachers reported that students were interested in designing a biological life support system for a crew in space, but their interest greatly increased when they were using the BaBS simulator. Some teachers asked the design team whether there was a way to get the students to the model-building simulator without having to work through all the component simulator exercises. One software solution to this 'time crunch' problem was to design four 'samplers', which provide an abbreviated exploratory, research and model-building experience. Each of the four samplers has a content theme (plants, humans, resource recycling and integrated system) and is designed to be completed by students within five 40-minute class periods.

Refinement to designing cognitive guideposts

Teachers wanted the software to guide students more when they first started working through it. In response, the designers created a Launch Sequence that directs students through an introductory sequence of software experiences and that can be completed within a 40-minute class period.

Based on teachers' desire to guide students as they worked through the simulations, a discussion board was created for teachers. The 'whiteboard' is modelled after the message board scientists were using at NASA research centres to give short message updates across teams regarding the status of system tests. It gave teachers a similar capability to call attention to events or assignments (by group or by class). One teacher used the message board to communicate all assignments to her students. This feature functioned similarly to the research journal (shown in Figure 3.3) but was password protected so that the teacher could maintain control of what, to whom and when messages were posted.

The following adjustments were made to the simulator interface based on both observations of students using the simulators and suggestions from teachers who helped field-test the software with their classes:

- Students wanted more detailed text descriptions of failures that occurred with the BaBS modelling system. Additional information was provided that included tips for interpreting parameter settings.
- Teachers requested dynamically generated graphs in the component simulators so that students could see the data represented in line graphs as well as summary tables. In addition, the presentation format of the component simulator exercises was modified to match the hands-on laboratory activities so that students would easily see the connection between the hands-on labs and data output from the simulators.
- Teachers reported that students did not know how to use the research journal and that the teachers did not have time to individually address this problem. The beta and final versions of the program include sample journal entries as illustrated in Figure 3.3. Students could then see how other students used the journal and how observations could be summarized as journal entries.

Refinement to scientific reasoning and inquiry

From proof of concept to final published version, much time was spent modifying the presentation of exercises, guides and assignments to keep them manageable and doable within the school time frame. The more structured simulation exercises presented with the component simulations were trimmed so that they could be completed within a class period. Observation of classes using the program demonstrated across schools that a few students would master the introductory run almost straight away while other groups required all three class sessions to complete the basic criteria for success. Therefore, the guidelines and suggestions for running the modelling system were divided into two parts: a basic design, test and run procedure and an 'optimized run' procedure for more advanced students.

Summary and recommendations for future research

The virtual reality presentation of a problem scenario provided a way to support student inquiry through a process of whole-to-part-to-whole problem solving. The inquiry experiences offered via the simulation exercises guided students through ordered epistemological tasks to increasingly complex applications of the core scientific concepts. The structured exercises that accompanied the simulators moved students through interactive models of expert problem-solving strategies. Student experiences with the final model design and testing system required them to apply what they learnt from the component simulations and journal activities. Thus, the designers conclude that graphical, interactive simulations within the context of a carefully designed learning environment can be used to model scientific problem solving and promote scientific inquiry. We have three suggestions for future simulation designs.

First, incorporate use of dynamic assessment – a procedure that determines whether substantive changes occur in examinee behaviour if feedback is provided. This could help teachers and instructional systems developers better understand the learning potential of model-building programs. Using dynamic assessment exercises across networked learning environments offers increased opportunities for instructional designers and classroom teachers to gauge how students are progressing as they work in cooperative teams to complete a multitask challenge. The network assessment tools can also help students get some measure of how they are progressing in comparison with teacher expectations. This technique, according to Swanson and Lussier (2001), especially helps under-achieving learners.

Second, incorporate network e-learning tools. This offers potential for giving students some exposure to presenting their findings within a community of apprenticing scientists. Children and adults enjoy comparing and competing in networked games in which they can compare scores. The simulated model-building software also offers areas for sharing and comparing outcomes without giving away complete solutions. Adding a network-based 'scoreboard' in which students compare components of their design solutions would increase student competition and would motivate some gaming experts to get involved.

Third, for greater use of network learning environments, build electronic connections between teachers, both for professional development and for comparison of results using different teaching strategies (Cain, 1999). Throughout the development of software programs, teachers' input is crucial for design development and testing. Teachers also need continued opportunities to communicate with other teachers using the software and to be able to give feedback to the development team as new issues arise. Having an easy-to-use network discussion system would help new teachers as they implement a program for the first time and would also provide a dynamic documentation system for providing ongoing support for professional development, system support and system upgrades.

References

Bransford, J D, Brown, A L and Cocking, R R (2000) *How People Learn: Brain, mind, and school,* National Academy Press, Washington, DC

Brown, J S, Collins, A and Duguid, P (1989) Situated cognition and the culture of learning, *Educational Researcher,* **18,** pp 32–41

Cain, J (1999) Simulation-based learning activities in a hypermedia curriculum supplement for high school biology: a case study at NASA's classroom of the future. Unpublished doctoral dissertation, Florida Institute of Technology, Melbourne

Germann, P J, Aram, R and Burke, G (1996) Identifying patterns and relationships among the responses of seventh-grade students to the science process skill of designing experiments, *Journal of Research in Science Teaching,* **33** (1), pp 79–99

Hofer, B and Pintrich, P (1997) The development of epistemological theories: beliefs about knowledge and knowing and their relation to learning, *Review of Educational Research,* **67** (1), pp 88–140

Jacobson, M J, Maouri, C, Mishra, P A and Kolar, C (1996) Learning with hypertext learning environments: theory, design, and research, *Journal of Educational Multimedia and Hypermedia,* **5** (3/4), pp 239–81

Kuhn, D (1997) Constraints or guideposts? Developmental psychology and science education, *Review of Educational Research,* **67** (1), 141–50

Matthews, M R (2000) Appraising constructivism in science and mathematics education, in *Constructivism in Education: Opinions and second opinions on controversial issues: 99th yearbook of the National Society for the Study of Education,* ed D C Phillips, Pt 1, pp 161–92, University of Chicago, Chicago IL

National Research Council (1996) *National Science Education Standards,* National Academy Press, Washington, DC

Park, I and Hannafin, M J (1993) Empirically based guidelines for the design of interactive multimedia, *ETRandD,* **44** (3), pp 63–85

Penner, D E (2001) Cognition, computers, and synthetic science: building knowledge and meaning through modelling, in *Review of Research in Education,* ed W G Secada, **25,** pp 1–35, American Educational Research Association, Washington, DC

Schoenfeld, A (1992) Learning to think mathematically: problem solving, metacognition and sense making in mathematics, in *Handbook of Research on Mathematics Teaching and Learning,* ed D A Grouws, pp 334–70, Macmillan, New York

Swanson, H L and Lussier, C M (2001) A selective synthesis of the experimental literature on dynamic assessment, *Review of Educational Research,* **71** (21), pp 321–63

Chapter 4

Optimizing domain knowledge representation with multimedia objects

Kinshuk and Ashok Patel

Introduction

The success of the learning process in an educational system depends on how the system presents the domain knowledge to the learner and changes its presentation in terms of complexity and granularity according to learners' progress. Tutoring strategies are the major source of taking decisions regarding domain knowledge presentation. A set of effective and efficient tutoring strategies leads to the creation of educational frameworks.

The need for suitable educational frameworks in the use of multimedia technology in educational systems has been emphasized by many researchers. Educational software is expected to be not only a teaching and learning resource, but also a carrier of the instructional strategies (Adams *et al*, 1996). Therefore, the design of such a system and its presentation should consider learning theories and concepts, the pedagogies that apply to those concepts, and how they impact instructional design and practice. A large number of multimedia-based educational systems in current existence have placed too much emphasis on the affective and psychomotor aspects and lured the learner by using spectacular effects provided by images, animations, video and sound (Pham, 1997). In such systems, the emphasis has shifted from adequate learning outcomes and cognitive development, and the goal of knowledge acquisition seems to have diluted. It should not be assumed that simply adding a visual or audio component will enhance learning (Ellis, 2001).

Multimedia technology can contribute to the success of learning only if it can adequately represent the tasks and concepts of the domain knowledge. The Multiple Representation (MR) approach, presented in this chapter, is predominantly dependent on the framework of tutoring strategies in which it is being applied. This research work is focused on task-oriented disciplines where the major requirement is the acquisition of cognitive skills. The next section discusses the application of multimedia technology in cognitive skills acquisition and proceeds to discuss the implementation of MR approach under a Cognitive Apprenticeship framework.

Multimedia and cognitive skills

The use of multimedia objects such as pictures, animations and simulations in educational systems can enhance the efficacy of the system to present domain knowledge or domain competence. Various multimedia objects may facilitate various requirements of different learning tasks. However, just collecting and integrating multimedia objects in a system does not guarantee adequate learning (Rogers *et al*, 1995).

In the area of cognitive skills, the use of various multimedia objects in a suitable educational framework may satisfy different learning needs, which arise at different stages of cognitive skills acquisition. The Cognitive Apprenticeship framework (Collins *et al*, 1989) provides one such effective path. According to the Cognitive Apprenticeship framework:

- learners can study task-solving patterns of experts to develop their own cognitive model of the domain, ie about the tasks, tools and solutions (*modelling*);
- learners can solve tasks on their own by consulting a tutorial component (*coaching*);
- tutoring activity of the system is gradually reduced with the learners' improving performances and problem solving (*fading*).

Various tasks and stages of the Cognitive Apprenticeship framework have different requirements from a learning point of view and consequently they need different multimedia objects for learners' interaction with the domain content.

Multimedia objects and the Cognitive Apprenticeship framework

The first step in Cognitive Apprenticeship is the observation phase, where the learner observes the task pattern of an expert. Within a system, realization of receptive exploration is possible through reading of text, observing a picture, watching a video or animation (Payne *et al,* 1992), and listening to audio clips. Once the learner has basic understanding and is motivated for further complex observations, the system can provide the opportunity through image maps, interactive videos and pictorial virtual reality (VR) scenarios, where the learner actively engages in the observation process.

After the observation phase, the learner is required to imitate the observed tasks to get skills. Simulations and interactive flowcharts can provide an adaptive environment where learners can imitate the tasks under a system's expert guidance.

Table 4.1 presents examples of multimedia objects suitable for different tasks under Cognitive Apprenticeship framework. The list in the table is not exhaustive.

Table 4.1   *Tasks in cognitive skills acquisition and related multimedia objects*

Requirement	Example of suitable multimedia objects
Observation (receptive)	Text, Static pictures, Animations, Video, Audio
Observation (active)	Image maps, User controlled animations, Textual links, Interactive videos, pictorial VR
Exploration (imitation)	Simulations, Flowcharts

Given the variety of multimedia objects available for various tasks, it is not easy to select adequate objects in a particular context. A task becomes even more difficult when there is a need to integrate various objects for domain representation, or the objects are required to act as navigational aids within the system. The MR approach provides guidelines for manipulation of multimedia objects and ensures that the domain representation confirms the educational perspective of the system and facilitates adequate learning.

The MR approach

The MR approach tackles the presentation of domain content in three ways: multimedia objects selection; navigational objects selection; and integration of multimedia objects.

Multimedia objects selection

The MR approach facilitates the presentation of domain content to the learner with suitable multimedia objects as and when required according to the learner's current level of domain competence. Various recommendations are described below.

Task specificity and learner's competence

According to the MR approach, the selection of multimedia objects should be based on the tasks to be carried out. Different multimedia objects are suitable for fulfilling different purposes and tasks. For example, audio is good for stimulating imagination, video clips for providing action information, text for conveying details, whereas diagrams are good for conveying ideas (Alty, 1991). The selection of objects should also consider the level of the learner's domain competence in the current situation. For this purpose, the curriculum should follow a granular structure so that the measurement of competence level and allotment of tasks should be carried out on individual units (Adams *et al*, 1996). For example, an abstract concept could be introduced with the help of an animation of a concrete instance of the concept (Rogers and Scaife, 1997). This would facilitate a reduction in cognitive load on the novice learner. Later on, at a higher level of abstraction, the representations could be more complex requiring more cognitive processing.

Expectations

The selection of multimedia objects should take into account the expectations of the learner and the domain knowledge. For example, a learner who is looking for an overview of middle ear structure may expect to see just a graphic representation, but from the subject matter domain's point of view, textual details are also necessary to emphasize some intricate details. The system, in that case, should try to present graphical representation along with intricate textual details.

Reference and revisits of already learnt domain content

In the process of learning it is necessary and desirable to refer to already learnt domain content in different contexts. Spiro *et al* (1991) claimed that 'revisiting the same material, at different times, in re-arranged contexts, for different purposes, and from different conceptual perspectives is essential for attaining the goals of advanced knowledge acquisition'. The MR approach favours revisiting the same domain content in different contexts. The multimedia objects used in each case depend on the context although, if possible, the use of similar multimedia objects is favoured since it puts less cognitive overload on the user. Reference to previously learnt material provides the following advantages:

- it enforces links between concepts (the one currently being learnt and the referred one);
- it enhances the mental model of the previously learnt concept and helps in generalizing its applicability in multiple situated scenarios;
- it provides ease in learning the current concept by making familiarization with past learning experiences.

Use of multi-sensory channels

The selection of objects should adequately use the visual, aural and tactile senses of the learner. If any of the sensory channels is not being used at the time of learning, the chances of getting distraction due to this channel are high (Bagui, 1998).

Context based selection of multimedia objects

When there are more than one multimedia objects available for representation of the same task or concept, some of them would be more suitable for representation in a particular context than in another. The presentation should then use the most suitable object in the context. For example, a simulation permits learner interaction with the objects on the screen (Figure 4.1), and is appropriate for those who are learning about this subject for the first time. On the other hand, a more experienced learner might want to review the concepts without having to physically execute each simulation. In this case, a text-based multimedia object would be more appropriate (Rogers *et al*, 1995).

Authenticity of multimedia objects

The learner should be aware of the authenticity of the multimedia objects (Laurel *et al*, 1992). For example, schematic diagrams and animations of the processes may not show the real objects but they are helpful in understanding the underlying processes. The system should keep the learner aware of the authenticity of the representation by suitable messages. For example, learners can first learn about the basics of tympanic membrane using the simplified Figure 4.2(a) to get ready for the intricate details in Figure 4.2(b), but while showing Figure 4.2(a), the learner should be made aware that this figure is a simplified form of the actual membrane.

Navigational objects selection

The navigation in typical educational systems takes place through various links provided in the system. Rada (1995) pointed out that the link does not say what happens to the screen when the user activates the link. The important point to consider is the proper match of the learner's expectations of outcome while activating a link with the presentation of actual resulting interface connected to the link.

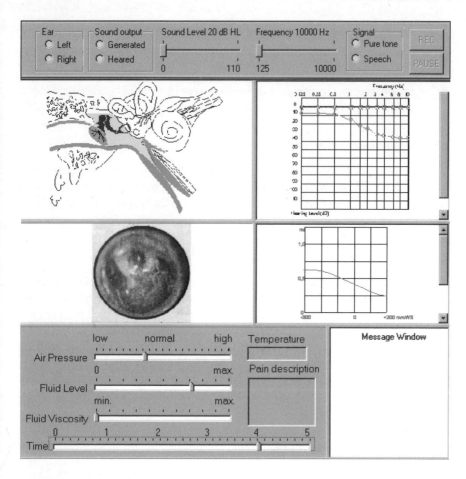

Figure 4.1 *Simulation of middle ear disease*

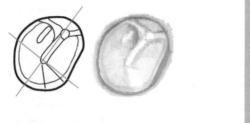

a. *Simplified view*   **b.** *Complete details*

Figure 4.2 *Tympanic membrane*

According to the MR approach, the selection of links should not detract the learner's attention from the main task of learning. The existence of a link should appear to the learner as transparent as possible. The MR approach identifies six types of navigational links concerning learning processes under the Cognitive Apprenticeship framework:

1. *Direct successor link* leads to the successive domain unit in the knowledge hierarchy. Such transfer should arise from current context, for example, the link to Ossicles-Incus in the bottom left message window in Figure 4.3.
2. *Parallel concept link* leads to the analogous domain unit for comparative learning or to the unit related to another aspect of the domain content currently being learnt. For example, clicking on the left side bones in Figure 4.3 will bring the user to that particular bone's unit. The learning of one bone does not automatically require transfer to another bone, but being analogous, it is helpful for the understanding if these bones are studied together.
3. *Fine grained unit link* leads to the fine details of the domain content once some missing information or misconceptions are identified in learners' understanding (Patel and Kinshuk, 1997). These transfers are very contextual and it is necessary to maintain the context during transfer. For example, double clicking on the highlighted Stapedius in the graphic of Figure 4.3 will lead to the fine-grained unit describing Stapedius in detail.
4. *Glossary link* leads to a pop-up 'spring loaded' module (Nielsen, 1996) in exploration process, which is available only while the learner is interested in it and is explicitly doing something to keep it active (such as pressing the mouse button).
5. *Excursion link* leads to a learning unit outside the current context (Kashihara *et al,* 1997). Excursion links are used to provide related learning of current context but the context in such case would not be as narrow as a term or a part of a picture.
6. *Problem links* lead to problems related to the current conceptual unit.

Different types of links should be clearly identified for their types (Benyon *et al,* 1997) and their representations should be consistent throughout the system.

Integration of multimedia objects

In many situations the presentation of the domain content demands more than one multimedia object at a time on the screen for suitable representation. There have also been many studies showing improvement in learning through more than one multimedia object for the same domain content compared to a single object. For example, Palmiter *et al* (1991) favoured the multi-sensory reception of instruction by suggesting that the presentation should include verbal, visual and motoric components. But not all possible combinations of multimedia objects are adequate from a learning point of view. Consideration should be given to how best to combine multiple multimedia objects in relation to different learning tasks (Rogers

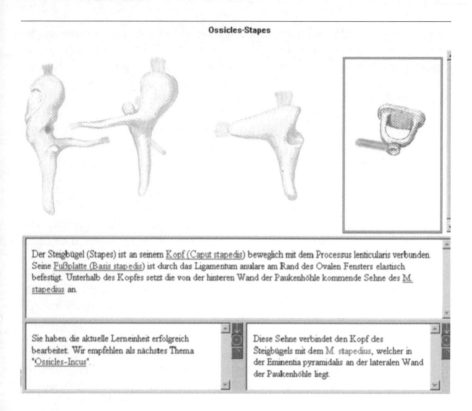

Ossicles-Stapes

Der Steigbügel (Stapes) ist an seinem Kopf (Caput stapedis) beweglich mit dem Processus lenticularis verbunden. Seine Fußplatte (Basis stapedis) ist durch das Ligamentum anulare am Rand des Ovalen Fensters elastisch befestigt. Unterhalb des Kopfes setzt die von der hinteren Wand der Paukenhöhle kommende Sehne des M. stapedius an.

Sie haben die aktuelle Lerneinheit erfolgreich bearbeitet. Wir empfehlen als nächstes Thema "Ossicles-Incus".

Diese Sehne verbindet den Kopf des Steigbügels mit dem M. stapedius, welcher in der Eminentia pyramidalis an der lateralen Wand der Paukenhöhle liegt.

Figure 4.3   *Various types of navigational objects*

and Scaife, 1997). Below are some recommendations regarding integration of multimedia objects to be observed during the design process of educational systems within the Cognitive Apprenticeship framework:

- There should not be more than one observation multimedia object at a time on the screen. The exception is the comparative study of two actions, where more than one active observation is recommended.
- The integration of multimedia objects should be complementary to each other and should be synchronized (IBM, 1991). For example, audio narration along with a diagram should direct the learner towards the salient parts of the diagram (Rogers and Scaife, 1997). Care should also be taken not to present the same material with more than one multimedia object.
- Decision-intensive objects such as flowcharts demand high cognitive loading. Therefore integration of such objects with any other multimedia object is not recommended.
- Integration of dynamic observation objects (such as animations) with static observation objects (such as text) should be such that the learner should not be forced to observe both of them by the same sensory channel at the same time.

The MR approach is implemented in the InterSim system described below.

The InterSim system

The InterSim system aims to facilitate competence in the subject matter by providing basic and advanced knowledge of the domain as well as associated cognitive skills. The Cognitive Apprenticeship framework (Collins *et al*, 1989) is adopted in the system for supporting learning. The InterSim system covers three areas of ear domain:

1. auditory system – structure, functionality and pathology of the ear;
2. physics of sound – basic and advance physics of sound related to the auditory system; and
3. audiometric measurements – various graphs and diagrams related to the auditory system and their interpretations.

In this way the system has its main focus on the auditory system and other areas are provided for better understanding of the main area. The learning state in the system is divided into four conceptual sub-processes to reflect the various stages of the Cognitive Apprenticeship framework:

1. coarse grained instruction dominated learning;
2. fine-grained knowledge construction;
3. cognitive skills development; and
4. application of the acquired knowledge and skills.

The MR approach in the InterSim system

The MR approach is used for domain representation in various states and sub-processes of the InterSim system as described below.

Multimedia objects selection

To select the appropriate multimedia objects for various parts of the system, the educational objectives served by each sub-process of the InterSim system are examined under the Cognitive Apprenticeship framework, as shown in Table 4.2.

Various multimedia objects are then selected on the basis of the educational objectives described in Table 4.2. The following section describes the rationale for using various multimedia objects based on the application of MR approach under the Cognitive Apprenticeship framework.

The receptive and active observation of the subject domain starts with the help of static pictures along with corresponding text. Three types of static pictures are

Table 4.2 *Educational objectives served by various states and sub-processes in the InterSim system*

States and sub-processes	Educational objective
Coarse grained instruction dominated learning	➤ Receptive and active observation of structure and functionality of healthy ear ➤ Observation of simple physics related to auditory system ➤ Observation of graphs and diagrams related to auditory system
Fine grained knowledge construction	➤ Exploration of structure and functionality of healthy ear ➤ Excursions to auditory system related topics in physics of sound and audiometric measurements ➤ Observation of diseases of ear
Cognitive skills development	➤ Exploration and diagnosis of diseases of ear ➤ Interpretation of graphs and diagrams related to auditory system
Application of the acquired knowledge and skills	➤ Learning by problem solving of healthy ear and diseases of the ear ➤ Repetitive training by practice in multiple contexts

used: normal static pictures, static pictures with sensitive parts (similar to image maps), and static pictures with semi-sensitive parts. Sensitive parts in the pictures represent those domain objects that are in the current domain hierarchy and are part of the current learning goal. Such objects respond for mouse over, single click and double click mouse actions. Semi-sensitive parts are those parts that do not belong to the current domain hierarchy but are explained somewhere else in the system. They are not part of the current learning goal. These objects react only to double click mouse actions and provide information about how to change the current learning goal and access the corresponding domain hierarchy to get more information on that part.

The next stage in the receptive observation process deals with the dynamic and functional behaviour of ear parts in the InterSim system. Animations are used in the system for such representations. They provide a close look at the effects that cannot be seen or are difficult to visualize in the real world (Towne, 1995). The animations are considered not as the art of *drawings*-that-move but as the art of *movements*-that-are-drawn (Baecker and Small, 1990). What happens between each frame is more important than what exists on each frame. Three types of animations are used in the InterSim system:

1. Regular phenomena are described with the help of *automatic animations*. Such animations run on their own without requiring any learner intervention and show the events in continuous loops.
2. Random or explicit actions (such as swallowing) within a running series of actions are explained with the help of *user-controlled animations*. In these animations, learners see a continuous regular action and they can generate a particular event by taking some explicit action (for example, pressing a button).
3. In situations where the initial state is static and an instantaneous action leads to a whole series of actions, *user-initiated animations* are used. Learners initially see the animation stopped in its starting position, and explicit action on the part of the learner leads to running the animation to show the complete process.

Once the learners have observed a phenomenon in an animation, simulations are provided to the learners for the acquisition of competence in skills. Simulations are helpful for the training of operational skills where the learners can apply the declarative and procedural knowledge acquired previously (Yacef and Alem, 1996). Learners can explore various scenarios and can get feedback on their actions.

To provide a more realistic learning environment where necessary (such as the structure of an organ or part of an organ), pictorial virtual reality (VR), also known as 'desktop VR' (Hobbs and Moore, 1994) is used, which presents and allows manipulation of three-dimensional objects and scenes. VR conveys reality through the computer hence eliminating the need to use metaphors in the learning process that fall short of reality and force the learner to make an internal translation in order to use the system successfully (Hobbs and Moore, 1994).

Even more realistic cases are provided with the help of videos, which show the actual phenomena in their reality, for example, a video sequence of treatment of a particular disease on a human patient.

Decision-making skills are also provided to the learners with the help of various flowcharts. Flowcharts represent and identify graphically the sequencing process, and the options and conditions that affect the execution of the domain content representation (Lara and Perez-Luque, 1996). In particular, flowcharts are used for observation and exploration of the diagnosis and treatment of various diseases by the students.

Navigational objects selection

In the InterSim system the navigation methods are selected following the MR approach. For example, in the partial screen of the Ossicle Chain learning unit in Figure 4.4, the navigation panel on the left side provides various combo boxes for explicit navigation among various learning units. The ossicle chain picture on the right behaves as an image map to allow navigation to successor units. The textual links pop-up glossary window explains the terms.

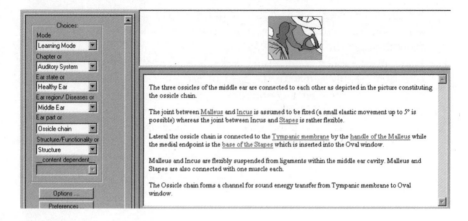

Figure 4.4   *Screen shot of ossicle chain learning unit in the InterSim ear system*

Integration of multimedia objects

The InterSim system follows the MR approach in integrating multimedia objects for domain content representation. For example, the concept of 'appropriate sound energy routing' is presented by two comparative animations. On another occasion, the structure of ossicles required representation both as a static picture and as pictorial VR. Since both multimedia objects have similar initial visual states (not recommended by the MR approach for simultaneous use) they are used as alternatives and the learner can explicitly switch between the two without being confused due to their initial similar states.

Concluding comment

Domain knowledge representation in learning systems requires adaptation to the needs and competence of the learners, and the specific attributes of the domain. Although multimedia technology provides an effective solution for representing the domain knowledge, serious consideration of educational pedagogy is required in the use of such objects for effective learning processes. The multiple representation approach described in this chapter attempts to guide the use of multimedia in learning systems. It provides recommendations for the selection of multimedia objects for content representation, navigational objects representation and integration of multimedia objects. The approach has been implemented in the InterSim system prototype that is designed for learning human ear structure and functionality.

References

Adams, E S, Carswell, L, Ellis, A, Hall, P, Kumar, A, Meyer, J and Motil, J (1996) Interactive multimedia pedagogies: report of the working group on interactive multimedia pedagogy, *Sigcue Outlook,* **24** (1, 2 and 3), pp 182–91

Alty, J L (1991) Multimedia – what is it and how do we exploit it?, in *People and Computers IV,* eds D Diaper and N Hammond, pp 31–46, Cambridge University Press, Cambridge

Baecker, R and Small, I (1990) Animation at the interface, in *The Art of Human-computer Interface Design,* ed B Laurel, pp 251–67, Addison-Wesley, Reading, MA

Bagui, S (1998) Reasons for increased learning using multimedia, *Journal of Educational Multimedia and Hypermedia,* **7** (1), pp 3–18

Benyon, D, Stone, D and Woodroffe, M (1997) Experience with developing multimedia courseware for the World Wide Web: the need for better tools and clear pedagogy, *International Journal of Human-Computer Studies,* **47,** pp 197–218

Collins, A, Brown, J S and Newman, S E (1989) Cognitive apprenticeship: teaching the crafts of reading, writing and mathematics, in *Knowing, Learning and Instruction,* ed L B Resnick, pp 453–94, Lawrence Erlbaum, Hillsdale, NJ

Ellis, T J (2001) Multimedia enhanced educational products as a tool to promote critical thinking in adult students, *Journal of Educational Multimedia and Hypermedia,* **10** (2), 107–23

Hobbs, D and Moore, D (1994) LMU experiences with design of computer-based multimedia learning systems. Paper presented at the Workshop on Complex Learning in Computer Environments, May, University of Joensuu, Finland

IBM (1991) *SAA CUA Guide to User Interface Design,* IBM Corporation, North Carolina

Kashihara, A, Kinshuk, Oppermann, R, Rashev, R and Simm, H (1997) An exploration space control as intelligent assistance in enabling systems, in *International Conference on Computers in Education Proceedings,* eds Z Halim, T Ottmann and Z Razak, pp 114–21, AACE, Virginia

Lara, S and Perez-Luque, M J (1996) Designing educational multimedia, *Lecture Notes in Computer Science,* **1108,** pp 288–97

Laurel, B, Oren, T and Don, A (1992) Issues in multimedia design: media integration and interface agents, in *Multimedia Interface Design,* eds M M Blattner and R B Dannenberg, pp 53–64, ACM Press, New York

Nielsen, J (1996) Features missing in current web browsers. Accessed February 2002, from http://wwwsuncom/950701/columns/alertbox/newfeatureshtml

Palmiter, S, Elkerton, J and Baggett, P (1991) Animated demonstrations vs written instructions for learning procedural tasks: a preliminary investigation, *International Journal of Man-Machine Studies,* **34,** pp 687–701

Patel, A and Kinshuk (1997) Granular interface design: decomposing learning tasks and enhancing tutoring interaction, in *Advances in Human Factors/Ergonomics Design of Computing Systems: Social and ergonomic considerations,* eds M J Smith, G Salvendy and R J Koubek, pp 161–4, Elsevier Science, Amsterdam

Payne, S J, Chesworth, L and Hill, E (1992) Animated demonstrations for exploratory learners, *Interacting with Computers,* **4** (1), pp 3–22

Pham, B (1997) Development of educational multimedia systems. Paper presented at the Australasian Association for Engineering Education, 9th Annual Convention and Conference, December, Ballarat, Australia

Rada, R (1995) Hypertext, multimedia and hypermedia, in *The New Review of Hypermedia and Multimedia,* ed P Baird, pp 1–21, Taylor Graham, London

Rogers, E, Kennedy, Y, Walton, T, Nelms, P and Sherry, I (1995) Intelligent multimedia tutoring for manufacturing education. Paper presented at Frontiers in Education Conference, November, Atlanta, GA

Rogers, Y and Scaife, M (1997) How can interactive multimedia facilitate learning? Accessed 3 February 2002, from http://wwwcogssusxacuk/users/yvonner/ecoihome/IMMIhtml

Spiro, R J, Feltovitch, P J, Jacobson, M J and Coulson, R J (1991) Cognitive flexibility, constructivism and hypertext: random access instruction for advanced knowledge acquisition in ill-structured domains, *Educational Technology,* **31** (5), pp 24–33

Towne, D M (1995) *Learning and Instruction in Simulation Environments,* Educational Technology Publications, Englewood Cliffs, NJ

Yacef, K and Alem, L (1996) Student and expert modeling for simulation-based training: a cost-effective framework, *Lecture Notes in Computer Science,* **1086,** pp 614–22

Part 2

Activation of learning

Chapter 5

Using interactive video-based multimedia to scaffold learning in teacher education

John Baird

Introduction

The purpose of this chapter is to show how information technology – expressly interactive, video-based multimedia – can enhance teacher education by stimulating intending teachers to engage more effectively in the process of productive professional learning.

The chapter centres on a discussion of the philosophical, conceptual and methodological bases for an interactive, video-based CD ROM program entitled 'QuILT: Quality in Learning and Teaching', developed for core professional studies subjects in three courses in the Faculty of Education, University of Melbourne. These courses are the four-year Bachelor of Education (Primary), the one-year Diploma in Education and the two-year Bachelor of Teaching. These bases will involve various theoretical perspectives, including situated cognition, cognitive apprenticeship, metacognition and guided reflection, and scaffolding of three main types (conceptual, metacognitive, and strategic). Then, some key metaphors that

...gn and navigation are described, in order to emphasize their
...ing cognitive and affective engagement and activation of
...gramme of teacher education.

...ultimedia within teacher education

In an environment of diminishing budgets and worsening staff-student ratios in
university faculties of education, teacher educators are increasingly pressed to
incorporate information and communications technology (ICT) within pre-service
education subjects. The nature of incorporation of ICT can vary depending on its
role in the subject. A 'passive', information-provision role is when examples of
recent software used in the school curriculum are presented to students, or when
ICT is used simply to deliver subject content. A more 'active' role for ICT is when
it is used to train students in its effective use in teaching or, as is the case in this
chapter, when it is used to drive change in students' thinking, feeling and acting
about their teaching and their students' learning.

Perceptions vary considerably regarding the extent and effectiveness of incorporation of ICT within teacher education courses. On the one hand it has been argued
that, notwithstanding the 'IT revolution' that has occurred over the decade, teacher
education and classroom teaching approaches and strategies often remain quite
traditional (eg, Albion, 2000) and teacher education is yet to benefit adequately
from ICT advances (Davis, 1997; Schrum and Dehoney, 1998). On the other hand
there is no doubt that, with the accelerating push to embed the 'digital revolution'
within university teaching courses, multimedia programs of increasing quality are
being designed.

Debate continues regarding the extent to which ICT should be incorporated
into, transform, or replace, more traditional instructional approaches (eg, Marx *et
al,* 1998; Willis, 1997). As one aspect of this debate, it has been argued that the
technology of new multimedia programs has sometimes overshadowed their
educational rationale and learning principles (eg, Brown *et al,* 1996). That is, the
affordances and constraints of the technology itself may drive the nature of the new
programs, rather than servicing them. In order to achieve genuine improvement
in educational quality, consideration must first be given to course aims, processes
and outcomes and then to how ICT may help realize these features. Such course
aims will be considered next.

Pre-service teachers should leave their course of professional preparation having
the confidence and competence to take informed responsibility and control over
their own teaching practice. In order to do this, they need to have assumed a basis
for principled action – action based upon personal values, beliefs, intentions and
purposes that are defensible, feasible and, above all, personally appropriate.
Elsewhere, I have argued that quality teaching and learning should centre on a
process of purposeful inquiry, comprising reflection (asking evaluative questions)
and action (to find out answers to these questions) (Baird 1991a, 1991b, 1999). An

outcome of this process of purposeful inquiry is productive metacognition regarding personal practice. I define metacognition in teaching as comprising three components (Baird, 1991a):

1. metacognitive knowledge – knowledge of the nature of teaching, of effective teaching techniques and strategies, and of personal teaching characteristics and habits;
2. metacognitive awareness – as I teach, understanding what I am doing and why I am doing it;
3. metacognitive control – based on this awareness, making productive decisions about my teaching and my students' learning.

As is described below, the QuILT program was directed to enhancing users' metacognition in teaching through a process of purposeful inquiry, centred on reflection and guided by various design and procedural components of the program.

General features of QuILT

QuILT: Quality In Learning and Teaching, has formed the basis for study in each course for the last three years, used each year by a total of over 800 students. As described above, its aim is to assist intending teachers to develop personal conceptions of quality in learning and teaching and to apply these developing conceptions to their own professional practice. The two-disk program contains over 300 QuickTime video clips of authentic classroom teaching and learning episodes and associated teacher and pupil interviews. The episodes are situated in six classes taught by seven teachers in one elementary school and one secondary school. The classes encompass 11 years of schooling – from the preparatory year to year 10. QuILT represents everyday, authentic classroom practices of practising teachers; its purpose is not to present scripted episodes of exemplary teaching.

In each of the three years, the program has been revised to improve aspects of program architecture, navigation and instructional clarity, but the aims and conceptual underpinnings of the program remain unchanged.

Philosophical, conceptual and procedural underpinning of the QuILT program

Constructivism

QuILT is based on a constructivist epistemology and its design reflects a funda-mental philosophical position regarding the nature of effective learning. This epistemological position is grounded in the belief that quality learning and teaching are fundamentally pluralist and relativist in nature (eg, Alexander, 1996; Baird, 1989). The position eschews the notion that there is one correct, or even best, way to teach or to learn, independent of the content or the human, societal, physical, or temporal context. Thus, looking for the 'right answer' (indeed, any simple answer to any complex question) by applying convergent, hypothetico-deductive thinking is usually inappropriate and unproductive. As there are potentially many ways to teach well, and teaching well in one subject, context or for certain purposes does not necessarily apply to other, different teaching conditions, the program fosters inductive logic to help the user explore, illuminate, articulate and justify a personal view of quality.

Situated cognition and cognitive apprenticeship

Situated cognition stresses the importance of learners observing and purposefully sharing the practices, contexts and culture in which concepts are located. Brown *et al* (1989) detail how 'knowing and doing' are frequently treated in education communities as separate entities, with 'doing' greatly undervalued in favour of beliefs that knowledge can be abstracted from the settings in which it is learnt and used. Situative theories of thinking, learning and knowledge argue that such conceptions of learning are reductive. A situative perspective posits that knowledge is most meaningfully understood when experienced through authentic contexts and authentic activities (Brown *et al*, 1989; Lave and Wenger, 1991).

Putnam and Borko (2000) acknowledge the roots of what is increasingly known as the 'situative perspective' in the work of Dewey and Vygotsky, and provide a summary of the perspective as three conceptual themes. These three themes emphasize that 'cognition is (a) situated in particular physical and social contexts; (b) social in nature; and (c) distributed across the individual, other persons, and tools' (p 4). For the situated theme, they emphasize the requirement for authentic activities; for the social aspect, they review research that highlights the need for 'enculturating students into various discourse communities' (p 5) and helping students learn how to learn; for the distributed aspect, they argue for a move away from individual competencies and recognition that cognition is shared across other individuals and the tools needed to achieve success. They consider the implications of the situative perspective for the learning of both pre-service and practising teachers, where cases 'provide shared experiences for teachers to examine together, using multiple perspectives and frameworks. . . (where some) interactive multi-media cases and hypermedia environments have the potential to provide even richer sets of materials documenting classroom teaching and learning' (p 8).

Metacognition, guided reflection and scaffolding

Asking evaluative questions and determining answers, and identifying problems and devising and managing solutions, are crucial competencies that cohere professional thinking, feeling and acting. These competencies require scaffolding. As noted elsewhere (McLoughlin *et al,* 2000), scaffolding of learning in QuILT takes three main forms: metacognitive scaffolding, conceptual scaffolding and strategic scaffolding.

Metacognition has its roots in Dewey's (1933) notion of learning to think, a process involving active monitoring, critical evaluation and purposeful seeking of meanings and relationships. Above, I related a process of reflection (based on asking evaluative questions and then determining answers to these questions) and an outcome of metacognition (as knowledge about, and awareness and control over, personal practice). Two seemingly conflicting features of QuILT are central to program design and manner of operation. These features are user metacognitive control and scaffolding of learning through guided reflection.

The first feature is that the user determines the nature and extent of approach, progress and outcome based upon personal needs, concerns and interests. Throughout the program, the user remains metacognitively in control, determining which video sequences to consider, in what order, and to what extent each is analysed. No 'theory' is presented directly anywhere in the program. Only when the user has formulated tentative values, beliefs, or perspectives by interacting with the program is 'theory' introduced through class discussion, lecture or assigned reading.

The second feature, however, is that video episodes and sequences are structured to foster a process of guided reflection by which key ideas and issues are progressively clarified and thus learning is scaffolded through enhanced metacognitive awareness and control.

Three aspects of the program contribute to this metacognitive scaffolding: screen questions, lenses and notepad. The user works through the program in the nature, manner and extent desired, but is continually confronted with screen questions that challenge understandings and invite links to personal prior knowledge and belief systems. The user is encouraged to attend to and clarify the problem or issue from different perspectives by returning to the classroom episode using the four different lenses. The electronic notepad enables users to record their thinking and feeling as they engage with the episodes, and induce educational principles from the specifics of the episode.

Two other sorts of scaffolding are attendant upon this metacognitive scaffolding. The process of inductive logic fosters conceptual scaffolding, where key concepts are generated actively by the user and then subjected to review and critique. Guiding principles for practice then build upon these key concepts. Strategic scaffolding occurs where alternative scenarios for development of classroom actions and events are provided. The user judges the effectiveness of each of these scenarios and uses this information to formulate strategic plans for dealing with each scenario.

According to this view, quality derives from coherence among the three aspects shown, so that thinking, feeling and acting are integrated, purposeful and productive. As already mentioned, this conception of quality allows for different representations of particular thoughts, feelings and actions, depending on the individuals concerned, the nature and purposes of the learning and teaching involved, and other contextual and societal features. Thus, quality is not defined by the actual knowledge, values and beliefs that are held, the intentions and purpose that are sought, or the approaches and practices that are enacted. What defines quality is the awareness and control of these aspects of personal practice that arise from their considered integration. This conception of quality that underpins QuILT is represented in the central metaphor of construction of a patchwork QuILT, and it is further imbued in the structural and procedural metaphors that direct the user's approach to and progress through the program, all of which is discussed next.

Metaphors used to frame the QuILT program

Overall metaphor of quilt construction

The goal of QuILT is represented metaphorically as a finished patchwork quilt: a metaphor for the user's coherent personal view of quality in teaching. It integrates the major aspects of teaching and learning, and comprises patches of nine types, each of which is a major 'Focus Area' or topic covered in the program, discussed below.

Construction of a patchwork quilt is considered a helpful metaphor to frame progress towards quality of personal pedagogical thinking, feeling and acting. A quilt is created through the weaving of fibres to produce material from which the patches are made, and the construction and then combination of these patches to create a harmonious and distinctive product. Quilt construction involves individual expertise, interpersonal and collaborative endeavour, societal norms and mores, and contextual and physical constraints that all come together to produce a product with both aesthetic and functional value. All stages of quilt construction involve purposeful thinking, feeling and acting. Constructing a considered, coherent position regarding personal professional practice involves similar attributes and processes.

Structural metaphor: patches of the quilt

As teacher education students move through the QuILT program they encounter a range of 'Focus Areas', or major topics, related to classroom learning and teaching. Metaphorically, each of these Focus Areas is a patch of the quilt (see Figure 5.1). As the user moves through the Focus Areas (in the manner and in the order that he or she chooses), opportunities are provided to link insights, conceptions or strategies in different areas, by which process the patches metaphorically are stitched together.

The nine Focus Areas featured in QuILT include such central components of pedagogy as 'Planning units for learning', 'Development of learners' and 'Questioning for learning'. When using Focus Area 4, 'Student and classroom management', for example, users analyse diverse classroom scenarios depicted in over 50 video clips. This analysis aims to interpret activities and behaviours, predict what actions might follow certain key points or critical episodes, propose and justify actions they

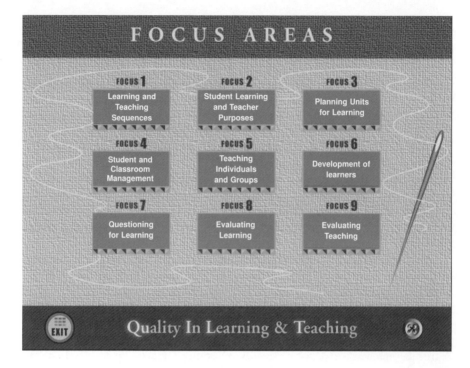

Figure 5.1   *Focus areas in QuILT*

would take themselves in such a situation, and draw inferences and conclusions about worthwhile, feasible teaching strategies that foster effective classroom learning. Throughout, the user infers the effectiveness and desirability of classroom actions and determines methods to employ in future personal practice.

Making and stitching the patches: balancing individual and group endeavour

The interdependent relationship between individual and group endeavour both in patchwork quilt construction and the operation of the QuILT program is the basis for this feature of the program.

While the goal of QuILT is essentially personal – a position regarding the nature of quality, generated through the program – the critical importance of groups for testing the viability of new understandings through interaction with peers (eg, Savery and Duffy, 1995) requires that collaborative work is an integral part of the program.

Each student is required to prepare for weekly class sessions by completing the Focus Area that is the topic for that week. For this preparation, the student inserts entries within an electronic notepad (outlined below), built into the program. The printout of this notepad is then brought to the face-to-face class session, where the entries are discussed, as outlined next.

Class work in the teacher education subjects in which QuILT is used is organized in student groups of approximately 30 students. Each class group is further divided into 'syndicate groups' of five to six students. Much of the class work is done through collaborative learning in these syndicate groups. In a given week, for instance, members of each syndicate group may be required to prepare a task for joint completion and presentation to the whole class group. This task usually requires the syndicate group to share and discuss diverse points of view arising from the QuILT Focus Area and summarized in their notepads, and decide upon and defend a consensual position regarding an aspect of the topic. In most class sessions, the lecturer displays selected segments of QuILT through data display in order to structure discussion and, when appropriate, to scaffold students' understandings by linking to relevant theory. Once again returning to the program's primary metaphor of quilt-making, collaboration is reinforced as an enabling condition for constructing the harmonious and coherent patterns and relationships that distinguish quality.

Next, three additional operational metaphors used in QuILT will be considered, in order to elaborate the philosophical and conceptual underpinnings of the program.

Operational metaphor: magnifying glass

A user begins work in a Focus Area by observing a video clip of the classroom actions of school pupils and their teacher. Metaphorically, the user opens the door to a teacher's classroom, and closely examines what is occurring within (Figure 5.2). Thus, a magnifying glass is presented as an operational metaphor for this process of close examination of people and events. Operated via a standard VCR type controller, users can play, replay or pause each clip as required and thus examine classroom episodes closely and methodically.

Through screen questions, the user is prompted to reflect upon the classroom sequence and assume a personal position regarding the extent to which it illustrates worthwhile and effective learning and teaching. Thus, screen questions are a stimulus for the user to induce from the specifics of the classroom episodes more general principles for personal thinking, feeling and acting. Through a simple point and click sequence, the user can insert each screen question within the electronic notepad (Figure 5.3), and then use the keyboard to type a response to the question.

The questions and responses recorded in the notepad can then be edited, saved to a file on a local disk or network, and printed, all in a fashion similar to a simple text document. As the subject proceeds, this notepad develops into a professional journal and progressive entries can be used to reflect on the nature of, and changes to, personal views about quality in classroom practices.

Operational metaphor: lenses

The metaphor of a magnifying glass to examine the behaviours of others is extended in QuILT through a related metaphor – that of coloured glass lenses.

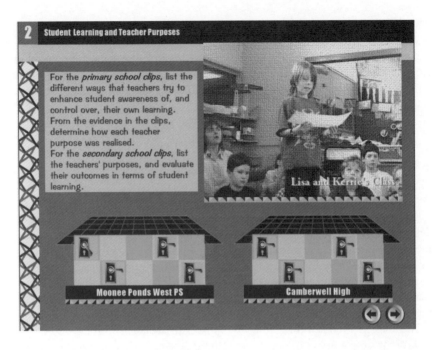

Figure 5.2   *'Entering classrooms' in QuILT*

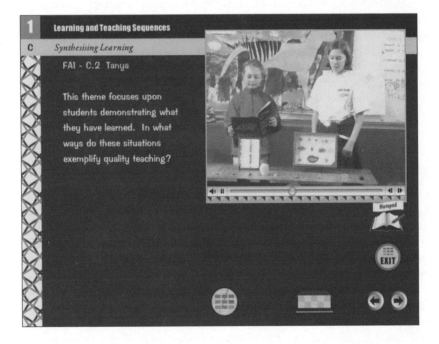

Figure 5.3   *Screen question and electronic notepad*

These lenses are introduced to scaffold progressive understanding of the meanings that underlie these behaviours.

Screen backgrounds on which clips appear are coded in four different colours, each of which signifies to the user a different way of observing and understanding what is happening. Each of the four lenses addresses a different question, as follows:

1. 'What is the teacher doing?'
2. 'What is the teacher thinking and feeling?'
3. 'What are the pupils doing?'
4. 'What are the pupils thinking and feeling?'

By progressively using the lenses, the user can reassess the same clip and move from observing behaviours to ascertaining meanings and purposes that underlie them. Through this process, the user's tentative evaluation of whether observed behaviours constitute quality learning and teaching is progressively supported, challenged or elaborated. Through the use of these lenses, the user comes to realize that adequate interpretation and evaluation of the nature and worth of a particular classroom episode may often only be achieved once the episode is considered from these four points of view.

In order to attend to the questions 'What is the teacher thinking and feeling?' and 'What are the pupils thinking and feeling?', the user views interviews in which teachers outline their classroom intentions and provide self-evaluations of their actions, and pupils provide their perceptions of lesson nature, progress and content, and of their learning and the teacher's teaching. These interviews provide insights regarding classroom interactions that are normally not available through classroom observation alone.

From the perspective of the over-arching program metaphor of quilt-making, each of the four lenses are the analogues of the coloured fibres that, through weaving, form the material's warp and weft. In this way, the pluralist and relativist nature of quality teaching and learning is reinforced as an intricate, complex design constructed from experience, reflection and action.

Operational metaphor: mirror

A second major operational metaphor complements that of the magnifying glass and its different lenses. Where the magnifying glass enabled the user to examine closely the values, beliefs, intentions and behaviours of others, this second metaphor is of a mirror, where such aspects are turned to oneself. The mirror is used to focus upon personal thinking, feeling and acting, in order to determine personal principles for future teaching approaches and actions.

The mirror metaphor is introduced at the end of each Focus Area through a task entitled an 'Action planner' (Figure 5.4). This task requires the user to identify and synthesize key issues or insights that emerged as he or she worked through the Focus Area, and then to determine a personal action plan for teaching, based on these issues and insights. Each Action planner is a Word document, opened by

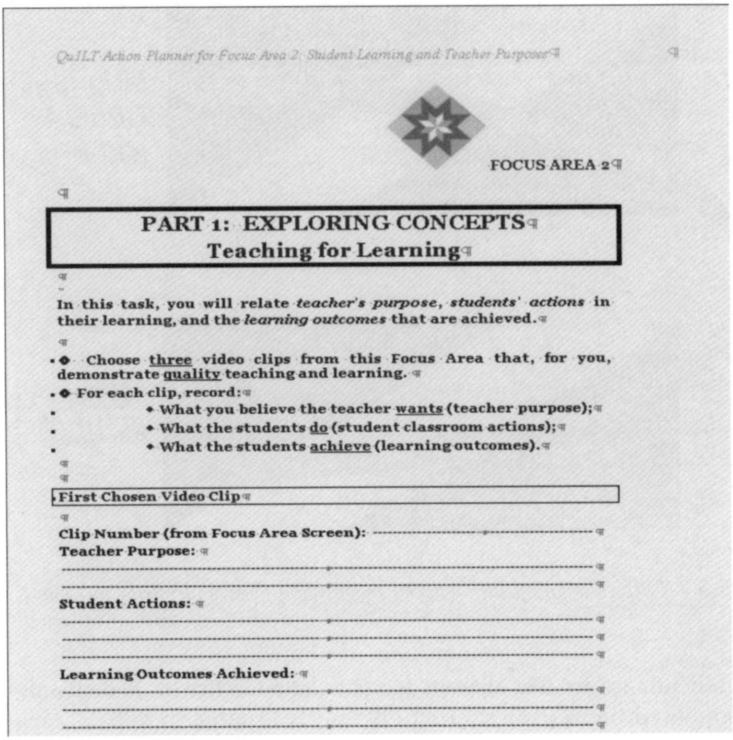
QuILT Action Planner for Focus Area 2: Student Learning and Teacher Purposes

FOCUS AREA 2

PART 1: EXPLORING CONCEPTS
Teaching for Learning

In this task, you will relate *teacher's purpose*, *students' actions* in their learning, and the *learning outcomes* that are achieved.

- **Choose three video clips from this Focus Area that, for you, demonstrate quality teaching and learning.**
- **For each clip, record:**
  - **What you believe the teacher wants (teacher purpose);**
  - **What the students do (student classroom actions);**
  - **What the students achieve (learning outcomes).**

First Chosen Video Clip

Clip Number (from Focus Area Screen): --
Teacher Purpose:

Student Actions:

Learning Outcomes Achieved:

Figure 5.4 *'Action planner'*

clicking on the Mirror icon. The user completes the activities in the planner by inserting text where indicated. Completed planners are used as part of the formal assessment in the subject.

Figure 5.5 represents diagrammatically the relationship between the magnifying glass and mirror metaphors in QuILT. For the magnifying glass, the user moves from a consideration of the teaching and learning actions of others to the thoughts and feelings that underlie these actions. For the mirror, personal thoughts and feelings about desirable practice are first elucidated, then appropriate actions to enact these thoughts and feelings are determined and rehearsed.

Some trends arising from program use

Over the three-year period, extensive and diverse data have been collected on students' perceptions of the program, of patterns of its use, and of learning and teaching outcomes. These data are not considered in detail here, but a summary is given of users' perceptions of the program's major strengths and shortcomings. The following aspects constituted major perceived strengths of the program:

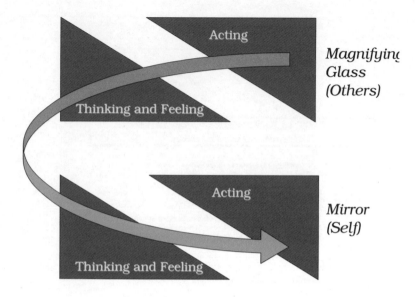

Figure 5.5   *QuILT: relationship between magnifying glass and mirror metaphors*

- its authentic nature that allowed access to 'real teachers in real classrooms' – commented upon strongly in 1999 and continued to appear each year thereafter;
- the high level of engagement that the program affords – also repeated strongly each year;
- the spread of effective and ineffective teaching and learning episodes that helped students focus upon personal perspectives of quality and strategies to develop a personal teaching approach and style;
- the four different 'lenses' and, particularly, the teacher and student interviews that directed attention to crucial aspects of teaching and learning that otherwise might not have been identified;
- the notepad and 'Action planners' that required students to record ideas and perspectives in a coherent and structured manner to support critical analysis and self-reflection.

Each of the following aspects were seen as major shortcomings:

- technological concerns of various sorts: lack of student (and staff) competence and confidence in using interactive multimedia; technical problems associated with incompatibility of the program with the capabilities of older computers; the imposition of requirements for levels of technological expertise and relatively high-end hardware. As mentioned above, this type of concern varied with the type of cohort in a given year and, for similar cohorts, diminished across the three years;

- a weekly workload associated with QuILT that many students considered excessive and, especially in the first two years, considered to be unduly emphasized in subject assessment;
- confusion associated with some screen questions and 'Action planner' tasks. This concern, attributable both to some poorly designed aspects and to students' unfamiliarity with the inductive approach, progressively diminished as the result of replacement of troublesome items and enhanced guidance and support.

Concluding comment

Teaching is a social art and science. As such, it is unlikely that interactive multimedia could or should replace the real world experiences of face-to-face instruction, group discussion and school-based teaching that form parts of most teacher education courses. Multimedia programs can, however, constitute engaging and powerful adjuncts to these real-time experiences by providing opportunities for systematic, focused reflection, for illumination of core educational ideas, and for enhanced metacognitive knowledge, awareness and control over personal teaching practice. In so doing, they will have achieved their goal of enhancing both cognitive and affective engagement in purposeful, productive teacher professional education.

Acknowledgement

I wish to acknowledge the crucial contribution of Keith Pigdon, Marilyn Woolley and Bradley Shrimpton to the design and production of QuILT, to the research outlined above, and to the writing of an earlier version of this chapter.

References

Albion, P R (2000) Interactive multimedia problem-based learning for enhancing pre-service teachers' self-efficacy beliefs about teaching with computers: design, development and evaluation. Unpublished doctoral dissertation, University of Southern Queensland

Alexander, P A (1996) The past, present and future of knowledge research: a re-examination of the role of knowledge in learning and instruction, *Educational Psychologist,* **31** (2), pp 89–92

Baird, J (1989) Intellectual and methodological imperatives for individual teacher development. Paper delivered at the annual meeting of the American Educational Research Association, Los Angeles

Baird, J (1991a) Individual and group reflection as a basis for teacher development, in *Teachers' Professional Development,* ed P Hughes, Australian Council of Educational Research, Victoria

Baird, J (1991b) Collaboration reflection, systematic enquiry, better teaching, in *Teachers and Teaching: From classroom to reflection,* eds T Russell and H Munby, Falmer Press, London

Baird, J (ed) (1999) *Reflecting, Teaching, Learning: Perspectives on educational improvement,* Hawker Brownlow Education, Melbourne

Brown, J, Collins, A and Duguid, P (1989) Situated cognition and the culture of learning, *Educational Researcher,* **18** (1), pp 32–41

Brown, T, Knight, B A and Durrant, C B (1996) Strategic teaching frameworks: an Australian perspective, *Journal of Information Technology for Teacher Education,* **5** (3), pp 219–32

Davis, N (1997) Do electronic communications offer a new learning opportunity in education?, in *Using Information Technology Effectively in Teaching and Learning,* eds B Somekh and N Davis, pp 167–82, Routledge, London

Dewey, J (1933) *How We Think: A restatement of the relation of reflective thinking to the educative process,* D C Heath, Boston MA

Lave, J and Wenger, E (1991) *Situated Learning: Legitimate peripheral participation,* Cambridge University Press, Cambridge

Marx, R W, Blumenfeld, P C, Krajcik, J S and Soloway, E (1998) New technologies for teacher professional development, *Teaching and Teacher Education,* **14** (1), pp 33–52

McLoughlin, C, Baird, J, Pigdon, K and Woolley, M (2000) Fostering teacher inquiry and reflective learning processes through technology enhanced scaffolding in a multimedia environment, in *Proceedings of Ed-Media 2000 World Conference on Educational Multimedia, Hypermedia and Telecommunications,* eds J Bourdeau and R Heller, AACE Publications, Charlottesville

Putnam, R and Borko, H (2000) What do new views of knowledge and thinking have to say about research on teaching learning?, *Educational Researcher,* **29** (1), pp 4–15

Savery, J and Duffy, T (1995) Problem-based learning: an instructional model and its constructivist framework, *Educational Technology,* **35** (5), pp 31–37

Schrum, L and Dehoney, J (1998) Meeting the future: a teacher education program joins the information age, *Journal of Technology in Teacher Education,* **6** (1), pp 23–37

Willis, E M (1997) Technology: integrated into, not added onto, the curriculum experiences in pre-service teacher education, *Computers in the Schools,* **13** (1–2), pp 141–53

Chapter 6

Using authentic patient encounters to engage medical students in a problem-based learning curriculum

Mike Keppell, Kristine Elliott, Gregor Kennedy, Susan Elliott and Peter Harris

Introduction

In this chapter we will examine how medical triggers utilized in clinical scenarios are used to activate student learning in a problem-based learning medical curriculum. Medical triggers represent the first point of contact for students undertaking problem-based learning tutorials. The role of the trigger is to begin to immerse the student in the context of the weekly problem. The chapter will examine the specific design strategies that have been enlisted to engage the student in contextualizing medical problems. This examination will focus on: the nature of problem-based learning (PBL), PBL cases, problem triggers, media deployed to address the problem triggers and the epistemological beliefs of designers who develop these learner interactions. The chapter will conclude with a number of recommendations for educators utilizing authentic learning resources in technology-enhanced environments.

Problem-based learning

Teaching and learning strategy

The increasing use of PBL as an instructional method reflects a current international trend away from teacher-centred delivery towards student-centred learning programmes. Such programmes commonly present students with a problem and require them to conduct their own inquiry, which involves formulating hypotheses, developing questions, gathering and interpreting data, and communicating their findings to peers and tutors (Brown *et al*, 1989; Linn *et al*, 1996; Schank, 1997; von Glasersfeld, 1987).

PBL is being widely adopted as a powerful teaching and learning strategy in medical education. In particular, PBL may address recognized deficiencies in traditional medical education and the way medical knowledge is applied in the clinical setting (Koschmann *et al*, 1997). Situated in a constructivist paradigm, PBL is a learner-centred pedagogical strategy, where the students themselves assume major responsibility for their learning. These are also considered to be real-world or authentic learning experiences. Authentic learning experiences are 'those which are problem- or case-based, that immerse the learner in the situation requiring him or her to acquire skills or knowledge in order to solve the problem or manipulate the situation' (Jonassen *et al*, 1993, p 235). Generally PBL is divided into several phases that involve small group work and independent study (Barrows and Tamblyn, 1980; Schmidt, 1993). Specifically, Albanese and Mitchell (1993) have described PBL as used in medical and health sciences curricula as 'an instructional method characterized by the use of patient problems as a context for students to learn problem-solving skills and acquire knowledge about the basic and clinical sciences' (p 53). PBL problems are unique because they are presented to students before their exposure to underlying basic science or clinical concepts (Albanese and Mitchell, 1993).

Activation

Essential to PBL is the concept that 'activation of prior knowledge facilitates the subsequent processing of new information' (Norman and Schmidt, 1992, p 559). Research on prior knowledge and the need to account for the learner's existing ideas and concepts in teaching and learning has a long history within the education and cognitive science literature. For instance Dewey (1938) examined experience and education; Ausubel (1960) examined subsumption theory; Mayer (1979) focused on assimilation theory; Rumelhart and Norman (1983) and Gordon and Rennie (1987) focused on schema theory. Little appears to have changed since

1979 when Mayer commented that 'it seems that one cannot read a textbook on learning and memory without finding a statement to the effect that learning involves connecting new ideas to old knowledge' (Mayer, 1979, p 136). Within the context of PBL, Schmidt (1993) suggests that the extent of prior knowledge is one of the major determinants of the 'nature and amount of new information that can be processed' (p 424). The importance of focusing on the concept of prior knowledge in the PBL process is that students soon realize that 'prior knowledge of the problem is, in itself, insufficient for them to understand it in depth' (Norman and Schmidt, 1992, p 557). PBL utilizes this inherent dilemma to motivate learners to seek an understanding of the clinical case and address the deficiency in their knowledge. Under the guidance of the PBL tutor, an exchange of ideas among students in the PBL session assists in activating their prior knowledge. This exchange needs to occur before students further investigate learning resources, for it creates a 'learner readiness' by asking the students to generate hypotheses for the problem.

PBL cases

One method of approaching the activation of learning in a PBL curriculum is to create weekly problems that address different clinical issues; these are called 'problems of the week'. Each problem begins with a visual and/or audio trigger. The aim of the trigger is to set the stage for the clinical problem by providing students with an image of the hypothetical patient and some of the circumstances surrounding the medical scenario. For example, the trigger shown in Figure 6.1 provides the context and setting for a lost mountaineer in a cold, high-altitude environment. In viewing the image the medical student needs to examine information that may be pertinent to possible medical issues. Does the mountaineer have sufficient food, water and clothing? How cold does the temperature get in this area? What would happen if the mountaineer were lost? How long can he survive without food? How could he protect himself from the elements without a tent? Each question encourages the student to examine physiological and psychological stress, the effects of altitude, hypothermia, dehydration and metabolism, etc.

Using the information elicited from the trigger text and image, students are instructed to list information about the patient, identify the presenting problems, list possible causes of each problem (hypotheses), provide a rationale for each hypothesis, prioritize the list of hypotheses, and then determine what other additional information (physical examinations, laboratory tests, etc) is required to differentiate between hypotheses. During this process students are progressively given supporting information in the form of a medical history, physical examination and investigation results.

Figure 6.1 *Medical trigger utilized to activate learning in nutrition, digestion and metabolism*

Medical triggers

One of the advantages of presenting clinical problems online is the capacity to enrich them with high quality graphics, photographs, Shockwave movies, audio and video. Students are also able to access the material and revisit the content as needed within the networked learning environment. Our aim in designing these triggers is to create images that 'suspend the disbelief' of students and allow them to approach each problem as if it were a real-life clinical case. Since the trigger represents the entry point to the problem, it could potentially influence student interaction with the problem by determining how realistic students rated the encounter (Elliott and Keppell, 2000). For instance, the trigger shown in Figure 6.2 was used to set the stage for a clinical scenario. Initial evaluation and student discussions with Elliott (co-author) suggested that we achieved our goal in this respect. Students viewing the medical trigger:

expressed great concern for a virtual patient who was experiencing severe pain. 'How could they have taken photos of somebody in so much pain?' The point to highlight here is that the hospitalized patient was an actor, the scenario was staged and the students had been taken in by the reality of the image. (Elliott and Keppell, 2000, p 280)

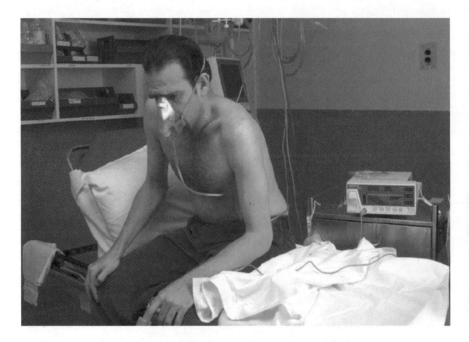

Figure 6.2 *Medical trigger utilized to activate learning in cardio-respiratory and locomotor systems*

In conjunction with the trigger, students are provided with information about the case:

> You are a medical student working in the Emergency Department of a hospital in central Victoria. The medical officer tells you that one hour ago, while Mentor was resting after painting one of the new accommodation huts, he suddenly complained of severe pain in the right side of his chest. The pain settled after a few minutes, but he has become increasingly more short of breath.

From this information it is possible to focus attention on the critical issues about Mentor. Key information includes that he is a 28-year-old male, is breathless, has severe chest pain and requires an oxygen mask. From this further information the medical student in conjunction with his or her colleagues and PBL tutor explore possible medical reasons for Mentor's shortness of breath. He or she is also encouraged to define symptoms and signs without necessarily having prior expert knowledge.

Elliott and Keppell (2000) have reported on the artificial nature of practice simulations, where a medical condition and/or scenario is presented to students as 'too neat and tidy' (Atkins and O'Halloran, 1995, p 6). This is in direct contrast to the complexity of real-life patient encounters, which may include unusual presentations and could involve missing or even erroneous data (Koschmann *et al*, 1996). Koschmann *et al* (1997) suggest that the 'mechanics of simulating an encounter with a patient. . . can be quite cumbersome' (p 1). The challenge of designing triggers for clinical problems is to ensure that the images clearly demonstrate sufficient detail to enable students to begin the process of formulating hypotheses about the scientific basis of a medical condition, without compromising on the complexity of reality (Elliott and Keppell, 2000).

For instance, the trigger shown in Figure 6.3 of an elderly lady lying on the floor demonstrated the importance of using 'physical props' (lights, ladders, streamers, etc) in the design of the trigger. What is the significance of the light and the time of day/night? Why is the ladder overturned? What was the woman doing to end up in this situation? What do the hat and bag suggest about the activity level of the woman? Is there anything peculiar about the right leg position as compared to the left? How long do you think the elderly lady has been lying on the floor?

Figure 6.3   *Medical trigger demonstrating the importance of setting and context*

A well-designed trigger can, for example, encourage the clinical-based reasoning skills of students. A poorly designed trigger that makes the medical condition too obvious, or alternatively distracts students with too much detail and causes the formulation of too many hypotheses, could inhibit this process. Observation of students engaged in PBL tutorials demonstrated how carefully students scrutinized the visual triggers looking for cues to begin the formulation of hypotheses. It was therefore critical that visual images were consistent, and that they matched the accompanying textual information (Elliott and Keppell, 2000).

Design considerations in creating medical triggers

Media deployed to create the medical trigger

Media are often deployed to create medical triggers because it is not always practical to access real patients for undergraduate education. Options include paper-based problems, 'trained patient surrogates' (Koschmann *et al*, 1996) and the media-based patient encounters examined in this chapter. In development, an attempt is made to match the nature of the medical condition or context to the appropriate media type (eg, static image, sequence of static images, video, audio, or Shockwave movie). A trigger that, for example, portrays a medical condition such as myasthenia gravis needs to show the progressive nature of skeletal-muscle fatigue. Consequently, video is the most appropriate medium to illustrate this progressive nature. Other triggers needed to demonstrate distinctive sequential changes in a process can be portrayed through a series of digitized photographs using a Shockwave or QuickTime movie. Often, a single digitized photograph conveys sufficient information to begin the problem-based learning approach (Keppell *et al*, 2001).

In creating triggers for the first three years of the medical curriculum we carefully considered the medical problem, the nature of the condition and the best way to portray an initial encounter that would activate student learning in relation to the information provided. Of the 60 triggers created, 64 per cent consist of still images or graphics, 27 per cent consist of Shockwave movies and 9 per cent consist of video. In creating the medical triggers, our focus was to 'apply each medium to the learning process it best supports' (Koumi, 1994, p 57). This required a careful analysis and attention to detail with the medical trigger. In addition we matched 'each topic/task with the medium whose characteristics would best benefit that topic' (Koumi, 1994, p 55). The medical trigger was an activating strategy, an attempt to initiate the student interaction with the clinical problem. In our design we exploited the 'distinctive presentational attributes' (Koumi, 1994, p 43) of the media in conjunction with an explicit teaching strategy in an attempt to match the media to the message. This approach focuses on improving learning by attempting to match the salient features/capabilities of the medium (photo, Shockwave movie, video) to the particular learning situation, tasks involved in the learning situation, the learners and the 'capabilities' used to enhance and optimize the instructional design (Nathan and Robinson, 2001). The trigger represents one micro-component of the PBL process. This approach is supported by Kozma (1991) who suggests that we need to consider 'micro-level decisions in the design of instructional programs and understand the moment-to-moment collaboration between the learner and the medium of the learning context' (p 76).

Matching media to the message

In approaching the creation of medical triggers it was essential that we utilized media for educational purposes rather than allow the technology/media to overpower the educational message (Koschmann et al, 1996). To guide the utilization of media in teaching and learning a number of design principles were considered. Norman's (1999) examination of the affordances and constraints of 'everyday things', Kozma's (1991) focus on exploiting the educational 'capabilities' of media and Koumi's (1994) examination of the 'comparative merits' of media appear to offer promise in this area.

'Affordances' refer to the perceived and actual properties that determine how a 'thing' can be used. Affordances also provide strong clues as to how the 'thing' should be used. Norman (1999) examined common day-to-day objects such as door handles: the salient features of the handle should signal whether we push or pull the door. In examining these principles in the use of media, Collins and Bielaczyc (2001) suggested that:

> affordances must be seen as more than just the kinds of information a medium can communicate well. Affordances also include the ways the content is presented, and the effect it has on the audience, and the room it allows for tailoring the impact of one's message. (p 2)

When the concept of affordances is applied to media in the medical trigger, PBL designers begin to consider carefully their choice of media in order to match the message to the media.

Kozma (1991) focused on exploiting the capabilities of media for enhancing the educational message. In particular, by emphasizing the design and the use of media from an instructional design perspective, good quality teaching and learning interactions can be optimized. Koumi (1994), in suggesting the concept of comparative merits of media, also provides a useful principle for creating micro-interactions like the triggers utilized in our curricula. Comparative merits examine the educational judgements that we need to make in deciding why one type of medium as opposed to another should be utilized to create the trigger. For instance, photographs may provide a realistic portrayal, affect attitudes, appreciations and motivations, and are relatively low cost as compared to video. Shockwave movies in which a series of photos can be used may provide more action/illusion of movement or sequential interactions as compared to an individual photo. Video allows pictures and sound to be synchronized, but is relatively high cost compared to photos or Shockwave movies. Video may provide a fluid and dynamic portrayal, which also utilizes the power of the spoken word to enhance the users' understanding of the setting. In fact this comparative merit of video may be 'easier to process because the viewers' senses are fed with stimuli that are realistic and are absorbed effortlessly and almost unconsciously' (England and Finney, 1999, p 155). On the other hand, static images may require viewers to contribute more to their interpretation of the context and setting because they do not necessarily have smooth transitions to different settings or the spoken word. Video is also useful for portraying social interactions, but it must be remembered that the field of view is predetermined, which provides selectivity that may enhance the micro-interaction or mislead the learner because it over-simplifies the process or social interaction.

Koumi's model also suggests that there will be other merits that will need to be individually considered depending upon the culture, institution, faculty and preferences in the development team. The principle of 'comparative merits' offers a means to customize media to the individual teaching and learning situation to assure 'pedagogical fit' of medical triggers.

Epistemological beliefs of designers

Another major factor that we must consider in designing learning interactions such as medial triggers is our set of epistemological assumptions in relation to the learning environment. As designers in virtual environments, Koschmann (2000) suggests that we have an obligation 'to make explicit our theories of teaching and learning. . . that motivate our work and that are embedded in our designs' (Koschmann, 2000, p 2). In other words, what were our explicit choices in deciding to use a photograph, Shockwave, video and audio as a teaching resource for activating student involvement with the clinical scenario? Vrasidas (2000) suggests that context and content are crucial in constructivist environments, and that the goal of constructivist educators is to assist students to 'think and act like experts' (p 350).

Epistemological beliefs of educators and designers of learning interactions have a major influence on student learning (Reeves, 1997). In fact, Bain et al (1998) suggest, 'the educational context in which students learn is heavily influenced by the epistemological and educational assumptions of their academic teachers' (p 49). In their research they found that academics differed on a wide range of beliefs about knowledge, which influenced the methods used in their teaching. They suggested that these different knowledge beliefs also influence the creation of technology-enhanced teaching and learning resources. Likewise we must also consider the epistemological values of our students. This is essential as good pedagogic design needs to consider where students 'are conceptually' (Laurillard, 1993, p 193). Students bring to studying their own epistemological values that have often been nurtured in previous educational settings. Students, like academic instructional designers, may also have a preference for a particular learning style for most of their academic tasks (Jones and Kember, 1994).

Academic instructional designers also need to carefully examine their own beliefs about teaching and learning and be aware of when different approaches may be necessary to achieve 'pedagogical fit'. 'There are times when a more instructivist approach is appropriate and other times when a more constructivist approach is appropriate. It always depends on the context, content, resources, and learners' (Vrasidas, 2000, p 358). In our approach to creating triggers, as well as considering the affordances, capabilities and comparative merits of different media, we need to examine the obvious constraints in relation to facilities, staff, budget, resources, bandwidth variations for Internet delivery and the place of the medical trigger in the context of the problem.

An initial evaluation was undertaken in relation to the 18 triggers utilized in semesters one and two and delivered in 1999 (Elliott and Keppell, 2000). The Director of the Faculty Education Unit was interviewed and asked about her perceptions in relation to the effectiveness of the triggers. She believed that 'the more authentic the trigger the more students were drawn in by the reality of the situation and the more effective it was as a tool to initiate discussion about the scenario' (Elliott and Keppell, 2000, p 280). Observation of students in a PBL setting yielded some surprising results. Instead of spending a great deal of time analysing the trigger 'at the beginning of the PBL session students would quickly (almost casually) look at the trigger'. After discussion the students would 'revisit the trigger (again reasonably quickly) looking for information that would further refine their ideas. The process was repeated several times' (Elliott and Keppell, 2000, p 281).

Recommendations

As constructivist educators in a PBL curriculum there are a number of principles that have assisted our use of media-rich resources to activate student learning. We have found that media in the form of graphics, photographs, Shockwave movies and video can be utilized to create authentic clinical encounters. Although it appears that 'the more media that are combined the harder it is to keep all the factors appropriate' (England and Finney, 1999, p 156), it seems that the more meticulous the design the more realistic and appealing the trigger is perceived to be by students (Elliott and Keppell, 2000). A great deal of thought is required in creating a trigger that does not simplify the clinical issue or make the clinical issue overly complex in PBL.

Burford and Cooper (2000) suggest that 'quality is judged in terms of the extent to which a product or service meets its stated purpose' (p 14). The use of media (graphics, photographs, Shockwave movies, video) should never overpower the educational focus. Matching the multimedia to the message (educational goal) is the crucial aspect of our approach. It is important to exploit the capabilities of the media by using instructional methods that make full use of their characteristics. One method of doing so is to weigh carefully the comparative merits of the different media when making your choice.

As educators and designers it is essential that we are aware of our own epistemological beliefs about teaching and learning as these views dramatically affect the nature of design and student interaction with online learning materials. By carefully designing authentic patient encounters through the judicious use of appropriate media, student interactions in a medical PBL curriculum have been enhanced.

References

Albanese, M A and Mitchell, S (1993) Problem-based learning: a review of literature on its outcomes and implementation issues, *Academic Medicine,* **68** (1), pp 52–81

Atkins, M J and O'Halloran, C (1995) Evaluating multimedia applications for medical education, *AMEE Education Guide,* **6**, pp 1–10

Ausubel, D P (1960) The use of advance organizers in the learning and retention of meaningful verbal material, *Journal of Educational Psychology,* **51** (5), pp 267–72

Bain, J D, McNaught, C, Mills, C and Lueckenhausen, G (1998) Understanding CFL practices in higher education in terms of academics' educational beliefs: enhancing Reeves' analysis, in *Flexibility: The Next Wave. Proceedings of the 15th annual conference of the Australasian Society for Computers in Learning in Tertiary Education,* ed R Corderoy, pp 417–24, University of Wollongong, Wollongong, NSW

Barrows, H S and Tamblyn, R (1980) *Problem-based Learning: An approach to medical education,* Springer, New York

Brown, J S, Collins, A and Duguid, P (1989) Situated cognition and the culture of learning, *Educational Researcher,* Jan/Feb, pp 32–42

Burford, S and Cooper, L (2000) Online development using WebCT: a faculty managed process for quality, *Australian Journal of Educational Technology,* **16** (3), pp 201–14

Collins, A and Bielazyc, K (2001) The role of different media in designing learning environments. Accessed March 2002, from http://wwwapcsrcncuedutw/apc/allanmediahtm

Dewey, J (1938) *Experience and Education,* Collier Books, Macmillan, New York

Elliott, K and Keppell, M (2000) Visual triggers: improving the effectiveness of virtual patient encounters, in *Learning to Choose. Proceedings of the 17th annual conference of the Australasian Society for Computers in Learning in Tertiary Education,* eds R Sims, M O'Reilly and S Sawkins, pp 275–83, Southern Cross University Press, NSW

England, E and Finney, A (1999) *Managing Multimedia: Project management for interactive media* (2nd edn) Addison-Wesley, Harlow

Gordon, C J and Rennie, B J (1987) Restructuring content schemata: an intervention study, *Reading Research and Instruction,* **26** (3), pp 162–88

Jonassen, D, Mayes, T and McAleese, R (1993) A manifesto for a constructivist approach to uses of technology in higher education, in *Designing Environments for Constructive Learning,* eds T M Duffy, J Lowyck and D H Jonassen, Springer-Verlag, Berlin

Jones, A and Kember, D (1994) Approaches to learning and student acceptance of self-study packages, *Education and Training Technology-International,* **31** (2), pp 93–7

Keppell, M, Kennedy, G, Elliott, K and Harris, P (2001) Transforming traditional curricula: enhancing medical education through multimedia and web-based resources, *Interactive Multimedia Electronic Journal of Computer-Enhanced Learning (IMEJ),* **3** (1). Accessed March 2002, from http://imejwfuedu/articles/2001/1/indexasp

Koschmann, T (2000) Tools of termlessness: technology, educational reform, and Deweyan inquiry, in *Virtual Learning Environments,* ed Tim O'Shea, Lawrence Erlbaum, Mahwah, NJ. Accessed April 2002, from http://edaff.siumed.edu/tk/articles/UNESCO.pdf

Koschmann, T D, Feltovich, P J, Myers, A C and Barrows, H S (1997) Implications of CSCL for Problem-based Learning. Accessed March 2002, from http://www-cscl95.indiana.edu/cscl95/outlook/32_koschman.html

Koschmann, T D, Kelson, A C, Feltovich, P J and Barrows, H S (1996) Computer-supported problem-based learning: a principled approach to the use of computers in collaborative learning, in *Computer Supported Collaborative Learning: Theory and practice in an emerging paradigm,* ed T Koschmann, Lawrence Erlbaum, Mahwah, NJ

Koumi, J (1994) Media comparison and deployment: a practitioner's view, *British Journal of Educational Technology,* **25** (1), pp 41–57

Kozma, R B (1991) Learning with media, *Review of Educational Research,* **61** (2), pp 179–211

Laurillard, D (1993) *Rethinking University Teaching: A framework for the effective use of educational technology,* Routledge, London

Linn, M C, Songer, N B and Eylon, B S (1996) Shifts and convergences in science learning and instruction, in *Handbook of Educational Psychology,* eds D C Berliner and R C Calfee, pp 438–90, Macmillan, New York

Mayer, R E (1979) Twenty years of research on advance organizers: assimilation theory is still the best predictor of results, *Instructional Science,* **8,** pp 133–67

Nathan, M and Robinson, C (2001) Considerations of learning and learning research: revisiting the 'media effects' debate, *Journal of Interactive Learning Research,* **12** (1), pp 69–88

Norman, D A (1999) *The Design of Everyday Things,* MIT Press, London

Norman, G R and Schmidt, H G (1992) The psychological basis of problem-based learning: a review of the evidence, *Academic Medicine,* **67** (9), pp 557–65

Reeves, T (1997) Evaluating what really matters in computer-based education. Accessed March 2002, from http://wwweducationaueduau/archives/cp/reeveshtm#ref1

Rumelhart, D E and Norman, D A (1983) *Representation in Memory* (ERIC Documentation Service No ED 235 770)

Schank, R (1997) *Virtual Learning: A revolutionary approach to building a highly skilled workforce,* McGraw-Hill, New York

Schmidt, H G (1993) Foundations of problem-based learning: some explanatory notes, *Medical Education,* **27,** pp 422–32

von Glasersfeld, E (1987) Learning as constructive activity, in *The Construction of Knowledge: Contributions to conceptual semantics,* ed E von Glaserfeld, Intersystems Publication

Vrasidas, C (2000) Constructivism versus objectivism: implications for interaction, course design, and evaluation in distance education, *International Journal of Educational Telecommunications,* **6** (4), pp 339–62

Chapter 7

Virtual learning in cultural studies: matching subject content and instructional delivery

Lee Wallace, Annamarie Jagose and Cathy Gunn

Introduction

Within the contexts of e-learning and technology-enhanced learning environments, the potentialities of the medium of delivery offer unique opportunities to match academic content and pedagogic form in previously unimagined ways. Using the example of the Virtual Shopping Mall project (VSM), this chapter will focus attention on the processes by which purpose-built Information and Computer Technology (ICT) platforms can be developed to activate and enhance content-specific learning. The challenge the VSM designers set themselves was to investigate how computer-assisted learning could augment the student's entry-point interaction with new subject domains, in this case contemporary cultural studies. This chapter evaluates the impact this 'matching' of academic content and instructional delivery has on student motivation and their engagement of learning.

Review of the literature

Educational software design is informed by a variety of instructional theories ranging from early behaviourist (Bloom, 1956; Merrill *et al*, 1991) to contemporary constructivist (Wilson *et al*,1997). While the pedagogy of the discipline and educational level of a product will determine the most appropriate theoretical basis, all approaches share the common objective of maximizing learning (Somekh, 1996), and most learning environments include a mix of mastery and constructive learning. Contemporary theories for university learning relevant to the work described in all four chapters in this section emphasize active, constructive and situated learning. These are variously described as Rich Environments for Active Learning (REALs) by Grabinger and Dunlap (1995), constructivist learning opportunities by Jonassen (1998) and authentic contexts for situated learning by Herrington and Oliver (2000). Activation of learning through engagement with authentic environments is discussed in some detail by both Keppell and Baird (see Chapters 5 and 6 in this book). While the VSM is not designed around problem solving activity such as that described by Keppell, the underlying principle applies equally to the analytical decision making model on which it is based. Students have 'signposted' access to a knowledge domain which represents an ill-structured view of an authentic scenario they must investigate, reach and support decisions about. The VSM scenarios also reflect the 'real life complexity' that is often missing in simulated environments. In Baird's chapter this complexity is provided through access to real teachers in real life situations with examples of both good and bad practice in teaching situations. While these attributes can be promoted in any learning environment, the ease of access as well as the sensory and interactive potential of Web-based multimedia provides far greater opportunities for the achievement of these 'higher level' pedagogical aims.

Creating interactive environments

Despite common use of the term 'interactive multimedia', multimedia itself is not inherently interactive. While the definition implies the presence of audio-visual as well as text-based content, it is possible to include these multimedia features in a product that is designed to do no more than transmit information – albeit multi-sensory information – to passive users. The interactive quality of any instructional resource is a function of the design, not the technology. A definition of interactivity drawn from the discipline of Human Computer Interaction (HCI) focuses specifically on the relationship between the user and the technology-based system. The basis of HCI design principles is to make the interaction, which is defined as a function of the input required by the learner while responding to the computer and the consequent reaction by the computer, both meaningful and engaging (Hutchings *et al*, 1993; Jones *et al*, 1995). Basic interaction in the form of 'point and click' and hyperlinked navigation is useful for some applications such as information kiosks, shopping or booking systems. Educational products, however, which are designed not simply to transfer information but to extend the conceptual competency of the user, require more complex forms of interactivity that must be indexed to the instructional strategy employed by the application. Interactivity is a necessary and fundamental mechanism for knowledge acquisition and the development of cognitive and physical skills. It is no longer adequate for the work of instructional designers to be limited to products where interactivity is trivialized to menu selection, clickable objects or linear sequencing. Real interaction is essential to successful, effective educational practice as well as to individual discovery (Sims, 1997). Increasing capacity to develop and provide access to Web-based multimedia environments supports articulation of the constructivist learning principles that underpin this notion of interactivity. The term coined by Evans and Swain in Chapter 8 in this book is a 'virtual practice situation'. The development of genuinely interactive environments, such as those described in the chapters in this Part, is necessary to create potential for deep learning to occur within these applications.

Cognitive flexibility, motivation and game-play protocols

One of the unique qualities of Web-based multimedia environments is the capacity to support multiple representations of complex domains through the provision of hyperlinks and user choice in navigation through knowledge spaces (Spiro and Jehng, 1990). Traditional methods of instruction have little option but to rely on linear media. This presents few problems when the subject matter is well structured and relatively simple. However, as complexity of content and structure increases, greater amounts of information are lost with linear media. The advent of random access instruction through hypertext addresses this problem and research into the educational benefits associated with opportunities to construct personalized views of subject domains is ongoing (Hutchings *et al*, 1993; Lemke, 1993).

The instructional design of educational multimedia needs also to ensure the motivation of learners. At an operational level, Keller (1987) describes five dimensions of motivation as:

1.   interest – arousing curiosity, capturing attention;
2.   relevance – connection of learning objectives to tasks and activities;
3.   engagement – active participation supported by meaningful feedback;
4.   expectancy – developing confidence and control;
5.   satisfaction – making measurable progress, achieving specified outcomes.

A recent current in computer-assisted learning research suggests that the developers of educational multimedia have much to learn from the design of computer games and the modes of cognitive interactivity and imaginative engagement they support

(Johnson, 1998). Game play protocols can 'enhance learning while affecting the motivation and retention of knowledge and skills positively' so that, in an optimal scenario, gaming 'becomes an intentional education tool (where) the rules which govern (play) demand the development and use of educationally valuable skills, the acquisition of important knowledge, or exploration of a worthwhile world of experience' (Kinikoglu and Yadav, 1995). The incorporation of game features into instructional design has the potential to enhance student motivation by amplifying aspects of challenge, discovery and control (Johnson, 1998). These motivational cues actively reinforce the instructional objectives of the module while game play also provides opportunities for self-test and feedback scenarios unhampered by the stress and anxiety associated with academic testing. Optimal learning occurs when instructional content and motivational features are in a balanced combination with neither dominating nor impeding the other (Kinikoglu and Yadav, 1995).

Usability issues determining engagement of learning

A challenge to designers of multimedia educational environments is to incorporate elements of feedback and assessment – preferably in the form of self-assessment – that are essential to the learning process and to the promotion of the learner's critical analysis skills, confidence and independence. They must, furthermore, ensure that the interactive protocols they devise are useable. Squires and Preece (1996) stress the importance of focusing on learning design and usability in the development of educational software. Their work in the area of multimedia design identifies the following specific features as essential to the usability of educational modules:

- user control;
- effective presentation of content;
- good navigation;
- feedback and progress monitoring;
- intuitive and consistent design;
- clear graphical representation;
- incorporation of useful metaphors.

Squires and Preece further identify the critical role of integration of technology-based resources into the overall structure and assessment of courses. This dual emphasis on good instructional design and the full incorporation of multimedia modules within wider (and more conventional) structures of learning and assessment is reflected in the evaluation of educational software with a focus on both usability and integration (Draper et al, 1996).

   Although the literature describes the potential of multimedia and Web-based learning to create environments that significantly enhance learning, it has also been noted that few implementations actually come close to achieving this objective

(Owston, 1997). The rest of this chapter describes the process of developing the VSM, an innovative multimedia module that has realized this potential and demonstrably enhanced learning among its users. The example of the VSM confirms what the literature suggests, that the development of genuinely interactive multimedia environments depends on the dovetailing of design and evaluation as well as the productive cross-fertilizing of pedagogic concerns and technological capacity.

Activating learning through the VSM

The VSM offers first-year cultural studies students access to a Web-based learning environment that motivates student learning through the strategic adoption of the architectures of computer games. The VSM adopts a hybridized form of learning and game structures in order to erase the traditional distinction between the spaces of pedagogy and the spaces of play and leisure. For as long as it takes to complete the assignment task, students are narratively anchored in a thematically coherent environment: the mall. Offering a range of sensory experiences (animation, QTVR, acoustic cues, etc) this simulated environment is designed to simultaneously provide the conditions for game play and situated learning. The VSM is not itself a game but its design incorporates the narrative structures, incremental incentives and end-directed focus of computer games to maximize self-motivated learning in a thematically consistent virtual environment.

Development of the VSM was motivated by a combination of belief in the power of multimedia to support the creation of effective learning environments and the perceived usefulness of emerging models of learning to provide an appropriate basis for the design of such environments. Although there was little explicit reference to educational theory at the start, articulation of the designers' objectives in terms of contemporary learning theory increased as the project progressed. The academic creators of the VSM concept had a deep implicit understanding of learning issues and, over the years, had promoted effective learning through strategies developed from an experiential rather than a theoretical basis. This example conforms to the observation made by Taylor (1998) about 'early adopters' of innovative teaching technologies being recognized as exceptional teachers before embarking on innovations in teaching. Initial discussion between the commissioning academics and pedagogical experts identified the theoretical basis of the design as relating to the provision of authentic contexts (Herrington and Oliver, 2000) and situated learning (Brown *et al*, 1989).

The academics involved had initially conceived an online module in which cultural studies students could interact with everyday scenarios related to the presence of different characters in a shopping mall. As it happened their preliminary design already included some of the critical characteristics of an authentic learning environment, namely:

- authentic contexts that reflect the way the knowledge will be used in real life (the mall);
- authentic activities (shopping);
- access to multiple roles and perspectives (a range of shoppers).

In the development and pedagogic design process they were able to extend the module to support authentic learning in further ways. These innovations included enabling:

- access to expert performances and the modelling of processes;
- support for the collaborative construction of knowledge;
- reflective analysis and enabling abstractions to be formed;
- the articulation of tacit knowledge as explicit knowledge;
- coaching and scaffolding to occur at critical times;
- authentic assessment of learning within tasks.

The final design of the virtual environment promoted the concept of situated learning in manifold ways. The reflection of a 'real life' context was supported by the inclusion of retail outlets and consumer items within the mall that students would recognize and be familiar with (Country Road, The Body Shop, Borders Books and Music, Adidas, Skechers and Airwalk).

The inclusion of a range of fully articulated real-life characters (Cyra, Lilly, Anton) with whom students might identify anchors learning within this authentic context and also introduces multiple perspectives to the learning process (Wilson *et al*, 1997). Through interaction with the VSM, students are given practical contexts in which to encounter relevant theories from the domain of cultural studies and can also access the analyses of experts in the field. The interactive nature of the module's design ensures that students play an active role in the learning process and so avoids the common criticism that many so-called educational innovations are simply expensive and technologically complex versions of transmission learning.

The realization of these fundamental principles (authentic contexts; situated learning; an over-riding emphasis on interactivity) critically informed the design process. In this way the development of the VSM carefully built on prior successful initiatives in Web-based multimedia but also extended the commissioning academics' sense of the further possibilities of Web technology. In addition to a strong focus on educational design for the VSM, the importance of well-designed software that meets user needs in the most efficient way was not underrated. Continuous evaluation during development and implementation of the module, including the testing of a fully operational prototype, provided the necessary checks on achievement of these objectives (Gunn, 2000). As well as ongoing evaluation within the multidisciplinary team and with target groups of students, expert reviews of the Software Specification Document (SSD) were used as an objective 'reality check' at all phases of the project.

The VSM scenario

A description of the VSM is now presented to illustrate how the conceptual design attributes detailed above were implemented in the module in ways that specifically assisted the activation of learning. The VSM is an educational resource designed to enable the critical analysis of commodity culture. As its name suggests, the VSM is a simulated environment, which students explore while learning about contemporary critiques of consumer identity, and in which they engage in situational interactions that draw on this developing skill base. The virtual mall resembles a computer game environment insofar as it provides a thematically consistent environment in which several different aesthetic experiences are available, each relating to different levels of competency and reward. The four component sections of the VSM are described in some detail below.

Sales Pitch

The opening splash screen, with its acoustic and visual cues (a cartoon silhouette of a skatechick, dislodged by a waterfall of fetishized commodities sliding down the screen to a cyber-lounge soundtrack), 'promos' this alternate world. After log-in, it is suggested the student proceed to Sales Pitch where they are inducted into this imaginary mallscape via a 90-second animation that recalls and explicitly cites the opening sequences of many popular computer games. The ambient feel of the cartoon is retro-futuristic and this is taken up and continued by visual and aural motifs throughout the entire module. On subsequent viewings the alert student may also notice that the scenarios in the orienting cartoon prefigure the module's conceptual content: subcultures, resistance, fashion, surveillance. The student then engages in a series of tasks (shopping), which relate to the mall situation and which enable the incremental development of both navigational and critical competency. The shopping exercise, involves specific retail objects rather than generic ones (Airwalk sneakers or Adidas, Skechers backless or three-stripe classic with leather upper) and so engages first at the level of consumer desire. Once the student has committed to a purchase a reflective protocol appears to support critical self-assessment and prompts the student mark the elements that informed his or her choice from the given list (gender, fashion, price, etc). Sales Pitch closes with a second sound and vision sequence that balances the first but now includes a video-montage of a diverse range of real people wearing their equally diverse street clothing. This photo-gallery sequence prefigures the character-based scenarios of the assessment task, which ask students to consider the motivations behind their own and others' patterns of consumption. When this sequence closes, the student is free to select and proceed to another wing of the module although it is clear that access to Retail Therapy is dependent on the successful completion of the Quiz Zone. The module thus encourages or allows for free-form navigation inside an overarching narrative structure and offers an experiential equivalent to shopping itself.

Just Looking

Just Looking provides an online resource to critical concepts in cultural studies and the critique of commodity culture. This section bundles together from a variety of printed sources key information about consumer culture and functions as an online encyclopaedic text for the study of consumer culture generally (see Figure 7.1). At the system level, this resource is organized by concept or theorist but hypertext connections encourage students to navigate the section independently, enabling them to construct their own pathway through the subject matter according to the line of interest they are pursuing.

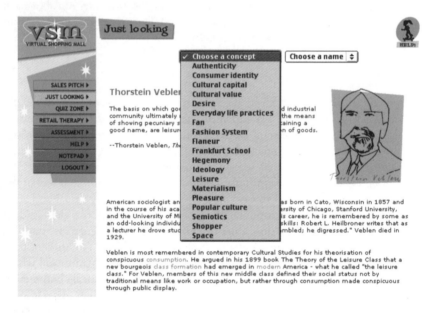

Figure 7.1 *Resource page with pull-down menu*

This wing of the module recalls traditional qualities of contemplative scholarship and research but learning is further augmented by the inclusion of television news clips, documentary footage, advertisements and photographs that illustrate the intersection of commodity culture and forms of citizenship (the opening of New Zealand's first shopping mall in the late 1950s; the Beatles being welcomed to NZ in the 1960s by Maori women in traditional dress; a 1970s NZ local punk rock band and their fans dressed in bin liners and Union Jacks; a Madonna look-alike competition staged in the late 1980s where most of the contestants are under 14, including the single male finalist). Obviously student learning via reading is thus enhanced by a sensory interaction, but as these examples suggest, the engagement is enriching of the learning experience in a number of ways, not least its ability to deepen a historical understanding of evolutions in commodity culture.

Throughout this section, a notepad function enables students to take notes online, in order to save them to a floppy drive, email them to themselves, print them out or simply refer to them when they next 'shop' at the VSM. As well as citing paper-based modes of learning, Just Looking also skills students in navigational techniques needed in Retail Therapy. Here they operate for the first time pull-down menus, a rollover glossary and video. In the larger context of the VSM, this traditional research activity is reformulated as the accumulation of 'knowledge-energy' undertaken by a player/character in a computer game in order to take on the next level of challenge or more advanced task.

Quiz Zone

The Quiz Zone comprises a self-testing gateway that enables students to amass sufficient 'knowledge-energy' to undertake the module's final challenge: Retail Therapy. At the start of the quiz the 'rules' are conveyed and the student is invited to select a prize for which they will play. Playing for a selected prize encourages students to associate this exercise with the consumer desire of commodity culture rather than the traditional academic process of testing acquired knowledge. This wing of the module has a slightly spacey, lounge sound that conveys the playfulness and 'theatre' of the quiz. As the student proceeds through the quiz committing answers, the win or lose factor is reinforced by further sound cues which accompany the 'gain' or 'loss' of pieces of the jigsaw prize. Secondary or 'reinforcing' information is also provided once an answer has been committed so that, when a student answers a particular question, some further contextualizing dialogue appears relating to why his or her response was correct or incorrect.

Once students have successfully answered five multi-choice questions in a row they can then claim their prize, which comes alive through sound and animation (the scooter turns over and drives off; the blender whirrs into action, and so on). At this point the students can proceed to Retail Therapy or elect to stay in the Quiz Zone longer, playing for other prizes, and working through the large and randomly generated question bank, testing and increasing their factual knowledge of cultural studies. The game-based learning environment functions as a productive alternative to the more conventional and achievement-driven pedagogies of competition and examination. The Quiz Zone also encourages a productive feedback loop to Just Looking, to which it may also provide the student's first point of entry. All the answers are contained in Just Looking, and links are provided between some correct and incorrect answers and related pages in the resource section, the browsing of which would allow the student to retool in the required subject matter and thus be better prepared to undertake that question again, or a later related task.

Retail Therapy

Retail Therapy contains three real-life retail scenarios structured, in the style of certain computer games, by character-based identification. These action-based scenarios unfold via QTVR and other visual and audio technologies.

Students/players imaginatively engage with each character in turn and proceed with them to explore and assess three authentic retail contexts via QTVR and other computer technologies: Body Shop, Country Road and Borders Books and Music. The VSM builds on the demonstrated capacity of game play to enhance deep learning by creating interfaces that encourage both imaginative immersion and reflective reasoning. In relation to each location, students undertake authentic tasks that draw on and extend the technical and cognitive skill base they have developed in the preliminary levels of the module. The students are initially asked to compose a profile of the character they have selected, judging by their appearance and the contents of their bag that they are able to examine in detail via QTVR technology. Once they have committed their assessment of this character, their response is displayed alongside the collated responses of their classmates and in this collaborative context they are prompted to reflect on and revise their original answer if desired.

The students proceed to shop with this character and to encounter learning exercises that are integral to this activity. They examine a shop window, and are invited to select among terms that they consider to describe the window display before working those terms into more complex sentences (see Figure 7.2). They are then prompted to compare their elaborated description to a supplied model answer (see Figure 7.3).

Shop window

The Body Shop represents itself as:

☐	elite	☐	sexually liberated	☐	good value
☐	humorous	☐	stylish	☐	sexy
☐	eurocentric	☐	egalitarian	☐	feminist

Select the terms you think best describe the window display

Figure 7.2 *Instructional protocol*

Retail Therapy

Shop window

Considering the model answer below, do you feel confident in your answer?

Model answer:

The close-up photograph of the model's face emphasizes her pouting mouth, glossy lips and falling veil of dark hair. This conventionally feminine sexiness is given a twist by the model's slightly masculine costuming and the lapel ID badge which reads CREW. This visual irony is verbally reinforced by the wordplay in the banner copy. Women moving into occupations traditionally associated with men (flight crew or film crew) is a "sign" of the times, and this image represents that professional advance as perfectly consistent with the feminine achievement of beauty.

Figure 7.3   *Reflective protocol*

Similarly, when considering an interior shop display the students evaluate their response in relation to three other supplied responses and must critically evaluate all four as persuasive or unpersuasive. This process is repeated in relation to the three characters and three store locations, although certain 'wildcard' activities are specific to each (an authentic CD listening post in Borders Books and Music, which plays five different sound bites as the students read the Borders copyrighted in-store reviews of each – Jimmy Buffet, Crowded House, The Jam, Yo La Tengo and Smashing Pumpkins; in The Body Shop a photographic archive of their recent billboard campaigns promoting Aboriginal reconciliation, etc). In this manner reflective reasoning and self-directed learning in cultural studies are supported by scenarios that ensure motivational engagement and authentic learning.

   In the Retail Therapy section of the VSM, the student actively engages, both imaginatively (via role-play) and critically (via instructional prompts), with a complex and realistic environment that advances reflective understanding and encourages revision. Throughout Retail Therapy, the learning activity is productively distributed across communicative interactions between a character role and an authentic environment. This counterweighted combination is designed to enhance the possibilities for situated learning in so far as the VSM's emphasis on narrative and thematic continuity secures the representational context necessary for engaged actions and meaningful experience (Laurillard, 1993).

Integration and evaluation

In terms of overall integration, the VSM is designed to support students through various aspects of the assessment for the target course. The Web-based module essentially plots a guided pathway across the virtual space with students required to complete specific evaluative tasks related to the shopping mall as an interface between public culture and private subjectivity. The module is designed so students are able to clearly identify the assessment goal (the critical mapping of social space demonstrating an engagement with contemporary theories of consumer subject-ivity) as it is embedded in the interactive task.

The learning outcomes associated with integration of the VSM do not differ significantly from those of the courses as they were previously taught. Rather the intention was to add richness to the learning experience through exposure to multiple perspectives including expert knowledge and student-generated views, self-selection of pathways through the knowledge domain and the encouragement of self-management throughout the process. On completion of the module students will have developed:

- the ability to demonstrate critical knowledge;
- exploration and analysis skills;
- autonomy in learning and the ability to self-assess;
- the ability to evaluate domain-specific information and situations.

The VSM was specifically designed to support achievement of these outcomes in the wider context of the host course. The outcome of continuous evaluation throughout the development and implementation phases demonstrates that these objectives are well articulated through the design and intended use of the VSM, and that considerable success in the achievement of these objectives resulted from its integration within the course structure.

The range of evaluative activities included expert reviews of the Software Design Specification (SDS) document (technical and pedagogical perspectives), student evaluation of a fully working prototype, attitude surveys, system log data and analysis of student performance on aspects of the course covered by the VSM. While the expert review process confirmed the relevance of the design objectives, student attitudes and performance are considered to be the real indicators of achievement of usability, integration and learning enhancement objectives.

Evaluation of the prototype was designed specifically to assess:

- the use of the designed exercises by students and whether this met with the designers' expectations;
- usability and functionality aspects of the site;
- the extent to which the exercises contributed to achievement of the learning outcomes.

The methods used for data collection at this stage were:

- observation records from student use of the VSM in a timetabled computer lab setting;
- an exit questionnaire included in the VSM site;
- analysis of student performance related to the learning objectives targeted by the VSM.

The observation schedule included technical, usability and learning incidents. These data, together with that from the exit questionnaire, identified issues that were modified in the final version of the program; see Table 7.1.

Table 7.1 *Technical, usability and learning issues identified during prototype evaluation*

Technical	Usability	Learning
Problems with plug-ins and bookmarks	Orientation issues – conceptual map of system, unclear objectives, where to go, what to do next, etc	Quiz zone requires completion before moving on is possible – students not sure how to answer questions or where the information should have been learnt
Student log-in problems	Low Web use ability made use of VSM problematic	Completeness of information on specific topics is questioned
Slow speed of operation of QTVR and animations	Double action required for certain functions	
	Screen size too small to see all function buttons and instructions	
	Sound is intermittent and students think it's not working when silent	

From a total of 156 responses to the exit questionnaire, it was evident that most students found the VSM easy to move around, well structured and offering relevant and complete information with clear instructions on how to proceed through the program. Constructive comments were offered on issues also identified through observation schedules confirming that some modification was required. Most of the students who did not find navigation easy cited orientation and lack of confidence as the reasons. On specific learning issues:

- 96 per cent of respondents reported some improvement in understanding of the subject following a short period of interaction with the prototype;
- 73 per cent of respondents reported some improvement in ability to reflect and revise ideas;
- 82 per cent of respondents reported some improvement in motivation. This is further supported by student comments related to the aspects of motivation defined in the literature review section of this chapter.

Comments on the best aspects of the program included the interactive aspects, attractive multimedia features and convenience of access to relevant information. These findings are entirely consistent with those reported by Baird (see Chapter 5 in this book), and suggestive of the fact that most problems encountered by students were either technical in nature or related to lack of competence and confidence with computers. Both these issues should disappear as computer and Web use increases across all disciplines and educational levels. For a first pass with the program, it was considered an overall success. Further evaluation of the VSM is currently being conducted to focus on specific ways that learning has been enhanced through the introduction of the program.

Summary and conclusion

One of the challenges faced in the development of the VSM was that the discipline of cultural studies, like many other humanities subjects, does not deal in quantitative or testable knowledge but in interpretative commentary. The goal was to design a module that was genuinely interactive from the student's perspective but did not simplify the complex skills required to frame and develop an interpretative argument. In the final module, through a series of interactive learning exercises that promotes both independence and self-reflexivity, the VSM enables students to develop and, perhaps more importantly, to evaluate their own skills of interpretation and critical argument. The demonstrated success of this module amplifies the potential of ICT to influence teaching and learning in the wider subject domain of cultural studies and confirms that content-specific developments in computer-assisted learning, such as the VSM represents, might also reconfigure our wider understanding of the activation mechanisms that trigger student learning.

References

Bloom, B S (ed) (1956) *Taxonomy of Educational Objectives: Cognitive domain (Handbook 1)*, Longman, Harlow

Brown, J S, Collins, A and Duguid, P (1989) Situated cognition and the culture of learning, *Educational Researcher*, **18** (1), pp 32–42

Draper, S W, Brown, M I, Henderson, F P and McAteer, E (1996) Integrative evaluation: an emerging role for classroom studies of CAL, *Computers and Education*, **26** (1–3), pp 17–32

Grabinger, S and Dunlap, J (1995) Rich environments for active learning: a definition, *The Association of Learning Technology Journal (ALT-J)*, **3** (2), pp 5–34

Gunn, C (2000) CAL evaluation: future directions, in *The Changing Face of Learning Technology*, eds G Jacobs, D Squires and G Conole, pp 59–67, University of Wales Press, Cardiff

Herrington, J and Oliver, R (2000) An instructional design framework for authentic learning environments, *Educational Technology, Research and Development*, **48** (3), pp 23–48

Hutchings, G A, Hall, W and Colburn, C J (1993) A model of learning with hypermedia systems. Paper presented at the HCI International Conference, Orlando, FL

Johnson, C (1998) Using cognitive models to transfer the strengths of computer games into human computer interfaces. Accessed November 20 2000, from http://wwwdcsglaacuk/~johnson/papers/ics/fun_and_gameshtml

Jonassen, D (1998) Designing constructivist learning environments, in *Instructional-design Theories and Models: A new paradigm of instructional* theory (2nd edn), ed C M Reigeluth, pp 215–39, Lawrence Erlbaum, Hillsdale, NJ

Jones, M, Farquar, J and Surrey, D (1995) Using metacognitive theories to design user interfaces for computer-based learning, *Educational Technology*, **35** (4), pp 12–22

Keller, J (1987) Strategies for stimulating the motivation to learn, *Performance and Instruction*, **26** (8), pp 1–7

Kinikoglu, Y T and Yadav, S B (1995) Determination of the features of instructional computer games. Accessed 25 October 2000, from http://hsbbayloredu/ramsower/acis/papers/kinikyhtm

Laurillard, D M (1993) *Rethinking University Teaching: A framework for the effective use of educational technology*, Routledge, London

Lemke, J (1993) Hypermedia and higher education, *Interpersonal Computing and Technology: An Electronic Journal for the 21ˢᵗ Century*, **1** (2). Accessed July 2001, from http://januccnauedu/~ipct-j/1993/n2/lemketxt

Merrill, D, Li, Z and Jones, M (1991) Second generation instructional design (ID2), *Educational Technology and Society*, **30** (1 and 2), pp 7–11 and 14–17

Owston, R D (1997) The World Wide Web: a technology to enhance teaching and learning?, *Educational Researcher*, **26** (2), pp 27–33

Sims, R (1997) Interactivity: A forgotten art? Accessed 10 July 2001, from http://introbaseorg/docs/interact/

Somekh, B (1996) Designing software to maximize learning: what can we learn from the literature?, *Association of Learning Technology Journal (ALT-J)*, **4** (3), pp 4–16

Spiro, R J and Jehng, J C (1990) Cognitive flexibility and hypertext: theory and technology for the non-linear and multidimensional traversal of complex subject matter, in *Cognition, Education and Multimedia: Exploring ideas in high technology*, ed D Nix and R J Spiro, pp 163–205, Lawrence Erlbaum, Hillsdale, NJ

Squires, D and Preece, J (1996) Usability and learning: evaluating the potential of educational software, *Computers and Education*, **27** (1), pp 15–22

Taylor, P (1998) Institutional change in uncertain times: lone ranging is not enough, *Studies in Higher Education,* **23** (3), 269–79

Wilson, B, Teslow, J and Osman-Jouchoux, R (1997) The impact of constructivism and postmodernism on ID fundamentals, in *Instructional Design Fundamentals: A review and reconsideration,* ed B B Seels, pp 137–57, Educational Technology Publications, Englewood Cliffs, NJ

Chapter 8

Replicating practice complexities – multimedia innovation in social work education

Stuart Evans and Phillip Swain

Introduction

The essence of social work education is that it prepares students for professional practice in the human services, in direct and indirect practice, policy and community development, and advocacy, working from individual, family, group or community perspectives. The domain of welfare and social work practice consists of 'the interaction between individuals and social arrangements. . . (that is) the many processes and relationships by which individuals and the social structure are produced and reproduced' (O'Connor *et al*, 1995, p 9). Social work thus focuses on the interface between the individual, family, group and community and the structures and institutions of society. It draws together the social, the political and the cultural influences on individual, group and community behaviour, and as a discipline has at its core the fundamental commitment to the pursuit and maintenance of human well-being (AASW, 1999a, Clause 1).

The pursuit of that well-being necessitates working towards more equitable access to social, political and physical resources. It is thus critical for social work practitioners, and those seeking to educate future practitioners, to 'not simply (be) seeking to adapt to the present, but also trying to anticipate the future, and to educate students to be adaptable, flexible, and able to see possibilities beyond the constraints of the present practice environment' (Ife, 1997, p 26). A critical ethical obligation of professional practice is to continue to develop competencies across the range of frameworks and intervention strategies relevant to particular fields and spheres of practice (AASW, 1999a, Clause 3.5; Swain, 1996) – thus the competent practitioner needs to do more than simply understand the situation faced by a particular client – whether individual, group or community. The practitioner must also be able to facilitate a structural analysis of client difficulties and to develop appropriate strategies for change with that client, using language that has meaning for all the involved parties, and skilfully facilitating a critical analysis of alternative strategies and sites of intervention (Fraser and Strong, 2000). The essence of social work is, then, engagement with both the client and the wider society and its influences or, to put it another way, with both the micro and macro dimensions of the human experience.

Hence social work education needs to mirror the myriad practice settings into which its students will graduate, and yet anticipate developments in those settings. The integration of theory and practice, usually associated with fieldwork place-ments, is itself a core requirement of approved social work courses of training, (AASW, 1999b). Such integration requires that what is taught in classrooms away from the field be as close a fit to practice reality as is possible, but simultaneously be amenable to change to meet the contextual developments and practice realities that may arise.

How can what is taught in the relative sterility of the classroom, even using practitioners as teachers and role models, match the reality of the vast range of experiences and complexities of practice in the field? This chapter outlines the pedagogical and practical implications of an explicit attempt through the use of multimedia to bring practice reality into the classroom experiences of social work students, as an integral part of learning and in the preparation of students for professional practice.

The context

Professional social work education is committed to the preparation of qualified practitioners by provision of a teaching and learning environment that develops knowledge, values, commitment and skills in working with people in need. Social work graduates are expected to be informed, skilled, caring and compassionate practitioners, who will work towards securing a more just, fair and equitable society in which social inequalities, discrimination and disadvantage are eliminated.

Apart from the range of interpersonal, group and community skills that graduates are expected to demonstrate, it is an increasing expectation of even beginning social work practitioners that they will be competent in the use of multimedia, familiar with computer technologies and comfortable in the use of the Internet for research and enhancement of practice skills. Such competency is also often essential for the maintenance of the detailed records that is demanded by professional practice, where adequate records may be critical to meeting the accountability demands practitioners face (Royce *et al,* 1993). Students need to develop such skills and confidence before beginning their practice, simultaneously with the continuing tasks of integrating practice with classroom teaching, and of implementing into their practice the frameworks and intervention strategies taught for classroom purposes across the different subjects offered within social work curricula. Across that curricula the essential functions of the theory offered to students in micro and macro-based subjects is the 'description; explanation; prediction; and control and management of events or changes' (Mullaly, 1997, p 100). However, the social work educator must also assist students to see that practice is not composed of discreet and unrelated parts, but of complex interactions between many individuals, structures and institutions in society. So, too, practice education – if it is to be education for practice reality – must mirror that complexity, but in ways that enable the student to engage with the materials presented.

In addition, within academic circles generally and in professional education in particular, there are strong imperatives to focus upon competency-based learning (Evans *et al,* 2001; Hopkins and Cooper, 2000). For that, curricula aptly character-ized as 'acquisition' learning – the learning of information, facts or data, the narrative media of lectures, print handouts, overheads and video – is generally appropriate to 'acquisition' of knowledge. Arguably, however, 'negotiation', decision making and assessment skills (for example) are better learnt through discursive interaction between student and teacher, and between students, in tutorials, role-play activities and other interactive modes, such as can be provided by multimedia developments (Evans *et al,* 2001; Laurillard, 1995; Murranka and Lynch, 1999). Competency-based learning requires attention and commitment to the develop-ment of behaviourally stated objectives, individualized learning, to interactivity, and to student-paced learning. Social work practice, too, is essentially not a unitary activity, as interdisciplinary practice is central to professional practice. Hence education for practice must emphasize interdisciplinary collaboration and team-work (Charlesworth *et al,* 2000, p 339).

The problem – replicating practice in the social work classroom

Within this academic and professional context, the development of LaSWoP (Law and Social Work Practice) at the University of Melbourne represented an attempt to move away from separation of teaching into discrete subjects and towards integration between content and assessment requirements of complementary subjects. The breaking up of curricula into subjects or units, though necessary for the practical delivery of content, is often seen by students as reflective of different concepts and frameworks of practice, so the ideas and concepts relevant and critical to one subject are not necessarily perceived as having a place in another, even related, subject. Not only does this not mirror the usual experience of practice, where professional social workers draw seamlessly from the range of knowledge bases to which they have been exposed, but such segregation of content further divides the twin domains of the classroom and the field. The development of the LaSWoP program attempted to replicate the integration of theory and practice through the integration of a theory-based subject (interpersonal skills with individuals and families) with a practice-based subject (the legal context of social work practice). Its development reflected a commitment to a focus on the core professional expertise that graduates require, along with the need to ensure that students had the opportunity to develop decision making skills in core practice areas. This was done within a reflective practice environment, which provided a degree of safety in anticipation of the many high-risk and public profile settings in which even beginning graduates often practice.

The LaSWoP project

The LaSWoP project was developed over 1999–2001 as a multimedia option within two core subjects (in interpersonal practice and in legal practice) within the social work degree. Funded by small university multimedia development grants, the project has evolved to become a central practice skill development component of the social work degree. It attempts to replicate within the relative safety of the classroom and multimedia environment the complex and multidisciplinary decision making with which practitioners have to become familiar, comfortable and competent.

To achieve this was no small aim. The LaSWoP program thus incorporated:

- The development of a series of interactive multimedia resource modules, each built around a case scenario incorporating a range of individual, familial and systemic characteristics which the practitioner might reasonably expect to regularly face. The program was designed to stand alongside regular classroom teaching, so as to encourage development of decision making and assessment skills in such complex practice areas such as child protection and juvenile justice (the practice settings initially developed under LaSWoP).
- Other practice dimensions such as domestic violence, social security and family law, can also be incorporated into the scenarios with which students engage.
- A commitment to the development of teaching case materials that are representative of contemporary thematic issues faced by social work practitioners, including different notions of family definition and parenting, issues of sexuality and sexual orientation, ethnicity, Aboriginality and immigrant intergenerationality. In LaSWoP this is achieved via visual, oral and text (refer-

ence) presentation of data, from which students must elicit appropriate indicia of behaviour, relationships and the like, which are then used in formulating their assessments and intervention strategies. Figure 8.1 shows one example of such information, presented both in text and with visual cues, which the student practitioner must incorporate into their completed assessment.

● An explicit commitment to the enhancement of student familiarity with Internet use as a research tool in law, social policy, and overseas and interstate practice developments (Evans *et al,* 2001, p 34). The LaSWoP project requires students to familiarize themselves with the use of the Internet, email and computer data programmes, and to develop the facility to craft assessments and submit information electronically.

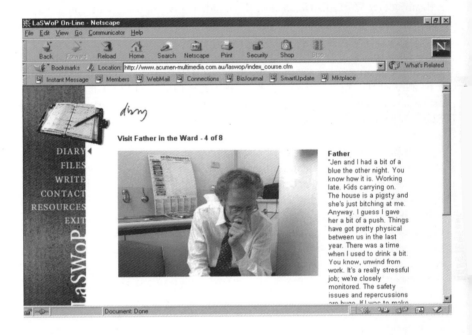

Figure 8.1   *Father visits the children's ward*

Within LaSWoP, students function as beginning staff members in a given practice setting (a child protection unit, a juvenile justice programme, an aged care programme, etc). They are then assigned a 'case' by their supervisor in respect of which they must utilize whatever frameworks of understanding and information they have, to make an interpersonal person-in-situation assessment.

They also need, over a notional period of time (a five-day period was used in the first two scenarios, but the days over which the scenario develops could be lengthened or shortened) to reach a conclusion as to an appropriate legal course of action and outcome. This must be done within the confines and requirements of the relevant law and with reference to the protocols and practice requirements of the appropriate jurisdiction. In making their assessments and recommending an outcome, students have access to a bank (library) of computer-based information and resources, to material presented in classroom-based course teaching, and to whatever they can locate through their own Internet research. They can also draw upon the situational and contextual information provided through LaSWoP about the particular agency, network and community setting in which the agency to which they are attached is located. The LaSWoP program allows the student-practitioner to make and edit case notes and preliminary assessments, and reports for both agency and court use, and prompts him or her to draw upon information from a range of other professional frameworks, or approaches or practitioners.

> Example: Has a paediatrician seen the child? Have you sought an opinion as to how the injury occurred?

As the tasks for each day are completed, more information becomes available and new information sources are introduced as the notional 'days' develop. The depth or paucity of the information can be manipulated by teaching staff – case notes can be incomplete or irrelevant, or staff may be unavailable in actual practice to expand upon or clarify what their assessments might have been. Often the practitioner must rely upon the best information that is available, rather than what might ideally have been sought, in making an assessment.

A key critical interactive component of LaSWoP is that students have access to other 'players' within the particular practice setting, from whom they can seek advice or further information via email. These 'players' could be other professionals within the particular agency, from other agencies within the relevant network, or colleagues with whom the practitioner has a line or accountability relationship, such as a supervisor or legal adviser. These key players add to the information from the practitioner by providing either computer-generated responses to frequently asked questions or by information in response to particular prompts. By allowing teaching staff to take particular roles, however, it is also possible to provide individualized responses in real time through email. This replicates the supervisory and information supports that the beginning practitioner ought to expect from such persons as supervisor, other key professionals working in the particular setting (the paediatrician and charge nurse in the hospital setting, the probation officer or school year coordinator in a juvenile justice setting, etc), legal advisers, and the like. Thus the capacity of the LaSWoP program to be 'self-authoring' allows – within the limits of availability and time! – the teacher-practitioner to respond to the individual needs of each student, rather than attempting to anticipate electronically the information needs, beginning competencies and learning styles of the student cohort as a group. Not only this, but the self-authoring capacity of LaSWoP allows for additional key personnel to be added to a scenario at any time (for example, a family support worker in another agency) with whom the student can then interact via email, just as would be possible (within ethical and practical limits) for the practitioner. Alternatively, if desired, a new piece of information can be introduced for students to consider, even while the programme is running (so, for example, in a hospital setting a new assessment by a doctor of a child at risk could be introduced into the scenario), or personnel can be withdrawn (the charge nurse is ill and so no longer available to clarify her case notes) or introduced (a new speech pathologist has been appointed and takes a different view of the appropriate assistance required by the family). Students can also be allocated to small learning groups to enhance their interactive learning opportunities.

In summary, LaSWoP has attempted to support student learning by mirroring the reality and complexity of social work practice through providing students with an interactive case-based simulation incorporating:

- multiple virtual day case evolution;
- the capacity to receive and respond to incoming system and email messages;
- the stimulus of learning 'prompts';
- the capacity to interact with peers;
- the opportunity of email contact with teaching staff;
- the opportunity of email contact with other characters within the scenario;
- access to files, resources, guides, exemplars, etc;
- support and advice regarding report and assignment writing;
- links to other Web-based resources.

The response – strengths and limitations of interactive technology

The initial development of LaSWoP – and continuing maintenance and further development to ensure the retention of current practice accuracy and relevance – took and is taking a great deal of time. This is particularly so as the 'authors (of the LaSWoP project) were simultaneously not only educators but also researchers, software co-developers, practitioners and field supervisors' (Evans *et al,* 2001, p 32). University contract and copyright issues regarding the ownership of the product (that is, the self-authoring scenario development potential of LaSWoP) remains complicated. The time taken and the costs involved (both direct, in software development, and indirect, in commitment of time to the project) were far greater than anticipated. As Morris and Naughton (1999) note, the costs of both initial development and ongoing maintenance are significant and often underestimated in these developments.

The project confirmed the considerable student differences in beginning competencies, comfort and familiarity with computer and Internet technology, highlighting that the 'paradox of interactive media is that being a user-control medium the learner expects to have control, and yet a learner does not know enough to be given full control' (Laurillard, 1995, p 185). Despite this and the inevitable concerns associated with software and hardware incompatibility, the project has received very strong affirmation from students. In 2000–01 approximately two-thirds of the social work student cohort chose to undertake LaSWoP as part of their participation in the two subject areas that the project incorporated. The evaluation of the project in 2000–01 showed that students clearly valued the diversity and depth of practice perspectives available to them, the attempt to replicate (more closely) the realities of practice, the explicit linking of theory and practice, and the opportunity to practise skills (in making assessments, in preparing court reports, in summarizing evidence coherently in the light of legislative requirements and criteria) which were seen to be directly relevant to practice. In addition, students greatly appreciated the study economies available through the combining of subjects, readings and assessment tasks. They responded positively to the link provided through LaSWoP between interpersonal practice assessment and the demands of situational context and time:

> Example: What is happening in this family? What this family needs is not available for a month, but I have to make a recommendation in a week!

There were – and continue to be – costs and difficulties associated with this important development. Apart from time factors, the exponential development of hardware and software has meant that developments at the forefront of available technology will, almost as soon as testing and implementation are completed, be at least partially superseded by new technological developments. Students also bring with them a variety of technological knowledge and resources, and will be considerably disadvantaged if unable to participate in programs such as LaSWoP if only those with the most up-to-date hardware and software could do so. Hence, for example, LaSWoP does not to this point include video streaming or audio information, although visual information is available in each scenario. Students are often working with outmoded hardware, often from home or outside of the access hours for university-based computer laboratories. In the absence of funding for system upgrades for such students the computer-based resources offered to them must be compatible with what they have, or some will be disadvantaged and excluded from these learning opportunities.

For the authors, the attempt to replicate the access expectations of real practice proved very time-consuming. While email access was not offered to students 24 hours a day, student expectations of access meant that replies from the various 'roles' undertaken by the authors through email contact (as senior social worker, legal adviser, and other roles) could not be delayed for more than a day or so without considerable anxiety on the part of students. A large cohort of students, undertaking the project over several weeks at their own pace, meant an unprecedented level of email activity associated with the project over most of the relevant teaching period – with, of course, more pressing and frequent demands from the less confident and less competent students. A clear indication to students as to their access to the support persons in each scenario, and of the likely delays in replies to requests for information and assistance, is critical – and even then some student concern cannot be avoided. Like the student-practitioner who writes the court report at 4 am who cannot expect the legal adviser to be available until the next working day, so those undertaking LaSWoP cannot always expect advice to be a few keystrokes away.

Critical attributes of multimedia developments within social work education

If learning in social work is to be enhanced and made to mirror and represent practice, then attention to several critical attributes is essential. How the LaSWoP project attempted to deal with these attributes is important in reflecting upon its adequacy as part of a professional practice-based education process.

First, case materials and exemplars utilized within educational processes must be authentic, relevant and current. Case scenarios must be reflective of current practice realities but, as shown in Figure 8.1, the advantage of interactive authoring is that text and other content can be easily replaced or amended to meet developments in practice – even those that occur while the program is running with a particular group of students. In social work and similar disciplines prerequisite experience and concurrent placement opportunities mean that students have a ready point of comparison for university-based teaching materials that are out of date. They will quickly identify (and comment upon) case and course materials that no longer reflect the practice, policy or organizational realities in the field. The organization that has merged with another, or that no longer exists, the practice setting that has been reorganized into new units of service delivery, the practitioner titles (and roles) that have been modified, the policy arrangement or legislative provision that are known to have been amended, will be likely to be known to at least some students, many of whom will already have some practice experience when they commence their social work education. Unless teaching materials reflect such developments students will quickly identify that the materials presented to them might have been relevant and current in the past, but are no longer so.

If case materials are to be current and authentic, it is imperative that they be developed (and maintained over time) with the active participation of the practitioners who are most familiar with them. Even the academic with extensive practice experience, but who is no longer working actively in a particular field of practice, will quickly develop romanticized or unrealistic notions of current practice in those fields. In the LaSWoP example, each case scenario has been developed in close consultation with practitioners from the various disciplines represented in the examples used. Current practice guidelines, manuals of procedures, established inter-agency protocols and acknowledged policies formed the underpinning of the case examples. Where possible these resources were formally incorporated into the case examples themselves, or were provided through direct online access. This, too, replicated the frequent experience of many practitioners who rely upon computer or online access to agency protocols and manuals of procedures:

Example: Why is this matter to be referred to the relevant child protection authority? Because first, there are legislative requirements (check the relevant legislation in your State – click here) supported by agency protocols and working agreements. (You should read the Agency-Hospital protocol – click here.)

Just as the new or inexperienced practitioner should in practice be able to access the relevant manual from the agency manager's office, or by asking a colleague or supervisor what the agency expectations are, or by seeking information from a library or electronic database, so the multimedia representation of practice needs to incorporate such opportunities. Given that more and more of practice involves the use of email as a communication medium, the potential for classroom-based interactive multimedia to replicate practice in the same way is high. The key is to ensure that the current realities of practice are replicated, and here close collaboration with the field is essential.

Multimedia developments, particularly where self-authoring is possible (as in LaSWoP) have a distinct advantage over fixed modes of case delivery (the written document or text, for example). With self-authoring and virtual case evolution, data, relationships, titles, roles, availability, relevance and completeness of information and the like, can be redeveloped between semesters of teaching, or even during the time when a particular student cohort is utilizing the program, if necessary. In the LaSWoP program, the nature of repeated (and clearly appropriate) student email enquiries seeking expert orthopaedic information in a case where a child showed some evidence of repeated fractures, suggested the addition to the scenario of a new role. Hence the introduction to the scenario of the hospital orthopaedic surgeon, who announced his 'involvement' to student practitioners via an email file note indicating that the request by the social work staff for an orthopaedic assessment had been noted, and that this would be undertaken within 48 hours, after which a report on the child would be placed on the hospital file. This new role introduction was both relevant and reflective of what would occur in practice in a major hospital setting where child abuse concerns were at issue.

Self-authoring multimedia allows 'staff' to go off after their roster ends, or when the weekend comes, or to return to work unexpectedly when someone is ill. It lets them write sloppy, unprofessional, detailed or minimal case notes – as also occurs in practice from time to time – requiring the student practitioner to seek clarifications of meaning, or evidence, or the basis upon which apparent conclusions are drawn. Similarly, particularly in settings where staff are rostered, time limits can be built into scenarios to reflect the demands of practice:

Example: Too busy to clarify with the Charge Nurse what her case note meant? Sorry, she's off duty for three days.

In this example, the social work report that is due will have to be prepared without any additional information this particular professional might have been able to give. Again this is reflective of practice reality – people do get ill, take leave, not reply to email messages, or reply with limited or irrelevant information.

Secondly, multimedia components of social work education must maintain the integration of theory and practice and contribute to the development of beginning practitioner expertise. The primary site of practice learning for student social workers is, arguably, the field placement where under skilled and accessible supervision they are exposed to what practice is really like. The students must be challenged to draw upon information sources relevant to the particular practice setting – the specialist medical report in the hospital setting – but to then apply to the information provided the frameworks and disciplinary understanding acquired through professional education.

A key task of professional education is to integrate what occurs in the field with what is offered to the student in the classroom – otherwise practice becomes no more than ill-informed (if well intended) intervention based on the individual's unique but ungrounded sense of what might be appropriate in a particular situation. In part, such theory-practice integration is made more possible by the very currency and relevance of the practice examples used for teaching purposes, as noted above. In the LaSWoP program, this integration was enhanced and empha-sized through the key roles of 'senior social worker' and 'legal adviser' taken by teaching staff, whose task was to both direct students to appropriate information sources and also to foster critical reflection upon their practice and those of others presented in the scenarios. The use within the LaSWoP project of reflective diary and file entries, which the student-practitioner could edit, provided a stimulus for better understanding of both practice and personal responses to the case materials presented. Enabling subject teachers to view and contribute to these reflective entries further fostered a critical environment where practice and theory were seen as two sides of the same coin, rather than as separate spheres of reality.

Thirdly, response systems need to be timely, at least to the extent of mirroring the time constraints likely to be actually encountered in practice:

Example: 'Remember that the case is set for tomorrow afternoon in the Children's Court. Your report must be logged by midday.'

The difficulty, as noted above, is that a central characteristic of both email and multimedia is speed – the email arrives moments after it has left the sender. The student-practitioner undertaking a case assessment late at night or at weekends (as students are likely to do, given the competing demands of employment, study, family and personal lives which almost all must somehow balance), needs to be reminded that responses to queries will be timely but not necessarily immediate. In the LaSWoP example, the understanding was that email queries would be checked at least once each day during the week, but not always outside regular business hours (although, given that one case involved rostered staff at a hospital, a late email from a registrar or charge nurse finalizing case notes before the end of a shift would not have been inappropriate). Nevertheless, even with this limitation, student demand for immediacy of response did place considerable pressure on teaching staff to be more available than would be the practice reality, with both time (and, so, cost) implications for all those involved:

'Guided discovery' relies upon readily available teacher input to guide, advise, to respond to uncertainties, to comment on progress, and to offer explanations. This accessibility is the richest mode of learning but, of course, the most expensive, requiring both the intimate involvement of the teacher, and the 'teacher-constructed world' (Evans *et al*, 2001, p 38).

Pressures for immediate response and access to information became increasingly the case as the time demands built into the scenarios to reflect the realities of practice ('your court report is due by the end of the week') became more pressing – but this too reflects what is likely to be the practitioner experience of working with limited resources of information and time.

Fourthly, multimedia educational systems need to recognize, take account of and value the differential attributes (life and employment experiences, qualifications, interests and preferred modes of engagement with learning materials), which different students bring to the task of learning and experiencing. Social work education is characterized by a diverse student population in terms of age, previous educational experience across a range of disciplines, cultural background, experience of tertiary study, and familiarity with computers and the Web. Within LaSWoP, the capacity for interactive self-authoring meant that the system was able to respond, on the one hand, to the student who is naïve in the use of a computer:

Example: 'Unsure what to do? Try starting with. . . Still not sure? Make an appointment to see your tutor.'

and on the other, to the student who is already experienced in practice and reduces what had been anticipated to be a task requiring several hours of work over several sessions, to a brief engagement and generation of outcomes based on previous experience:

Example: 'Have you carefully read all the reports available to you? Don't just follow the guidelines – the Magistrate will expect you to canvass ALL the possible outcomes, not just those you are familiar with or which you most frequently utilize.'

The interactive and self-authoring nature of LaSWoP meant that both extremes of response could be accommodated, by differential email responses to the individual student. Thus the more experienced student-practitioner could be prompted to question the basis of apparent wisdom derived from past practice experience and to consider new or unfamiliar approaches to (for example) an assessment task, while the inexperienced or unconfident new practitioner could be gently encouraged to complete the required task on a step-by-step basis, with affirmation along the way, until greater confidence developed.

Conclusions

Social work's greatest strength has been described by Ife (1997, p 159) as 'its ability to ground its understandings and its practice in the reality of the oppressed and the disadvantaged'. In order to support and optimize learning opportunities in social work, teaching materials and the formal educational environments must reflect and engender that reality by incorporating the realities of practice – in its acknowledgment and use of approaches and frameworks of understanding, its essentially interdisciplinary nature, its basis in networks of groups and agencies, and the time and other constraints that impact upon practice.

Although risk and uncertainty are key characteristics of social work practice (Camilleri 1999), and so need to be elements of the practice to which students are introduced, students also need to be able to step into practice in a controlled way, with access to learning supports and advice, and with the opportunity to make mistakes without facing the potentially serious repercussions of errors in practice (Swain, 1996). With careful development, attention to the demands of particular practice settings, and a commitment of resources to development and maintenance of relevant practice-based materials, use of interactive multimedia has shown through such developments as LaSWoP that it has great potential to supplement classroom-based learning and to reproduce the vagaries of direct interpersonal practice.

References

Australian Association of Social Workers (1999a) *Code of Ethics,* AASW, Canberra

Australian Association of Social Workers (1999b) *Guidelines for Accreditation,* AASW, Canberra

Camilleri, P (1999) Social work and its search for meaning: theories, narratives and practices, in *Transforming Social Work,* eds B Pease and J Fook, Allen and Unwin, Sydney

Charlesworth, S, Turner, J N and Foreman, L (2000) *Disrupted Families: The law,* Federation Press, Sydney

Evans, S, Petrakis, M and Swain, P (2001) Experiencing practice complexities via computer: multimedia innovation in social work education, *New Technology in the Human Services,* **13** (3–4), pp 31–42

Fraser, H and Strong, D (2000) Teaching structural social work skills to beginning students, *Advances in Social Work and Welfare Education,* **3,** pp 27–36

Hopkins J and Cooper L (2000) The competency approach, in *Fieldwork in the Human Services,* eds L Cooper and L Briggs, Ch 5, Allen and Unwin, Sydney

Ife, J (1997) *Rethinking Social Work,* Longman, Sydney

Laurillard, D (1995) Multimedia and the changing experience of the learner, *British Journal of Educational Technology,* **26** (3), pp 179–89

Morris, D and Naughton, J (1999) The future's digital, isn't it? Some experience and forecasts based on the Open University's Technology Foundation course, *Systems Research and Behavioural Science,* **16** (2), p 147

Mullaly, B (1997) *Structural Social Work,* 2nd edn, Oxford University Press, Ontario

Murranka, P A and Lynch, D (1999) Developing a competency-based fundamentals of management communication course, *Business Communication Quarterly,* **62** (3), p 9

O'Connor, I, Wilson, J and Setterlund, D (1995) *Social Work and Welfare Practice* (2nd edn), Longman, Sydney

Royce, D, Dhooper, S and Rompf, E (1993) *Field Instruction: A guide for social work students,* Longman, Sydney

Swain, P (1996) Social workers and professional competence: a last goodbye to the Clapham omnibus?, *Torts Law Journal,* **4,** pp 41–59

Part 3

Providing socialization support

Chapter 9

Technology and second language learning through socialization

Robert Debski

Introduction

The past several decades have seen a significant shift in the conceptualization of language. From perceiving the laws of language as an external phenomenon in and of itself worth study, through positing them in the human mind, we have come to understand language as closely interwoven with society and social semiotic systems. Our understanding of learning has undergone a similar change. Learning a second language (L2) no longer seems to be about memorization of rules and discrete language items. Increasingly, it is perceived as a two-tiered phenomenon: individual and cognitive on the one hand, and socially-situated, collaboratively-constructed and inseparably connected with other semiotic systems such as gesture, customs and rituals, and social and cultural artefacts on the other. Consequently, there has been an evident shift from the learner as individual to the learner as a member of the social group actively involved in goal-oriented activity and in co-constructing the learning process. Socialization has become a desired feature of the L2 classroom and a viable area of learning research.

Applications of information and communications technology (ICT) in L2 learning have also undergone an evolution, both responding to and assisting the advancement of current beliefs about language learning and classroom practices. The use of computers to dispatch information has first been complemented by approaches underscoring exploration and discovery by students, and more recently by instructional practices involving electronic social interaction in simulated (Murphy and Gazi, Chapter 12, this volume) and naturalistic settings. In fact, social computing (Debski *et al*, 1997) has probably been the single most important factor changing L2 learning and teaching practices in recent time. Second language students are asked to communicate and collaborate in the target language with overseas partners, to search for information on the Internet, create Web projects and share them with online communities.

Despite the growing popularity and intuitive appeal, the position of computer-supported collaborative learning is however still far from settled and exactly what and how students learn through such practices is still unclear (Koschmann, 1996; Koschmann *et al*, 2002). The critics for instance point out the reliance of that approach on individual student and teacher variables (Debski and Gruba, 1998) and the student anxiety caused by technological instruments (Lewis and Atzert, 2000). The proponents argue that computer-supported collaborative learning can make L2 learning purposeful and meaningful, as networked machines help learners participate in social environments where their L2 can serve as a vehicle for carrying out 'collective intentionality' (Searle, 1995). ICT can also help build learning environments in which the process of reconstruction of social reality and identity in the L2 can be carried out. Taking these premises as a point of departure, the aim of this chapter is to demonstrate how technology can effectively support various second language acquisition (SLA) approaches that feature social interaction as an important vehicle of language learning.

The subsequent part of this chapter presents several SLA concepts illuminating the role of social interaction in the L2 classroom. These notions are viewed here as complementary, addressing the central issue at different levels and from differing standpoints, and together better capable of explaining the role of social interaction for language development. This is followed by a description of the Project-Oriented Computer-Assisted Language Learning (PrOCALL) project conducted in the School of Languages at the University of Melbourne (Debski, 2000), taking social constructivism (Vygotsky, 1978) as its theoretical base and exploiting social computing as a medium of L2 learning. In the final part, several themes explaining the significance of modern technology for situating language learning in social contexts are discussed. In summary, the chapter provides evidence that ICT can facilitate L2 pedagogy based on socially-oriented SLA theory by:

- enabling activity functioning as a catalyst for social interaction;
- supporting negotiation of meaning in communication;
- increasing learner audience awareness and agency;
- aiding development of cross-cultural skills;
- changing power relations;
- supporting identity development.

Examples drawn from various studies of the PrOCALL classrooms are used to illustrate these themes. Where possible, this evidence is triangulated with the results of other studies.

Socialization and language learning

Different perspectives on second language acquisition accentuate the importance of social interaction for L2 learning; these are discussed below.

Interactionist SLA

Interactionist SLA emphasizes the significance of environments supporting the resolution of communicative breakdowns and negotiation of meaning for promoting learning (Gass, 1997; Long, 1983; Pica, 1994; Swain and Lapkin, 1998). Negotiation of meaning occurs when learners engaged in interactions experience difficulties in understanding each other (Long, 1983). Speakers resort to it in order to put the exact communicative message across (Swain and Lapkin, 1998). This concept is derived from the input hypothesis (Krashen, 1981, 1985) stating that learner output modified through negotiation of meaning provides comprehensible input to learners as well as feedback on their production (Gass, 1997). Thus, negotiation of meaning assists learners in producing comprehensible input and output, and draws their attention to their inter-language and to different target language forms (Gass, 1997). Learner attention or 'noticing' also facilitates learning (Schmidt, 1990). The concepts of noticing and negotiation of meaning bring together the cognitive and the social to form the foundation of the prevailing view of second language learning.

More recent interactionist positions stress the significance of naturalistic social discourse for creating situations that abound in opportunities to learn through negotiation of meaning and noticing. L2 learning tasks should thus provide opportunities for consensus building, planning, discussing controversy and outcomes, and all linguistic functions present in naturalistic goal-oriented discourse. An important underlying assumption is that learning is facilitated by use of the target language in content-rich and purposeful ways while an active awareness of the forms and functions of language used is maintained (Schmidt, 1990). Such opinions close the gap between interactionist SLA theory and views of SLA inspired by sociocultural theory (Vygotsky, 1978, 1981; Wertsch, 1985).

Socio-interactive SLA theory

Socio-interactive SLA theory is a more holistic perspective on L2, one that includes consideration of the learning task as well as of the complexity of individual and social conditions surrounding it. According to the socio-interactive approach, L2 learner constructs first emerge at the intra-psychological, social level supported by the process of scaffolding (Bruner, 1975) and only later at the inter-psychological platform through the processes of internalization. To better explain interaction, researchers have thus begun to study how L2 learners collaborate with one another as they work on language learning tasks and projects. Studies demonstrate that learners working collaboratively can guide themselves through linguistically complex tasks that would be far too complex for them if they were working individually (Donato, 1994; Ohta, 1995). In such a view, the boundaries between individual interacting learners become somewhat unclear, as they produce jointly owned language in response to goal-oriented activity. Language development can be viewed as a form of gradual socialization among individuals.

By drawing on Vygotsky's (1978) assumption that mental activity is organized through socially constructed artefacts, socio-interactive SLA emphasizes the significance of collaborative, goal-oriented learning. Interacting groups of learners generate contingencies or affordances (van Lier, 2000) that can be turned into learning that is socially situated and meaningful. Socio-interactive approaches also draw our attention to how social activity is mediated by various tools. Internet mediation thus not only carries learning activity, but also interacts with it by changing learning conditions. Researchers argue that Internet mediation changes student speech behaviour, for example by affecting power relations and creating in them a greater sense of freedom to express controversial opinions (Thorne, 1999; Warschauer, 1996) or removing barriers caused by shyness (Kern, 1995).

Van Lier (2000) allies socio-interactive SLA with ecological theory. His approach presumes that language cannot be reduced to a system of simpler phenomena, since at every level of linguistic complexity new properties emerge that cannot be broken down into those of lower levels. It also assumes that the social activity of the learner does not facilitate learning but in fact constitutes learning. Consequently, language learning is not a process of representing linguistic objects in the brain. We do not 'own' language, we learn to live in it. The ecological perspective on SLA 'places a strong emphasis on contextualizing language into other semiotic systems, and into the contextual world as a whole' (van Lier, 2000, p 259). What ramifications does this theory have for the creation and study of language learning environments? Language is learnt in semiotically rich environments such as natural social contexts. Such environments will provide opportunities for meaningful linguistic action and help language emerge out of semiotic activity involving language, social norms, gesture, artistic creativity, etc.

SLA, acculturation and identity

Social and cultural distance between the learner and the target language group is regarded as a predictor of success in L2 learning. Traditionally, learner motivation and personality interact with this predictor, either inhibiting or enhancing the learning process (Schumann, 1976, 1978). Peirce (1995) argues that social distance is a phenomenon that is dynamically constructed, and she considers power relations as a decisive factor in this process. She also holds that SLA needs to develop a concept of the language learner as having a complex social identity that must be understood with reference to larger inequitable social structures.

Networked, project-oriented L2 classrooms

The PrOCALL project restructured units within eight language courses at the University of Melbourne to integrate large-scale projects created and published by students in a technologically rich environment. Within these units, project-oriented negotiations, online research, computer-mediated communication (CMC) with local and overseas partners, and Web creation and publishing replaced or complemented syllabus-driven role-playing, composition writing and discussion. Supported by the Global Learning Environment (Figure 9.1), this transformation involved classes in Chinese, ESL, French, German, Indonesian, Japanese and Russian.

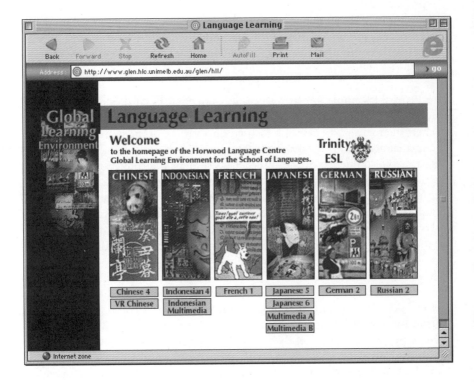

Figure 9.1   *The Global Learning Environment (GLEn)*

The motivation for the PrOCALL project can be traced back to the early teaching experiments conducted by John Barson at Stanford University. Barson organized a series of inter-university collaborations involving French students at Stanford, Harvard and the University of Pittsburg (Barson, 1991; Barson *et al*, 1993). Those early implementations of computer-supported project-oriented L2 learning relied on several fundamental principles:

- Engaging students in broad-scale collaborative activity is conducive to language learning. Repeated opportunities to link communicative acts to meaningful situations will result in enhanced language retention and availability for application in similar real-life situations.
- Learning must be meaningful to the learner. Students must take responsibility for designing, selecting and executing their tasks. Interaction in an environment where students manage their own affairs contributes to language learning.
- In a project-oriented CALL class, the role of the teachers is to initiate activity and interaction, and to help students sustain a level of engagement leading to the successful completion of work.
- The syllabus is conceived as a schedule of activity, which is negotiated and sensitive to the relationships evolving between the learners in the context of project work.
- Technology has an important role to help implement the proposed model by extending the boundaries of the classroom, which are now limited only by network configurations, and customizing access to and through learning material by hyperlinking and guided browsing. (Barson *et al,* 1993)

The PrOCALL implementation was accompanied by an evaluation/research project conducted by an independent evaluator, postgraduate students and the teachers themselves. The research focused on a variety of themes, such as patterns of target language use (Tanaka, 2000), management of student anxiety (Lewis and Atzert, 2000), influence of the Internet on student interpretation of the target language culture (Andrews, 2000), development of linguistic skills (Ewing, 2000), and learner factors influencing successful uptake of socio-collaborative CALL (Smith, 2000). Although most of the PrOCALL classes have undergone significant re-creation (Debski, 2000), overall the project has had a positive impact on second language study at Melbourne University and project-oriented learning with technology is still part of several curricula.

Smaller-scale 'sociocollaborative' (Meskill, 1999) projects have in recent years been conducted by other teachers and researchers in all parts of the world. Barson and Debski (1997) report on a project where students of Polish at Stanford and Jagiellonian University, Poland, collaborate using email to create Web pages about their respective campuses. Kubota (1999) describes a semester-long project in which students work in dyads to write research papers on Japanese culture, later published on the Web with images and links. Zhao (1996) designs an online magazine with his students. Kramsch *et al* (2000) analyse authorship online in a study of Hong Kong immigrants in California high schools. Makalapua and Hawkins (1997) discuss the significance of Web-based project-oriented L2 learning for the Hawaiian revitalization programme at the University of Hawaii.

L2 learning through socialization enabled by technology

This part of the chapter describes the socialization features of L2 interaction observed in the PrOCALL classrooms. The focus is on how various technologies interacted with L2 learning by supporting negotiation of meaning, the use of rhetorical structures, practice of literacy in forms specific to the target culture, changing power relations and impacting identity development.

Web-based projects as catalysts for social interaction

Ewing (2000) discusses the potential of project-oriented work with technology to provide students with an environment where they can use and develop linguistic skills in Indonesian that are not available in conventional classrooms. He records, transcribes and codes discourse generated by students working on computer-based projects and contrasts it with interaction transpiring a conventional teacher-led classroom, where introduction of material/problem is followed by a discussion. The most striking differences in his comparison are the rhetorical moves in the PrOCALL and conventional classrooms (Table 9.1). These rhetorical moves arise when hearers or readers perceive a relation between two units of a discourse, such as elaboration or cause (Mann and Thompson, 1986).

Table 9.1 *Frequency of rhetorical relationships arising from classroom discourse (Based on Ewing, 2000)*

Rhetorical Relation	PrOCALL (%)	Conventional (%)
Elaboration	26	53
Evaluation	19	18
Restatement	14	9
Sequence	10	1
Contrast	9	5
Circumstance	7	7
Cause	7	4
Background	4	0
Motivation	3	2

The feature of 'elaboration', where concepts in one part of the interaction are further specified in another part, was the most frequent rhetorical move in the conventional, lecture/discussion classroom. Ewing attributed this to the controlled progression of interaction in the conventional classroom, expressed as a series of elaborations used to build on what has been said previously. On the other hand, the distribution of rhetorical features in the PrOCALL classroom discourse was more balanced, with all the rhetorical moves except for 'elaboration' 'more present' in this setting. This greater range of rhetorical features presumably better resembles naturalistic activity-oriented interaction, although it is still unclear to what extent it can be attributed to the catalytic presence of computers (cf Piper, 1986; Seedhouse, 1995).

It is quite evident however that collaborative Web page creation requires the use of complex interaction, described by van Lier as 'triadic and dynamic'. In such interaction, to use his description of social interaction at the computer, 'gestures, pictures and objects all blend with language in the communicative context, and even first language can be seen as a semiotic system that supports emerging second language use' (van Lier, 2000, p 256; see also Brooks *et al,* 1997; Nathan, 2000). This remark allows seeing in a somewhat different light the extensive use of English in the PrOCALL classrooms, a feature often considered as problematic and running counter to the principles of project-oriented CALL (Debski, 2000). More research is required on the role of the first language for second language development in PrOCALL situations.

Negotiation of meaning in computer-mediated communication

In her study of the patterns of target language use in a Japanese class participating in the PrOCALL project, Tanaka (2000) describes instances of negotiation of meaning and peer correction. In this class, a Web discussion forum was set up for the Australian students to communicate with partners in Japan and discuss issues relevant to their Web-based projects. Negotiation of meaning in the target language was observed in social interactions around computers as well as on the screen. The excerpt in Table 9.2 is from a discussion that took place on the Web forum between SA, a native Japanese speaker (NS), and AN, a non-native speaker (NNS) in Australia, working on a project on martial arts.

A lot is going on in this short interaction. Negotiation of meaning and learning occur at lexical, pragmatic and cross-cultural levels. First, the NNS uses an incorrect word in Japanese for 'stereotype' (1). The NS does not understand the word or perhaps understands it but prompts the NNS to use the correct form (4). This triggers the NNS to correct the word (5) and to provide an extensive explanation of what he means by it. The NNS also reflects on the different meanings of the phrases 'significance of martial arts' and 'image of martial arts' and on how this may have led to the misunderstanding (6). The students also manage to explain to one another the meaning of martial arts in Japan and Australia (2, 3). Throughout this interaction, the learners prompt themselves by asking questions and expressing different opinions provoking discussion (4, 6, 8). The medium, by virtue of being asynchronous and written, assists the students in providing thoughtful and focused responses (Sengupta, 2001). Interactions such as these are evidence that negotiation of meaning, considered a positive condition of SLA, can be effectively supported by asynchronous computer-mediated communication (Blake, 2000; Sotillo, 2000; Toyoda and Harrison, 2002).

Table 9.2 *Excerpt from a Web forum interaction between a native (NS) and a non-native (NNS) Japanese speaker (English translation) (Based on Tanaka, 2000)*

1 AN (NNS)	SA-san, thank you for your opinion. I didn't think that both Japanese and foreigners would receive (1) *suterodau* (ステロタイプ) from the mass media. [. . .] (2) <u>By the way, in Australia, many people are practicing martial arts for their own safety.</u> This is the same in Japan, isn't it?
2 SA (NS)	This is SA. Well, (3) <u>I think more people practice martial arts as a hobby rather than to protect themselves from danger.</u> [. . .] (4) <u>By the way, what does *suterodau* (ステロタイプ) mean?</u>
3 AN (NNS)	To SA-san, thank you for your reply. Since you wrote previously that you had seen something about martial arts on TV and films, I started to think that everybody receive a (5) stereotypical (ステレオタイプ) image of martial arts. However, I think my opinion was wrong but even the image of martial arts may be the same but audiences react differently according to their experience in this area. [. . .] (6) <u>Maybe I should have asked you what was the significance of martial arts rather than what was the image of it.</u>
4 SA (NS)	To AN-san. (7) <u>I understand and I see what you mean [. . .]. In my opinion, the martial arts trains your spirit and mind.</u> While you are training your body, you are also training to control your mind. That is, when you practice martial arts, you also learn to live your life as a good person. (8) What do you think of my explanation?

Audience awareness and agency

Goal-oriented L2 language use was the cornerstone principle of the PrOCALL classrooms. How exactly to realize this guideline, however, was largely left to the individual classrooms and students. A number of students embarked on personally meaningful and motivating projects oriented towards electronic communities on the Web. Student audience awareness emerged as a strong theme in the data collected during the PrOCALL project, although the student projects were directed towards different audiences ranging from the global Web audience to family members and friends in Australia and overseas. This is illustrated by many student interviews:

'I did find that writing Web page is totally different from writing normal Japanese essays so I had to change the style of writing so that it would be interesting to the reader. . .' (Ai, Japanese class)

'We had to try to find various bits of information and relate it back to our topic and with that we created our own Web site which can, hopefully, be used by other people around the world. I definitely think that our Web site could be useful for a lot of people studying history.' (Mike, German class)

'I've got friends in Japan as well and it's nice to show them the page. They are friends I made in Japan.' (Louise, Japanese class)

The fact that Web writing is done for a real audience was on a couple of occasions brought home to the students in a sudden and somewhat surprising way. In 1998, a German class received an email from an irritated policeman in response to a student's Web page containing allegations of xenophobia in the German police force. Two years later, another PrOCALL class received an email from an irate Web citizen with a threat that he would sue one of the students for plagiarism. The citizen was appeased by the student, the author was given proper credit for his work, but the ethical issue of Web publishing became a matter of discussion for the whole class. Apart from instilling in students the feeling of authorship, contingencies like these also created opportunities for second language use in response to authentic communicative needs (van Lier, 2000). An important task for teachers is to create situations that abound in contingencies, to notice opportunities for goal-oriented language use and assist their students in responding to these opportunities and turning them into learning events.

Kramsch *et al* (2000) argue that authorship is closely related to the concept of agency: that is the power to make meaningful action. Agency was gained in the PrOCALL classes by a number of students who oriented their work towards electronic communities on the Web. Students not only were aware of their audience but also believed that their work had potential to impact the world outside the classroom.

Jasper, a student of French, sees the pages created by his class as contributions to overcoming the colonization of the new electronic world by the English language: 'students are creating Web pages to diversify what's available on the Web and also to overcome the colonization of the English language. . . It's really like claiming land in cyberspace if you like'.

Another student, Luke, experienced living in Indonesia and became profoundly interested in Indonesian culture. He was shocked by the hardships of living there and at the same time genuinely impressed by the continued effort of the Indonesian people to maintain a communal lifestyle with dignity. Luke created a Web project on child labour in Indonesia intending to air this issue to the wide Internet audience. When asked about the purpose of his page, he said: 'basically to raise the issue, just to get people to think about it and to say there is a problem and that people, normal people should have some responsibility as well'. Luke tried to make his Web page simple by avoiding technical terms, as he wanted to appeal to a broad worldwide audience.

Development of cross-cultural linguistic awareness

Debski (2000) in his analysis of the recreation of the PrOCALL innovation gives an example of a student who expresses concern about how communication tools were used in his Japanese class. The students were asked to email assigned partners and inquire about the topics of their Web-based projects. This is how Mark reacted to this task:

'Also, in terms of emailing people on the Web forum that was good in principle, but at our level, we know a lot of Japanese people. And if you say to us to email someone on this kind of thing, I'd rather email someone I know. Maybe that's a Japanese thing. You tend more to spend the initial stages working on the relationship and then you work on what you are going to do together, whereas the way it worked here, from the outset you were asking questions, which seemed very unnatural.' (Mark, student of Japanese) (Debski, 2000)

Mark feels uncomfortable asking his Japanese partner questions without the customary Japanese introductions. The electronic medium facilitates direct and prompt contacts, yet the student experiences a dilemma as he is not sure how to transfer behaviour characteristic of face-to-face communication to electronic interaction.

The student's intuitive apprehension finds support in recent research in cross-cultural computer-mediated communication (CMC). Sugimoto and Levin (2000) discuss the electronic literacy practices in the US and Japan and describe several differences between the norms of email writing in the two countries. The researchers report, for example, that although email messages are colloquial in both countries, many US messages start with 'Hi, how are you doing?' while many Japanese open their email stating their name and affiliation, for example: 'This is Takagi @ Waseda University'. They also discuss the differences in the use of emoticons and conclude that although their general function is similar, the specific forms and uses are different. Similar to other media, email undergoes acculturation: it interacts with the message in order to mirror the specific sociocultural contexts in which it is used, a process well described by Gottlieb (2000) in her study of word-processing in Japan.

The PrOCALL classes gave the students an opportunity to reflect on how they should apply the linguistic norms and customs of the target cultures in their use of the electronic media. They supported the development of student skills in the use of the new electronic genres in the target languages and cultures. Such sociolinguistic knowledge well complemented the support the Internet tradition-ally provides for the learning of cultural content (Andrews, 2000; Mueller-Hartmann, 2000; Osuna and Meskill, 1998).

Distribution of power and identity development

Recent research describes CMC as having an equalizing effect on students (Harasim, 1990). In L2 learning contexts, it has been proven that shy students tend to participate more in networked discussion and the ratio between teacher-talk and student-talk improves (Kern, 1995; Warschauer, 1996). On the other hand, teachers decide whether they can be contacted by email, whether to permit or restrict free online discussion and access to certain resources, making electronic networks instruments of either liberation or control (Warschauer and Lepeintre, 1997). It is evident that CMC influences power relations between various stakeholders in the learning/teaching process.

The role of CMC as a liberating gateway to information and authentic social networks is particularly amplified in the case of languages and cultures that are politically oppressed or isolated. A student of Indonesian in one of the PrOCALL classrooms praised the class for helping her develop a more authentic view of what Indonesians think about their government:

'I found discussion groups with people criticizing the government. The press over there is very controlled by the government so the Internet is another option that I can really know what the people think and feel about the government.' (Odo, Indonesian class)

The significance of technology as a factor affecting power relations and assisting identity development has recently been present in discussions of language revival and maintenance in different parts of the world. Almasude (1999) describes the new communications technology as a powerful force helping to preserve the identity of the Amazigh people of North Africa and the Thmazight language. Before the Internet, the Amazigh identity was a local issue for the various isolated subgroups, as the countries of North Africa censured information on the Amazigh culture. Through online discussion, the researcher argues, the isolated groups began perceiving themselves as members of one language culture and started making plans for implementing the Thmazight language in education, technology and science. Similarly, Warschauer (in press) describes the significance of the Internet for the Hawaiian revitalization programme in a tertiary setting. Interacting in Hawaiian in cyberspace provided language students with the opportunity to strengthen their sense of individual and collective identity. He concludes that the most important role of the Internet for language maintenance is in helping people see an endangered language as part of their future. This note is also present in Nathan's (2000) study of Aboriginal participation in the WWW in Australia.

Conclusions

In this chapter we have considered the significance of modern technology for situating language learning in social contexts and for implementing learning through social interaction, as advocated by current SLA theory. For this purpose, we have looked at evidence coming from various project-oriented classrooms utilizing networked computers as a tool supporting learning through interaction. Several cautious conclusions can be drawn from these analyses.

Web-based projects act as a catalyst for social interaction. Research demonstrates that classroom communication engendered by Web projects contains a wide range of rhetorical features, resembling naturalistic interaction. Today's computers provide space where manipulation and movement of electronic objects intertwines with language use driven by negotiation and collaborative planning. However, to date little evidence has been collected linking second language development directly to collaborative work at the computer. In view of the ecological perspective on SLA, new research must be undertaken describing how second language development can be related to navigation through and manipulation of electronic signs on the computer screen. Such research could perhaps benefit from mixing observation and discourse analysis with methods developed in software usability studies, such as screen capture, eye tracking and input logging to obtain the clearest possible image of activity at the computer.

There is a growing body of evidence that CMC supports negotiation of meaning, a positive condition of second language acquisition. The medium assists students in providing thoughtful and focused responses, as interaction is chronicled and student contributions are placed next to one another inviting critical analysis. There are many aspects of the effect of CMC on L2 speakers that require further investigation. For example, we need to know more about how flexibly L2 speakers respond to a change of bandwidth (Swan, Chapter 10, this volume).

Web-based projects often instil in students the feeling of authorship much more vivid than generally experienced in traditional classrooms. Students are challenged to weigh their Web contributions prudently, as these become part of a widely available store of information and affect stakeholders in various social processes. Such authentic communicative situations create opportunities for contingent goal-oriented L2 use. An important task for teachers is to assist their students in responding to these opportunities in order to turn them into learning events, for example by facilitating 'noticing' or providing the discrete linguistic units the students may need.

The new media affect the distribution of power in educational environments, both at the micro level of the classroom and the macro level of state policy. Research shows, for example, that shy students tend to participate more in computer-mediated interaction and the voice of the teacher becomes less overwhelming. Web-based interaction can assist the development of cultural and social identity in language learners by increasing in them cross-cultural awareness and extending access to language resources and social networks. This last aspect is of particular importance to learners of oppressed and/or threatened languages. Communication technologies have become a means of expression for oppressed voices that is less subject to government control than newspapers, radio and television. More research is required on the role ICT plays in the learning and teaching of indigenous and minority languages around the world.

References

Almasude, A (1999) The new mass media and the shaping of Amazigh identity, *Revitalizing Indigenous Languages,* eds J Reyhner, G Cantoni, R N St Clair and E P Yazzi, pp 117–28, Northern Arizona University, Flagstaff, AZ

Andrews, C (2000) Project-oriented use of the World Wide Web for teaching and learning culture, *Computer Assisted Language Learning Journal,* 13 (4–5), pp 357–76

Barson, J (1991) The virtual classroom is born: what now?, in *Foreign Language Acquisition and the Classroom,* ed B Freed, pp 365–83, D C Heath, Lexington

Barson, J and Debski, R (1997) Calling back CALL: technology in the service of foreign language learning based on creativity, contingency, and goal-oriented activity, in *Telecollaboration in Foreign Language Learning,* ed M Warschauer, pp 49–68, Second Language Teaching and Curriculum Center, University of Hawaii at Manoa Manoa, HI

Barson, J, Frommer, J and Schwartz, M (1993) Foreign language learning using email in a task-oriented perspective: an inter-university experiment in communication and collaboration, *Journal for Science Education and Technology,* 2, pp 565–83

Blake, R (2000) CMC: a window on L2 Spanish interlanguage, *Language Learning and Technology,* 4 (1), pp 120–36

Brooks, F B, Donato, R and McGlone, J V (1997) When are you going to say 'it' right? Understanding learner talk during pair-work activity, *Foreign Language Annals,* 30 (4), pp 524–41

Bruner, J S (1975) The ontogenesis of speech acts, *Journal of Child Language,* 2, pp 1–19

Debski, R (2000) Exploring the re-creation of a CALL innovation, *Computer Assisted Language Learning Journal,* 13 (4–5), pp 307–32

Debski, R and Gruba, P (1998) A qualitative survey of tertiary instructor attitudes towards project-based CALL, *Computer Assisted Language Learning Journal,* 12 (3), pp 219–39

Debski, R, Gassin, J and Smith, M (eds) (1997) *Language Learning through Social Computing,* Applied Linguistics Association of Australia (Occasional Papers No 16)

Donato, R (1994) Collective scaffolding in second language learning, in *Vygotskian Approaches to Second Language Research,* eds J P Lantolf and G Appel, Ablex Press, Norwood, NJ

Ewing, M (2000) Conversations of Indonesian language students on computer-mediated projects: linguistic responsibility and control, *Computer Assisted Language Learning Journal,* 13 (4–5), pp 333–56

Gass, S M (1997) *Input, Interaction, and the Second Language Learner,* Lawrence Erlbaum, Mahwah, NJ

Gottlieb, N (2000) *Word-processing Technology in Japan: Kanji and the keyboard,* Curzon, Surrey

Harasim, L (1990) *On-line Education: Perspectives on a new environment,* Praeger, New York

Kern, R (1995) Restructuring classroom interaction with networked computers: effects on quality and quantity of language production, *Modern Language Journal,* **79** (4), pp 457–76

Koschmann, T (1996) Paradigm shifts in instructional technology: an introduction, in *CSCL: Theory and Practice of an Emerging Paradigm,* ed T Koschmann, pp 1–23, Lawrence Erlbaum, Mahwah, NJ

Koschmann, T, Hall, R and Miyake, N (eds) (2002) *CSCL 2: Carrying forward the conversation,* Lawrence Erlbaum, Mahwah, NJ

Kramsch, C, A'Ness, F and Lam, W S E (2000) Authenticity and authorship in the computer-mediated acquisition of L2 literacy, *Language Learning and Technology,* **4** (2), pp 78–104

Krashen, S (1981) Effective second language acquisition: insights from research, in *The Second Language Classroom: Directions for the 1980s,* eds J E Alitis, H B Altman and P M Alatis, Oxford University Press, Oxford

Krashen, S (1985) *The Input Hypothesis: Issues and implications,* Longman, Harlow

Kubota, R (1999) Word processing and WWW projects in a college Japanese language class, *Foreign Language Annals,* **32** (2), pp 205–18

Lewis, A and Atzert, S (2000) Dealing with computer-related anxiety in the project-oriented CALL classroom, *Computer Assisted Language Learning Journal,* **13** (4–5), pp 377–95

Long, M (1983) Native-speaker/non-native speaker conversation and the negotiation of comprehensible input, *Applied Linguistics,* **4** (2), pp 126–41

Makalapua, K and Hawkins, E (1997) Incorporating technology into a Hawaiian language curriculum, in *Teaching Indigenous Languages,* ed J Reyhner, pp 151–7, Northern Arizona University Flagstaff, AZ

Mann, W C and Thompson, S A (1986) Relational propositions in discourse, *Discourse Processes,* **9** (1), pp 57–80

Meskill, C (1999) Computers as tools for sociocollaborative language learning, in *CALL: Media, design and applications,* ed K Cameron, Swets and Zeitlinger, Lisse

Mueller-Hartmann, A (2000) The role of tasks in promoting intercultural learning in electronic learning networks, *Language Learning and Technology,* **4** (2), pp 129–47

Nathan, D (2000) Plugging in indigenous knowledge: connections and innovations, *Australian Aboriginal Studies,* **2,** pp 39–47

Ohta, A S (1995) Applying sociocultural theory to an analysis of learner discourse: learner-learner collaborative interaction in the zone of proximal development, *Issues in Applied Linguistics,* **6,** pp 93–121

Osuna, M M and Meskill, C (1998) Using the World Wide Web to integrate Spanish language and culture: a pilot study, *Language Learning and Technology,* **1** (2), pp 71–92

Peirce, B N (1995) Social identity, investment and language learning, *TESOL Quarterly,* **29** (1), pp 9–31

Pica, T (1994) Research on negotiation: what does it reveal about second-language learning conditions, processes and outcomes?, *Language Learning,* **44** (3), pp 493–527

Piper, A (1986) Conversation and the computer: a study of the conversational spin-off generated among learners of English as a foreign language working in groups, *System,* **14** (2), pp 187–98

Schmidt, R (1990) The role of consciousness in second language learning, *Applied Linguistics,* **11** (2), pp 129–58

Schumann, J (1976) Social distance as a factor in second language acquisition, *Language Learning,* **26,** pp 135–43

Schumann, J (1978) The acculturation model for second language acquisition, in *Second Language Acquisition and Foreign Language Teaching,* ed R C Gringas, pp 27–50, Centre for Applied Linguistics, Washington, DC

Searle, J (1995) *The Construction of Social Reality,* The Free Press, New York

Seedhouse, P (1995) Communicative CALL: focus on the interaction produced by CALL software, *ReCALL,* **7** (2), pp 20–28

Sengupta, S (2001) Exchanging ideas with peers in network-based classrooms: an aid or a pain?, *Language Learning and Technology,* **5** (1), pp 103–34

Smith, M (2000) Factors influencing successful student uptake of socio-collaborative CALL, *Computer Assisted Language Learning,* **13** (4–5), pp 397–415

Sotillo, S M (2000) Discourse functions and syntactic complexity in synchronous and asynchronous communication, *Language Learning and Technology,* **4** (1), pp 82–119

Sugimoto, T and Levin, J A (2000) Multiple literacies and multimedia: a comparison of Japanese and American uses of the Internet, in *Global Literacies and the World Wide Web,* eds G E Hawisher and C L Selfe, pp 133–53, Routledge, London

Swain, M and Lapkin (1998) Interaction and second language learning: two adolescent French immersion students working together, *The Modern Language Journal,* **82** (3), pp 320–37

Tanaka, N (2000) Patterns of target language use in a Japanese project-oriented CALL class. Master of CALL dissertation, University of Melbourne

Thorne, S (1999) An activity theoretical analysis of foreign language electronic discourse. Unpublished doctoral dissertation, University of California, Berkeley, CA

Toyoda, E and Harrison, R (2002) Categorization of text chat communication between learners and native speakers of Japanese, *Language Learning and Technology,* **6** (1), pp 82–99

van Lier, L (2000) From input to affordance: social-interactive learning from an ecological perspective, in *Sociocultural Theory and Second Language Learning,* ed J P Lantolf, pp 245–59, Oxford University Press, Oxford

Vygotsky, L S (1978) *Mind in Society: The development of higher psychological processes,* Harvard University Press, Cambridge, MA

Vygotsky, L S (1981) The genesis of higher mental functions, in *The Concept of Activity in Soviet Psychology,* ed J V Wertsch, Sharpe, Armonk, NY

Warschauer, M (1996) Comparing face-to-face and electronic discussion in the second language classroom, *CALICO Journal,* **13** (2), pp 7–26

Warschauer, M (2000) Language, identity, and the Internet, in *Race in Cyberspace,* eds B Kolko, L Nakamur and G Rodman, Routledge, New York

Warschauer, M and Lepeintre, S (1997) Freire's dream or Foucault's nightmare? Teacher-student relations on an international computer network, in *Language Learning through Social Computing,* eds R Debski, J Gassin and M Smith, pp 69–89, Applied Linguistics Association of Australia (Occasional Papers No 16)

Wertsch, J V (ed) (1985) *Culture, Communication, and Cognition: Vygotskian perspectives,* Cambridge University Press, Cambridge

Zhao, Y (1996) Language learning on the World Wide Web: toward a framework of network-based CALL, *CALICO Journal,* **14** (1), pp 37–51

Chapter 10

Developing social presence in online course discussions

Karen Swan

Introduction

One of the more interesting findings arising from research on learning through asynchronous electronic networks is the importance that online discussion seems to play in its success. For example, in our empirical study relating course design factors to student perceptions of learning (Swan *et al*, 2000), we found that interaction with instructors, interaction with peers, and the value placed on participation in course discussions were the factors most significantly related to student perceptions. Other researchers have reported similar findings (Hawisher and Pemberton, 1997; Jiang and Ting, 2000; Picciano, 1998).

Indeed, asynchronous discussion seems both a significant factor in the success of online courses and significantly different from face-to-face discussion in traditional classrooms. In online discussion, all students have a voice and no students can dominate the conversation. The asynchronous nature of the discussion makes it impossible for even an instructor to control. Accordingly, many researchers note that students perceive online discussion as more equitable and more democratic than traditional classroom discussions (Harasim, 1990; Levin *et al*, 1990; Ruberg *et al*, 1996). Because it is asynchronous, online discussion also affords participants the opportunity to reflect on their classmates' contributions while creating their own, and to reflect on their own writing before posting it. This creates a certain mindfulness among students and a culture of reflection in online learning (Hiltz, 1994; Poole, 2000).

In addition, many researchers familiar with computer-mediated communication (CMC) have noted what Walther (1992) refers to as the 'hyperpersonalness' of the medium. Participants in online discussion seem to project their personalities into it, creating feelings of presence that build online learning communities (Gunawardena and Zittle, 1997; Leh, 2001; Poole, 2000; Rourke *et al*, 2001). In fact, our own research (Richardson and Swan, 2001) shows that this feeling of presence is significantly correlated with student perceptions of satisfaction with and learning from online courses.

This feeling of presence, however, is precisely what is most surprising in the online learning literature. In fact, both social presence theory (Short *et al*, 1976) and media richness theory (Rice, 1992) predict just the opposite. They suggest that the inability of text-based CMC to transmit the vocal and non-verbal cues found in face-to-face communications renders it a less 'immediate', colder, less personable experience.

This chapter explores the issue of the development of social presence in online course discussions and proposes an equilibrium model to account for that development. It describes a study that examined the affective, interactive and cohesive verbal immediacy behaviours of participants in an online course discussion, and extrapolates from this research to provide suggestions for online developers and instructors seeking to create online communities of learning in their courses.

Background

'Immediacy' refers to the perceived 'psychological distance between communicators' (Weiner and Mehrabian, 1968). In traditional, face-to-face classrooms, educational researchers have found that teachers' behaviours can lessen the psychological distance between themselves and their students, leading, directly or indirectly depending on the study, to greater learning (Christophel, 1990; Gorham, 1988, Richmond, 1990; Rodriguez *et al*, 1996). They have further distinguished between teachers' verbal immediacy behaviours (giving praise, soliciting viewpoints, use of humour, self-disclosure, etc) and their non-verbal immediacy behaviours (physical proximity, touch, eye-contact, facial expressions, gestures, etc), both of which have been shown to positively contribute to student learning.

The immediacy research in traditional classrooms has implications for online learning. Some communication researchers have argued that differing media have differing capabilities to transmit the non-verbal and vocal cues that produce feelings of immediacy in face-to-face communication. Short *et al* (1976) referred to these capabilities as 'social presence,' or the 'quality of a medium to project the salience of others in interpersonal communication'. They contended that media with limited bandwidth have a correspondingly limited capacity to project social presence (and by extension promote learning) than more broadband media. Media richness theory (Rice, 1992) reached a similar conclusion, as does Picard's (1997) more recent notion of 'affective channel capacity'. Researchers experienced with online teaching and learning, however, contest this view. Participants in CMC, they argue, create social presence by projecting their identities into their communications. Walther (1992), for example, argued that even participants in strictly text-based electronic conferences adapt their language to make missing non-verbal and vocal cues explicit and so develop relationships that are marked by affective exchanges. What is important, these researchers contend, is not media capabilities, but rather personal perceptions of presence (Gunawardena and Zittle, 1997; Poole, 2000; Richardson and Swan, 2001; Rourke *et al*, 2001).

Of course, as previously noted, online discussions can be quite different from discussion in face-to-face classrooms. In particular, the role of instructors often shifts from discussion leader to discussion facilitator, and students commonly assume more responsibility (Ahern and El-Hindi, 2000; Coppola *et al*, 2001; Poole, 2000). Research on immediacy in face-to-face classrooms has focused on teacher immediacy behaviours. Research on social presence/immediacy in online environments, however, must accordingly concern itself with the immediacy behaviours of all discussion participants.

Gunawardena and Zittle (1997), for example, developed a survey to explore student perceptions of social presence in computer-mediated conferences. In two separate studies, they found that students rated the asynchronous discussion as highly interactive and social. The researchers concluded that course participants created social presence by projecting their identities online to build a discourse community among themselves.

Our own research (Richardson and Swan, 2001) explored perceptions of social presence among students enrolled in 17 online courses using a survey adapted from Gunawardena and Zittle. They found that students' perceived learning, satisfaction with instructors and perceptions of social presence were all highly correlated. Indeed, direct entry regression revealed that students' overall perception of social presence was a predictor of their perceived learning in the courses.

To account for such findings, Danchak *et al* (2001) argue for an equilibrium model of the development of social presence in mediated educational environments (Figure 10.1). Equilibrium, in this sense, refers to an expected level of interaction in communications (Argyle and Cook, 1976). When communicative equilibrium is disrupted (as, for example, when one conversation partner moves closer to another), reciprocal actions to restore equilibrium usually result (as when the other partner moves backward or reduces his or her gaze). Danchak *et al* suggest that analogous behaviours preserve the expected (from face-to-face-experience) social presence equilibrium in CMC. They argue that when fewer affective communication channels are available to transmit immediacy via conventional vocal and non-verbal cues, participants in mediated communications will increase their verbal immediacy behaviours to the extent needed to preserve a sense of presence.

To further explore the function of verbal immediacy behaviours in the development of social presence in online discussions, Rourke *et al* (2001) distinguished among three kinds of verbal immediacy responses. These are: *affective responses,*

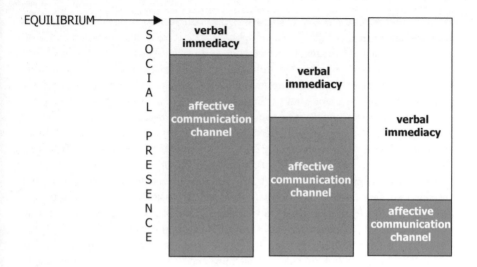

Figure 10.1   *Equilibrium Model of Social Presence*

personal expressions of emotion, feelings, beliefs, and values; *cohesive responses*, behaviours that build and sustain a sense of group commitment; and *interactive responses*, behaviours that provide evidence that the other is attending. They tested these categories in a pilot analysis of online discussion and found them quite reliable.

Verbal immediacy behaviours of participants in online course discussion

This section describes a study undertaken to better understand the kinds and uses of verbal immediacy behaviours in online course discussions based on the categories developed by Rourke *et al* (2001) and the equilibrium model of Danchak *et al* (2001).

Data were collected from the discussions that took place in a graduate level course in educational computing given entirely online in the Spring 2001 semester. The course consisted of four modules that ran sequentially across the semester. In each module, there were three discussions initiated by instructor questions. Students were required to submit at least one response to the instructor prompt and at least two responses to their classmates in each discussion. They could, of course, submit as many responses as they liked, and many participated a good deal more than required.

Data collected consisted of all discussion strands from the first discussion in each module initiated in the first five days each module was open. Two hundred and thirty-five postings in 39 discussion threads, or approximately 10 per cent of all postings in the course discussions, were examined. The average number of words per posting was 82.4 (range = 5 to 562); the average number of responses per thread was 6.05 (range = 0 to 30); and the average interactivity (measured as the depth of responses) was 3.63 (range = 1 to 10).

Students participating in the course ranged in age from 23 to 48 and were about two-thirds female. The majority were practicing K-12 teachers, but course participants also included post-secondary educators, librarians and educational technology specialists.

In order to examine the verbal immediacy behaviours of students participating in these course discussions, a coding schema was developed (Swan *et al*, 2001) based on the classroom-based immediacy literature, the CMC social presence literature and on indicators emerging from the data. Three categories of indicators were identified following the work of Rourke *et al* (2001):

1. *Affective indicators* are personal expressions of emotion, feelings, beliefs, and values. The affective indicators we coded for included the use of paralanguage, expressions of emotion, statements of values, humour and self-disclosure. These are listed in Table 10.1, which gives the code used for the indicator, its definition, examples from the discussion, and research sources for its inclusion in the coding scheme (note: 'emergent' references refers to categories emerging from the current data).
2. *Cohesive indicators* are verbal immediacy behaviours that build and sustain a sense of group commitment. Cohesive indicators coded for included greetings and salutations, the use of vocatives, group reference, social sharing and course reference. They are given in Table 10.2.
3. *Interactive indicators* provide evidence that others are attending. They support interactions among communicators. Indicators we coded for included acknowledgement, agreement, approval, invitation and personal advice. They are given in Table 10.3.

Hardcopy transcriptions of online discussions were coded by multiple researchers for each of the 15 immediacy indicators. Discrepancies between coders were resolved by consensus and reference to the discussion transcripts. Data analyses consisted of compiling and reviewing raw numbers of indicators across modules and reviewing the findings for patterns of indicator use.

Overall findings

Figure 10.2 shows the raw numbers of responses and indicators across modules. We found a great many immediacy indicators in the online discussions we reviewed, a total of 1,336 in 235 postings, or an average of almost six indicators per posting. We believe these findings provide evidence that participants in the online discussions we studied made up for the lack of affective communication channels by employing more immediacy behaviours in those channels that were available to them (Danchak *et al,* 2001).

Table 10.1 *Affective indicators*

Indicator (code)	Definition	Examples	References
paralanguage (PL)	features of text outside formal syntax used to convey emotion (ie, emoticons, exaggerated punctuation or spelling)	*Someday . . . . . .; How awful for you :-(; Mathcad is definitely NOT stand alone software; Absolutely!!!!!!*	Poole, 2000; Rourke *et al*, 2001
emotion (EM)	use of descriptive words that indicate feelings (ie, love, sad, hate, silly)	*When I make a spelling mistake, I look and feel stupid; I get chills when I think of . . .*	Christophel, 1990; Gorham, 1988; Richmond, 1990; Rourke *et al*, 2001
value (VL)	expressing personal values, beliefs and attitudes	*I think that it is a necessary evil; I feel our children have the same rights*	Emergent
humour (H)	use of humour – teasing cajoling, irony, sarcasm, understatement	*God forbid leaving your house to go to the library*	Christophel, 1990; Gorham, 1988; Richmond, 1990; Rourke *et al*, 2001
self-disclosure (SD)	sharing personal information, expressing vulnerability	*I sound like an old lady; I am a closet writer; We had a similar problem*	Christophel, 1990; Cutler, 1995; Gorham, 1988; Richmond, 1990

A closer look at the data supports this notion as well. For example, the most frequently used verbal immediacy behaviour (254 instances) was the use of paralanguage, the use of text to convey emotion or emphasis. It seems reasonable to assume that discussion participants were using paralanguage to take the place of gestures, facial expressions and aural cues in their conversations. At the other extreme, humour was the least used immediacy behaviour. This may be because humour really does necessitate more affective communications channels.

Affective immediacy indicators

Affective verbal immediacy behaviours might be thought of as ways of projecting personal presence into online discourse. Not surprisingly (given the equilibrium

Table 10.2 *Cohesive indicators*

Indicator (code)	Definition	Examples	References
greetings & salutations (GS)	greetings, closures	*Hi Mary; That's it for now, Tom*	Poole, 2000; Rourke *et al*, 2001
vocatives (V)	addressing classmates by name	*You know, Tamara, . . .; I totally agree with you Katherine*	Christenson and Menzel, 1998; Gorham, 1988
group reference (GR)	referring to the group as 'we', 'us', 'our'	*We need to be educated; Our use of the Internet may not be free*	Christophel, 1990; Gorham, 1988; Rourke *et al*, 2001
social sharing (SS)	sharing information unrelated to the course	*Happy Birthday!! to both of you!!!*	Bussman, 1998; Rourke *et al*, 2001
self-reflection (RF)	reflection on the course itself, a kind of self-awareness of the group	*I would never have imagined that we could have been having a discussion like this when we first started this course*	Emergent

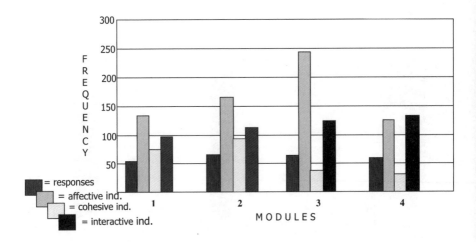

Figure 10.2 *Responses and immediacy indicators in each module*

Table 10.3 *Interactive indicators*

Indicator (code)	Definition	Examples	References
acknowledgement (AK)	referring directly to the contents of others' messages; quoting from others' messages agreement	*Those 'old machines' sure were something; we won by a landslide – 'landslide'* (next response)	Rourke *et al*, 2001
disagreement (AG)	expressing agreement or disagreement with others' messages	*I'm with you on that; I agree; I think what you are saying is so right*	Poole, 2000; Rourke *et al*, 2001
approval (AP)	expressing approval, offering praise, encouragement	*You make a good point; Right on; Good luck as you continue to learn*	Rourke *et al*, 2001
invitation (I)	asking questions or otherwise inviting response	*Any suggestions?; Would you describe that for me, I am unfamiliar with the term*	Christophel, 1990; Gorham, 1988; Rourke *et al*, 2001
personal advice (PA)	offering specific advice to classmates	*Also the CEC website might have some references*	Emergent

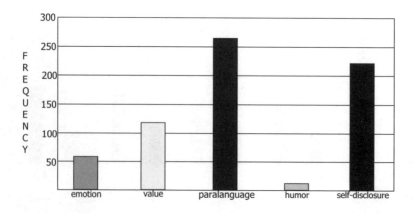

Figure 10.3 *Affective indicators across modules*

model), they were the most commonly used type of indicator. Across all modules, we found an average of 2.8 affective indicators per response. Figure 10.3 shows the raw numbers of affective verbal immediacy indicators found across all the discussion coded. The most frequently used affective indicator was paralanguage with an average of over one indicator per response. As previously noted, the use of paralanguage can be seen as an attempt to reproduce in text some of the affect conveyed in gestures, intonations and facial expressions.

The second most frequently employed affective indicator, with almost one indicator per response, was self-disclosure. Self-disclosure is the sharing of personal information, usually of a vulnerable nature. Self-disclosure is a verbal immediacy behaviour frequently noted in the immediacy research as employed by teachers to lesson the gap between themselves and their students (eg, Gorham, 1988; Rodriguez et al, 1996). It seems to have been employed similarly in the discussion threads we coded. Indeed, self-disclosure seemed to evoke the greatest number and depth of response from other participants. However, humour, another behaviour noted in the immediacy research was very little employed, perhaps because many forms of humour are easily misinterpreted in text-based communication. This finding points to differences between face-to-face and computer-mediated communications.

Figure 10.4 gives the raw numbers of affective immediacy indicators found in the discussion threads we coded. It thus shows the use of these indicators across time. It is interesting to note in this regard the pattern of usage across the modules. It can be seen that the use of affective indicators in general, and paralanguage and self-disclosure in particular, seemed to grow to a peak usage in the third module and drop precipitously after that. This usage seems to mirror the pattern of discussion in the course in general (Figure 10.2). The finding suggests that affective immediacy behaviours are an integral part of the social interaction that supports learning, but that in the online environment they take the only available, verbal, form.

For example, the excerpt that follows was taken from the first module. The discussion was about advertising on the World Wide Web. Notice the extensive use of affective verbal behaviours and the ways in which these uses of personal expression seem to be picked up by consecutive speakers:

WOW! (TD) – 1/25
Every Web site that I come upon has crazy advertising. It is almost getting to be too much. There are screens popping up on top of what you are doing and it gets to be a *pain in the butt! I think* it is good for the companies but it is *a pain for people like me* who use the computer for research and don't want to be interrupted. Maybe the advertising topic should only pop up if you are looking for that type of item. This might, *I mean MIGHT,* work. What do you think?

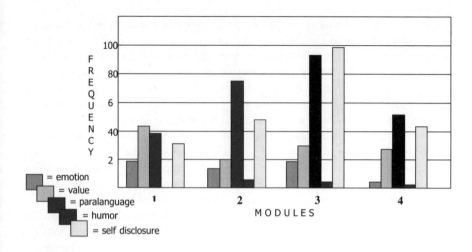

Figure 10.4 *Affective indicators for each module*

Advertising (DO) – 1/25
The problem with that is that the advertisers make most of their money selling us things we don't need so therefore they would never agree to this. Think about the times you get to the check out line and pick up stuff that is there that you weren't thinking of purchasing. They know what they are doing *believe you me!!!!*

Agree (TD) – 1/29
I agree with you. *There are times when I am told that I need this and that but as it turns out I really didn't need it. I am intelligent but I don't know everything and there are times when I get burnt. I hate it when people turn to pull the wool over your eyes and you are helpless.*
    Advertisements are great but don't sell me something that I really don't need.

Advertising (DO) – 1/31
I've heard that if you are to make a purchase for something you think you 'NEED' that if you wait one week and ask yourself again if you really need it your thoughts may differ and your wallet may stay intact!!!

Great idea (RR) – 2/03
I like this philosophy. My mother also has a similar take on this. She always says that 'nothing is a bargain unless you need it'. *I have stuck with this and my wallet has stayed relatively intact. I wish my mother-in-law would learn to do this. Thank God she does not have or know how to use a computer or her house would be full of things that were 'on sale'.*

Cohesive immediacy indicators

Cohesive verbal immediacy behaviours build and sustain a sense of group commitment to support the development of a discourse community. Figure 10.5 shows the raw numbers of cohesive immediacy indicators found across all the discussion postings we coded. Cohesive indicators were the least used of verbal immediacy behaviours in the discussion postings we coded. None the less, across all modules, we found an average of one cohesive indicator per response. The most frequently used cohesive indicator was group reference, the use of words such as 'we', 'our', or 'us' to refer to the class as a group. It is interesting to note in this regard that the use of group reference declined across the modules. It seems possible that the use of such reference became less necessary as a clear classroom community was formed.

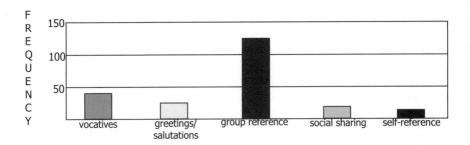

Figure 10.5   *Cohesive indicators across modules*

Figure 10.6 gives the raw numbers of cohesive immediacy indicators found in threads coded in each of the modules of the course. It shows a significant decline in all cohesive indicators by the third and fourth modules, except perhaps in the use of greetings and salutations and vocatives. Greetings and salutations and vocatives are immediacy indicators that refer to conversational partners by name. It may be, then, that some of the use of group reference was replaced by personal reference as participants learned and became comfortable using each other's names. This shift in behaviours does not account for the significant decline in most cohesive behaviours across modules. The most plausible explanation remains that discussion participants felt less need to employ cohesive indicators as they felt a greater organic cohesion amongst themselves.

A very interesting example of the use of social sharing occurred in the second module of the course. The discussion had been about computers then and now, when one student mentioned that they were turning 40 the next day (social sharing). The occasion became a very cohesive one for the class; there were a total of 30 responses in the whole thread, and students began to reflect on online discourse and community building process itself.

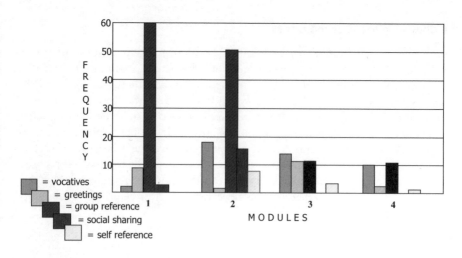

Figure 10.6 *Cohesive indicators for each module*

The excerpt that follows was taken from the discussion in the first module on the commercialization of the World Wide Web. Notice the use of group reference in all of the postings and the beginning use of greetings and vocatives.

Web wariness (CA) − 1/29
T, while I am a supporter of public radio and television, I also realize that *we* live in a world in which *our* children will be bombarded by commercials and it is *our job as teachers (and parents)* to teach them to be discriminating. The web offers an additional challenge to parents and teachers in that it solicits participation in 'contests.' My 10-year-old is bonkers about signing up for these, believing that he will win free things, etc. Our house rule is that he may not enter the contests—we tell him that it is just a way to solicit him, that it is highly unlikely that he will win, and that I refuse to allow our computer to be a receptacle for more unwanted advertising. So, web advertising can be used as a 'teachable moment' at home, or in the classroom.

Teachable moments (KS) − 1/29
Good point, *C.* Commercials won't go away. The best *we* can do is make them into teachable moments.

Just say no (CA) − 1/31
I also think the concept of 'just say no' to *our* children has been lost on *our* generation of parents. If a child or student doesn't understand that he or she is being manipulated by the advertiser, then, as adults, *we* simply have to say, 'no, you cannot have this.'

Learn (TD) – 2/05
We never stop learning and when *we* do *we* have given up on life. I learn
something new and everyday I am thankful for learning. Commercials *we* can
definitely learn from.

Interactive immediacy indicators

Interactive immediacy behaviours support communicative interactions by providing evidence that others are attending. Figure 10.7 shows the raw numbers of
interactive immediacy indicators found across all discussion postings coded. Across
all modules, we found an average of two interactive indicators per response. The
most frequently used interactive indicator was acknowledgement, which refers to
direct reference to the contents of others' messages. Discussion participants
employed almost one use of acknowledgement in every response. Agreement/
disagreement and approval, taken together, were used almost as frequently. These
findings seem to indicate that acknowledgement, agreement and approval are the
glue that holds asynchronous discussion together, an interpretation given further
credence by the fact that the use of all interactive indicators continued to increase
across modules.

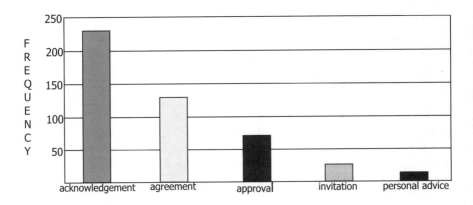

Figure 10.7 *Interactive indicators across modules*

Figure 10.8 gives the raw numbers of interactive immediacy indicators found in
the discussion threads coded in each of the modules of the course. It shows a
consistent increase in the use of interactive immediacy behaviours across time. The
pattern seems to indicate, at least within the course studied, a growing awareness
among course participants of the importance of the use of these indicators. Thus,
while cohesive behaviours became less important as the online community came
together, the importance of interactive behaviours seemed to grow over time as
participants became aware of their usefulness in linking the discussion into a
coherent whole.

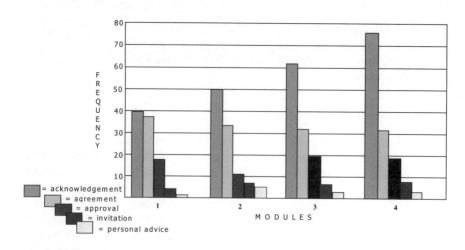

Figure 10.8 *Interactive indicators for each module*

For example, the excerpt that follows was taken from a discussion of computer-based tools in the third module. Participants in this thread had been talking about PowerPoint and word processing software and how they could be used to produce exciting presentations and documents. The excerpt begins with someone bringing in the point that sometimes the power of these tools can be overused. Notice that ED first agrees with the previous speaker before disagreeing slightly. In a similar vein, CA in the fourth response shown here begins by stating 'How about another perspective' rather than saying 'I disagree'.

Also notice the way the word 'glitziness' from the first posting here has been picked up in the subject lines of the next three postings. Likewise, the fifth posting picks up 'pictures and sounds' from the fourth posting as its subject line. The use of acknowledgement, as well as agreement and approval, continues through the texts of all the postings. This helps to link the postings together, and makes possible the creation of knowledge that seems to be taking place.

Cringe (ED) – 3/22
Yes, computers have made typewriters and BandW slides totally outdated. The new technology can make me cringe as well, especially when the presenter has over animated and added so many sound effects and moving text. I've gotten 'seasick' watching some presentations! Sometimes the glitziness takes away from content.

Great point – Beware of glitziness! (MO)
You make a great point and I agree that sometimes the use of technology can be overdone. We really have to think about the technology. . . is it really adding a benefit to the learner or is it a distraction.

Glitziness (WO) – 3/22
You've got a great point, and likewise with student papers and presentations. Sometimes a student's project report will have a stunning cover sheet (which I never require, anyway) and close to zero content.

Glitz – maybe not (CA) – 3/23
How about another perspective: Perhaps some learners who are more visual jump at the chance to use pictures and sound to express themselves. Sure, some students may be taking the 'easy' way out. But I suspect that other students who have problems expressing themselves in language, now have an alternative. Perhaps there is a way to work with them to deepen their understanding using the so-called 'gimmicks.' What about an essay in pictures and sound?

Pictures and sound (WO) – 3/23
It's a tough issue. In my posting I was thinking about a number of project reports I've received in the last few years that had lovely covers with interesting graphics but which really failed to address the issues in the project I'd assigned (first semester calculus).

However, I've been thinking a lot about exactly the issues you raise – how to present mathematics, and give students options for presenting it, in ways that appeal to other intelligences. I'm developing a liberal-arts math class. . .

Math alternatives (CA) – 3/27
W*, I can see that you are facing a difficult issue. I can imagine that it is not easy to find alternative ways to express math competency.*

Notice also the use of affective and cohesive immediacy behaviours in this excerpt. There is a lot of paralanguage, personal opinions and self-disclosure expressed, as well as group reference, vocatives, and greetings and salutations. It seems that all the immediacy indicators work together to make the discussion work.

Discussion

The findings from our analyses of the online course discussions suggest that the students participating in the course we investigated strove to create a community of learning by employing text-based, verbal immediacy behaviours to reduce the psychological distance amongst themselves. The findings support an equilibrium model of social presence (Danchak *et al*, 2001) that suggests that participants in mediated communication employ whatever means are available to them to create a feeling of presence similar to what they expect from their face-to-face experiences. In addition, the analyses reveal that although the use of affective indicators mirrored the general flow of the course discussions as the course progressed, cohesive indicators declined in importance, while the importance of interactive indicators increased. These findings suggest that different kinds of immediacy indicators perform different functions in the development of social presence and that the importance of these functions varies across time.

The research on teachers' immediacy behaviours in face-to-face classrooms shows links between teacher immediacy behaviours and students' learning. Although some scholars have argued that the lack of affective communication channels in CMC leads to a loss of immediacy and a corresponding loss in learning, more recent research suggests otherwise. This study supports the latter research and extends it by examining online discussion participants' use of particular kinds of immediacy behaviours across time.

Of course, this research only looks at a single course and it is impossible to generalize from it. Future research should examine discussion in other course contexts. It would be interesting, in this vein, to examine courses covering different subject areas and involving differing groups of students. Of particular interest, of course, are the roles of instructors and instructional design in providing support for the development of social presence.

In the educational computing course investigated, participation in the discussions was required. Indeed, it counted for almost a quarter of the course grade. Discussions were initiated by open-ended instructor questions that solicited discussion participants' opinions and experiences and allowed for their exploration of aspects of issues that were meaningful to them. The instructor was an active participant in the discussions, giving positive reinforcement to students that modelled the use of immediacy behaviours. Other chapters in this book (see Smith and Stacey, Murphy and Gazi, and McLoughlin) provide evidence that these sorts of discussion structures and instructor behaviours lead to greater socialization and the development of social presence and community. This chapter gives some insight into how students' verbal immediacy behaviours support that development within such an environment.

References

Ahern, T C and El-Hindi, A E (2000) Improving the instructional congruency of a computer-mediated small-group discussion: a case study in design and delivery, *Journal of Research on Computing in Education,* **32** (3), pp 385–400

Argyle, M and Cook, M (1976) *Gaze and Mutual Gaze,* Cambridge University Press, Cambridge

Bussman, H (1998) Phatic communion, in *Routledge Dictionary of Language and Linguistics,* eds G Trauth, K Kazzazi and K Kazzazi, Routledge, London

Christenson, L and Menzel, K (1998) The linear relationship between student reports of teacher immediacy behaviors and perceptions of state motivation and of cognitive, affective and behavioral learning, *Communication Education,* **47** (1), pp 82–90

Christophel, D (1990) The relationship among teacher immediacy behaviors, student motivation and learning, *Communication Education,* **39** (4), pp 323–40

Coppola, N W, Hiltz, S R and Rotter, N (2001) Becoming a virtual professor: pedagogical roles and asynchronous learning networks, *Proceedings of the 34th Hawaii International Conference on Systems Sciences,* IEEE Computer Society Press, Los Alamitos, CA

Cutler, R (1995) Distributed presence and community in Cyberspace, *Interpersonal Computing and Technology,* **3** (2), pp 12–32

Danchack, M M, Walther, J B and Swan, K (2001) Presence in mediated instruction: bandwidth, behavior and expectancy violations. Paper presented at the Sloan Conference on Asynchronous Learning Networks, November, Orlando, FL

Gorham, J (1988) The relationship between verbal teacher immediacy behaviors and student learning, *Communication Education,* **37** (1), pp 40–53

Gunawardena, C and Zittle, F (1997) Social presence as a predictor of satisfaction within a computer mediated conferencing environment, *American Journal of Distance Education,* **11** (3), pp 8–26

Harasim, L (1990) *On-line Education: Perspectives on a new environment,* Praeger, New York

Hawisher, G E and Pemberton, M A (1997) Writing across the curriculum encounters asynchronous learning networks or WAC meets up with ALN, *Journal of Asynchronous Learning Networks,* **1** (1), pp 52–72

Hiltz, S R (1994) *The Virtual Classroom: Learning without limits via computer networks,* Ablex, Norwood, NJ

Jiang, M and Ting, E (2000) A study of factors influencing students' perceived learning in a web-based course environment, *International Journal of Educational Telecommunications,* **6** (4), pp 317–38

Leh, A S (2001) Computer-mediated communication and social presence in a distance learning environment, *International Journal of Educational Telecommuni- cations,* **7** (2), pp 109–28

Levin, J A, Kim, H and Riel, M M (1990) Analyzing instructional interactions on electronic message networks, in *On-line Education: Perspectives on a new environ- ment,* ed L Harasim, Praeger, New York

Picard, R W (1997) *Affective Computing,* The MIT Press, Cambridge, MA

Picciano, A (1998) Developing an asynchronous course model at a large, urban university, *Journal of Asynchronous Learning Networks,* **2** (1), pp 1–14

Poole, D M (2000) Student participation in a discussion-oriented online course: a case study, *Journal of Research on Computing in Education,* **33** (2), pp 162–77

Rice, R E (1992) Contexts of research in organizational computer-mediated communication, in *Contexts of Computer-mediated Communication,* ed M Lea, Harvester Wheatsheaf, New York

Richardson, J and Swan, K (2001) An examination of social presence in online learning: students' perceived learning and satisfaction. Paper presented at the annual meeting of the American Educational Research Association, Seattle, WA

Richmond, V P (1990) Communication in the classroom: power and motivation, *Communication Education,* **39** (3), pp 181–95

Rodriguez, J L, Plax, T G and Kearney, P (1996) Clarifying the relationship between teacher nonverbal immediacy and student cognitive learning: affective learning as the central causal mediator, *Communication Education,* **45,** pp 293–305

Rourke, L, Anderson, T, Garrison, D R and Archer, W (2001) Assessing social presence in asynchronous text-based computer conferencing, *Journal of Distance Education,* **14** (2), pp 50–71. Accessed 17 April 2002, from http://cadeathaba scauca/vol142/rourke_et_alhtml

Ruberg, L F, Moore, D M and Taylor, C D (1996) Student participation, interaction and regulation in a computer-mediated communication environment: a qualitative study, *Journal of Educational Computing Research,* **14** (3), pp 243–68

Short, J, Williams, E and Christie, B (1976) *The Social Psychology of Telecommunications,* Wiley, Toronto

Swan, K, Polhemus, L, Shih, L-F and Rogers, D (2001) Building knowledge building communities through asynchronous online course discussion. Paper presented at the annual meeting of the American Educational Research Association, Seattle, WA

Swan, K, Shea, P, Fredericksen, E, Pickett, A, Pelz, W and Maher, G (2000) Building knowledge building communities: consistency, contact and communication in the virtual classroom, *Journal of Educational Computing Research,* **23** (4), pp 389–413

Walther, J B (1992) Interpersonal effects in computer mediated interaction: a relational perspective, *Communication Research,* **19** (1), pp 52–90

Weiner, M and Mehrabian, A (1968) *Language within Language: Immediacy, a channel in verbal communication,* Appleton-Century-Crofts, New York

Chapter 11

Socialization through CMC in differently structured environments

Peter Smith and Elizabeth Stacey

Introduction

Computer mediated communication (CMC) has changed the nature of learning at a distance from an individual experience that is largely remote and isolated from other students, to one in which the technology can enable more ongoing interaction with fellow students. The potential of using online technology such as computer conferencing to provide students with a means of developing and sharing their construction of knowledge of their course, while they socially construct group knowledge within a collaborative learning environment, is one of the greatest advantages of CMC.

It is clear, however, that for the social construction of learning to take place there must be established comfortable online socialization among students to provide a platform for learning construction to occur. That socialization must move beyond the unfocused interaction that Klemm and Snell (1995) have observed can be easily trivialized both by learners and their teachers, such that the interaction never moves beyond the entirely social. Establishing social presence, the ability of online participants to project themselves into a textual environment, which has few visual or contextual cues, is an important phase in an online course for students forming a learning community (Rourke *et al,* 1999; Stacey, 2001).

The provision of a course structure to enable online socialization to be used effectively so that students can learn collaboratively has received comment throughout the literature and forms the focus of our chapter in this book. We are interested here in exploring the effects that different forms of pedagogical structure can have on the encouragement towards comfortable socialization through CMC, and its progression towards becoming a tool for collaborative learning.

Constructivism

The importance to learning of the opportunity to participate in a social construction of knowledge has been researched by cognitive psychologists such as Piaget, Vygotsky and Bruner, who emphasized the social nature of learning, particularly when learners are confronted with problems that they cannot solve on their own without the resources of a group. More importantly, the process of discussion, listening to other group members and receiving feedback on ideas, provides the cognitive scaffolding these constructivists see as essential to higher-order thinking (Slavin, 1994). The development of knowledge and understanding within conceptual frameworks, it is argued by the constructivists (eg, von Glasersfeld, 1987), is an ongoing interpretive process, which is reinforced by past and ongoing experiences. As Rogoff (1995) has argued, the appropriation of knowledge and understanding is not just the internalization of externally derived stimuli, but also the individual's construction of those stimuli. Individuals collaboratively construct a common grounding of beliefs, meaning and understandings that they share in activity (Pea, 1993) through a culture, or community, of practice (Lave and Wenger, 1991). As Stacey (1996, 1998) has argued, these constructions depend largely on a socio-cultural and communicative context for their development.

Collaborative learning

Through her interview-based and content analysis research with three large groups of learners in differing contexts, Stacey (1998, 1999) has shown the importance of group collaboration in learning. Her discussion of CMC, from a social constructivist perspective, focused on interactive online group discussion as central to the learners' effective construction of new conceptual understandings. The research found that, in the social context of group interaction, the collaborative group develops a consensus of knowledge through communicating different perspectives, receiving feedback from other students and teachers and discussing ideas, until a final negotiation of understanding is reached. Drawing on Vygotsky's (1978) theory that conceptual understandings are developed through verbal interaction, Stacey found that a socially constructed learning environment is essential for effective learning. The social conversation provides the learner with a context and stimulus for thought construction and learning, which is the means by which the group contributes more to each learner's understanding than they are able to do individually.

Beckett (2000) has pointed to the potential for online learning to disembody learners and their instructors such that the important social construction of learning becomes lost. Effectively structured CMC that develops collaboration between learners and between learners and their instructors can serve to reduce the effects of that potential disembodiment and enable a more effective appropriation of meaning to be derived through interaction. Research by Baker and Dillon (1999) has also shown the importance of technologically mediated student-led and student-centred communication in developing the confidence of learners participating in online programs of instruction.

Socialization and community

The necessity for socialization to be established as an enabler for the social construction of knowledge to proceed has been identified in the online learning literature by Salmon (2000). In her staged model for effective computer mediated learning, Salmon adopts as its first stage the development of socialization among participants. The argument here is simple and straightforward – comfortable communication has to be established between students prior to more focused discussions occurring that assist with the construction of knowledge. More recently Smith and Smith (2002) have questioned the notion that socialization is an enabler that needs to be established among students prior to engaging them with the social construction of knowledge. Drawing on their previous research with Chinese students, Smith and Smith (1999) have suggested that for some students socialization is best developed contiguously within a structure of learning tasks that are designed to develop socialization as the task is addressed. Other work by Smith (2000) with vocational students points to the same conclusion, such that Smith (2001), and Smith and Sadler-Smith (2001) have developed a set of suggested strategies for the development of CMC-based socialization within a community of practice (Lave and Wenger, 1991) for learners in workplaces.

This notion of a community of practice is used in a different form by McAlpine (2000) in his research on computer-mediated learning that uses, in part, the establishment of special discussion groups for students to work together on common focused problems. Consistent with the Jonassen (1999) suggestion of Constructivist Learning Environments (CLEs), the technology enables collaboration and social construction of knowledge. CLEs engage students in investigation of a problem, critiquing related cases and reviewing information resources. Learners develop needed skills and collaborate with others, using the social support of the group to learn effectively (Morphew, 2000). Jonassen et al (1999, p 52) claim that 'the key to meaningful learning is ownership of the problem or learning goal', some component of which the learners must define.

Stacey's (2001) research found that the teacher's role was important in structuring and providing models of messaging. Although most students were comfortable with the Internet as an information source, computer conferencing was new to many and most needed to observe the teacher's social presence skills before attempting to socialize online. The literature on CMC provides a wealth of research on differently structured CMC experiences among students and their teachers (Collis *et al*, 2000; Housego and Freeman, 2000) but there is a lack of research that undertakes a comparative analysis of different forms of structure.

Some empirical observations on different structures

In previous research on CMC among postgraduate coursework students, Stacey *et al* (2001) have investigated different forms of structure and their effect on student communication between themselves and with their lecturer. In this research study we examined three forms of structure in CMC-supported subjects of study provided for distance education students. In each of our three forms of structure, students also received printed study materials that formed the basis of content, and CMC was used to develop student understanding through collaboration. Each of the different structures required different levels of interaction between students, and between students and their lecturer:

- One structure encouraged interaction but did not require it and, although the lecturer actively facilitated discussion between students, there was no relationship between level of interaction and assessment requirements.
- A second structure required students to participate online in specific tasks, but did not link that participation to formal assessment.
- A third structure required students to participate regularly throughout the semester and linked participation to the formal assessment of the subject.

As would be expected, interactivity was by far the greatest in the subject that linked participation to assessment. The mean number of interactions per student across the semester in that subject was 89. The subject that made no such formal link, but expected participation in online tasks, showed a mean number of interactions per participant at 10.8, while the encouraged but unstructured subject showed a mean of 4.1 interactions per participant across the semester.

The role of socialization was examined in the two subjects that differed most – the unstructured one, and the subject that required participation as part of the assessment. The unstructured subject was characterized by early socialization strategies of introduction and information sharing about self. Quite quickly though, participants moved into discussions of content and ideas, such that socialization continued but changed in nature to become more associated with encouragement of each other's inputs to the discussion. A similar pattern was observed in the assessment-linked subject, but the participation among students was much higher. The difference in online participation densities yielded naturally higher amounts of social interaction between students, as well as higher amounts of cognitive engagement. Qualitative data indicated students in both units liked the experience of CMC interaction. The evidence with the assessment-linked subject was that the required interaction had forced them to develop online relationships with their peers, and provided for a powerful opportunity for the construction of knowledge through that interaction.

A comparison of two distinct structures

As a result of the previously described research and our reflections on practice, we took the opportunity to develop a somewhat different form of structure in a new subject being offered for the first time, again to Masters degree by coursework students. We could then make some comparisons with an already existing subject that used a different collaborative structure. That development of a new structure enabled us to make detailed comparisons between the two structures focused on in this chapter. Table 11.1 provides a brief overview of the structures used in the two subjects compared here. Students undertaking each of these two subjects are drawn from the same pool of Masters degree students and are similar in many ways. Indeed, any of the students could just as likely been enrolled in the other subject. Additionally, the subjects each conform to a similar paradigm in terms of their workload demand, their styles of assessment and the provision of print-based materials as well. All students accessed the same groupware system (FirstClass) used for CMC in these two subjects. The FirstClass architecture provided to students is also very similar in both subjects.

Subject A

The previous research, together with McAlpine's (2000) findings, encouraged us to develop smaller discussion groups, focused on specific issues related to the subject. Collectively, students represented four general areas of interest, reflecting their work contexts and the challenges that they faced in their everyday practice. Accordingly, the new structure was based on these four communities of practice that were identifiable among the student group. For each specialized area of interest an application problem was generated, such that the subset of students in the focal area were expected to work together as a group of consultants to solve the problem that had been posed. The role of the lecturer was to act as the customer for the consultant group, and to supply information to the group as they requested it from the 'customer'. Additionally, a general space was available to all participants in the subject, such that they could engage in broader discussions of the subject and its content. As is the case in subject B, the architecture provides for specifically focused smaller group discussion spaces, but what is important here and described below, is how students are expected to, and do engage with these focused discussions.

In subject A student participation in the CMC discussion was strongly encouraged but was not compulsory, and participation had no direct impact on assessment. Participation was not made compulsory on a basis that CMC skills were not

Table 11.1 *Summary of collaborative structures in subjects A and B*

Feature	Subject A	Subject B
Compulsory participation	No	Yes
Participation part of assessment	No	Yes – students moderate then summarize an online discussion, gather and post online resources and work collaboratively on an online group assignment.
General discussion space	Yes – students use this space to socialize across the group, and to discuss across-subject issues.	Yes – students use space for administrative and whole group social interaction.
Specialized discussion space	Four different problem solving exercises were generated. Students selected two of these and worked together to solve the problem posed.	Four major areas with sub conferences within them. These relate to the online tasks and course structure with a student social area designed by student request.

part of the learning outcomes of the subject, and the student cohort varied in their degree of access to the CMC discussions.

The development of socialization within this model is interesting to follow. First, the lecturer invited students to enter the general space and introduce themselves, and to state what their particular interests were. Whenever a student entered that space the lecturer would respond within 24 hours to welcome the student, to acknowledge the participation, and to guide them towards the selection of a specialized conference that might best engage their interest. Students typically responded to that message in the general space again, advising that they had been to the specialized space and read the problem and had decided to engage with it, or had decided to engage with a different problem in another of the specialized spaces. At that point students invited others to join them in the specialized space, and then moved from the general space and into the chosen specialism. Once in the specialized spaces, student interaction began with considerable focus on the problem to be solved. However, it was clear that early communications between students were focused more on housekeeping matters of how they would organize themselves, what common ground and experience they had and what general perspectives they had on the problem to be solved. Also evident from the interactions between students was an early emphasis on such things as concern over the budget to be applied to the problem, and how the solution to the problem might be presented to the customer. It was clear that what was happening here was that students were developing socialization through the structure of the course, by focusing on the problem to be solved (Smith and Smith, 2002).

Also interesting in this structure was that the interaction between students began, by week three of the semester, to be characterized by a considerable reduction in socialization. Interactions became very task-focused, with students posting ideas and strategies that would serve to solve the problem they had been set. Most of these messages were succinct and very much to the point of the exercise. There appeared a sense of urgency among students to move towards task completion, and some impatience was displayed towards students who were not seen to be participating sufficiently. Communication flow in the CMC component of the subject was brisk at an early stage. These findings are similar to those of Rourke *et al* (1999) and Hara *et al* (2000) who found that purely social interaction, not focused on the content of the course, declined as the conference progressed, which they concluded was because students got to know one another better.

What became evident as the semester progressed was a decreased interest in the scenarios among students. Fewer students participated in the discussion, which became dominated by a committed few who were keen to reach a 'solution' to the problem posed. Some discussion with students on this reduction in interest indicated that a number felt excluded by the process as the problem moved towards solution, because the discussion had moved beyond their level of experience and knowledge of the issue, and they felt somewhat intimidated by the students who were more experienced with addressing the implementation issues demanded by the scenarios provided. Additionally, there appeared to be a related matter that the problem was not 'owned' by them (Jonassen *et al,* 1999) but had been developed by the course team. That lack of ownership was exacerbated by the convergent nature of the problems to be solved, which required the student group to reach agreed conclusions. There was evidence that the problems posed would have been more successful had they required divergent thinking and input on the part of students, such that they could each raise and explore issues, rather than converge to an agreed position.

Subject B

In subject B, students were required to share resources they had researched and evaluated through searching the World Wide Web, to moderate discussions about issues they had chosen about online learning, and to work in collaborative groups for an assessed task on researching the theory and process of learning collaboratively online. The subject has a needs-based curriculum, which is constructed to suit the varying levels of skills and experiences of each semester's group of students. The discussion is essential to developing the content of the subject and with such an authentic reason, online interaction is high as the learners demand it.

In this subject the teacher also explicitly established and modelled techniques of social interaction so that the social presence of the participants was established consciously in an environment that encouraged trust and supportive response.

Initially students were asked to introduce themselves to the group with specific points of discussion such as professional role, purpose for course choice and previous conferencing experience. At the beginning of the semester the teacher responded to each new student encouragingly and used this initial period to teach the students social practice and use of the software elements that encourage socialization.

The structure of the course required task-based small group discussions to be established in the early stages of the semester. After the introduction phase, students communicated in conference spaces with fewer participants who shared a content focus they had suggested or chosen. Moving into a small group collaborative environment meant that students could establish small group relationships in a more informal space and this was conducive to social comments being included in most content messages whatever their complexity of cognitive content. The structure of the tasks of the subject required the students to break into subgroups by choice of issue for discussion. Subsequently, common issues were grouped and used as the basis of the formation of the small collaborative groups in which students worked for the second assessment task. Such smaller group conference discussion spaces encouraged even more continuing socialization as the group members interacted socially before beginning the group task. Cohesive factors as defined by Rourke *et al* (1999), such as addressing each other by name, communicating in purely social ways such as greetings and farewells, and interactive aspects such as the reply and quote functions of the software, and asking questions and complimenting others' ideas were often used. The small group space was also a place for humour and emotional expressions and disclosing details of their lives, responses categorized as affective responses.

Though online participation was a requirement of this subject, the smaller collaborative group spaces continued to be used for socialization as well as the required content construction of the final group assignment. Though there was a high rate of cognitive message content, the social presence factors also continued to be important in the communication of the group, with high frequencies of interactive and cohesive comments in particular continuing to appear within messages. Levels of social presence frequency rose towards the end of the semester, contradicting the results predicted from the literature that there would be less social interaction over time, and challenging the notion of electronic conferences as depersonalized and task-oriented, with lessening social interaction over time (see Walther, 1996). It supports and confirms Walther's (1996) findings that though interpersonal impressions were formed more slowly with CMC, relationships developed in the same way as in face-to-face situations, even becoming more socially oriented in the online context. Walther proposed that relationships require longer to develop in an electronic medium, and even in the later part of the semester, members of the small groups were motivated to continue their social interaction and their social relationships. This enabled a social construction of knowledge to be developed into the collaborative group assignment, which was the focus of the small group online discussion.

Discussion

An important contrast between the two subjects of study under discussion here was not just the required participation, but also the flexibility of the problem, as well as students learning to define the problem for themselves in their own context. In the assessment-linked subject, students define the issues for discussion, find and share the resources, then socially construct their ideas in online discussion. Consistent with the Jonassen (1999) Constructivist Learning Environments (CLEs), the use of technology in subject B enabled collaboration and social construction of knowledge in that students were actively engaged with identification of issues for discussion, the investigation of a problem, critique-related cases and the review of information resources. These activities were developed by the group with teacher guidance. Learners developed collaborative skills with others, using the social support of the group to learn effectively. The ownership of the problem was strong in this subject, providing support to the Jonassen *et al* (1999) claim that ownership is a key to meaningful learning through technology mediation.

The observations on ownership by participants of the issue under discussion is given considerable support by our comparative observations in this chapter. In subject A the students were provided with the problem to be discussed and addressed through convergence in their discussion to an agreed solution. There was no strong opportunity for students to adapt or change the problems to become more personally meaningful, although there was an expectation that they would use their own experience and their reading to assist in the solution of the problems. However, the convergent nature of the required discussion was not as generative, nor as personally engaging, as discussion of a more divergent nature might have been.

Although compulsory participation obviously increased the participation rate in subject B, our observation is that there was an interaction between the compulsoriness and the nature of the discussions in the focus groups. Were compulsoriness the only explanation for the higher participation rate, it could be expected that there would be a minimalist approach to it among students. In fact, the frequency of the participation and the nature of the interactions were much more than minimalist, indicating interest among students in the discussion that went beyond serving the requirements of the subject.

Socialization was used largely by students in subject A to establish early comfort in communication with each other, and to establish some knowledge about each other's work contexts and interests in the problem being addressed. Subsequent to that establishment of comfort and mutual knowledge, socialization was rather limited and discussion was very task-oriented, and focused on completing the problem solving exercise. In subject B socialization was maintained throughout the subject and actually increased as the semester progressed, and embedded within the ongoing discussion that formed the learning component of the focused discussion.

In our view, this study has provided strong support to the development of problem and issue ownership as a crucial component of effective and sustained socialization that engages consistently with the learning intents of the subject. As a consequence of our research on these two structures, future development will change the problems posed from being defined closely by the course team and convergent in nature, towards providing greater opportunity for ownership through a more open problem definition allowing for more divergent engagement by students. A more constructivist learning environment will give purpose and importance to continuing socialization through CMC and establish a more effective environment for collaborative learning.

Within a context of the increasing importance of e-learning and networked learning environments, the research also provides some insights into the role of structure as an important variable in the development and maintenance of socialization and collaborative learning. The establishment of structure as an important variable provides considerable incentive for researchers and practitioners to experiment with and vary structures in CMC to result in a considerably more systematic body of knowledge and understanding than is currently available. This chapter provides but one set of insights into what is an important issue in e-learning and networked learning contexts that are based in CMC.

References

Baker, J, and Dillon, G (1999) Peer support on the web, *Innovations in Education and Training International*, **36** (1), pp 65–70

Beckett, D (2000) Eros and the virtual: enframing working knowledge through technology, in *Working Knowledge: The new vocationalism and higher education*, eds C Symes and J McIntyre, pp 66–83, Open University Press, Milton Keynes

Collis, B, Winnips, K and Moonen, J (2000) Structured support versus learner choice via the World Wide Web (WWW): where is the payoff?, *Journal of Interactive Learning Research*, **11** (2), pp 131–62

Hara, N, Bonk, C J and Angeli, C (2000) Content analysis of online discussion in an applied educational psychology course, *Instructional Science*, **28** (2), pp 115–52

Housego, S and Freeman, M (2000) Case studies: integrating the use of web-based learning systems into student learning, *Australian Journal of Educational Technology*, **16** (3), pp 258–82

Jonassen, D (1999) Designing constructivist learning environments, in *Instructional Design Theories and Models*, ed C M Reigeluth, Lawrence Erlbaum, Hillsdale NJ

Jonassen, D, Prevish, T, Christy, D and Stavrulaki, E (1999) Learning to solve problems on the web: aggregate planning in a business management course, *Distance Education*, **20** (1), pp 49–63

Klemm, W R and Snell, J R (1995) Instructional design principles for teaching in computer conferencing environments. Accessed 2 May 2000, from wwwcvm tamuedu/wklemm/instructhtml

Lave, J and Wenger, E (1991) *Situated Learning: Legitimate peripheral participation*, Cambridge University Press, Cambridge

McAlpine, I (2000) Collaborative learning online, *Distance Education*, **21** (1), pp 66–80

Morphew, V (2000) Web-based learning and instruction: a constructivist approach, in *Distance Learning Technologies: Issues, trends and opportunities*, ed L K Lau, pp 1–15, Idea Group, London

Pea, R D (1993) Learning scientific concepts through material and social activities: conversational analysis meets conceptual change, *Educational Psychologist*, **28**, pp 165–77

Rogoff, B (1995) Observing sociocultural activity on three planes: participatory appropriation, guided participation, apprenticeship, in *Sociocultural Studies of Mind*, eds J W Wertsch, A Alvarez and P del Rio, pp 139–64, Cambridge University Press, Cambridge

Rourke, L, Anderson, T, Garrison, D R and Archer, W (1999) Assessing social presence in asynchronous text-based computer conferencing, *Journal of Distance Education*, **14** (2), pp 50–71

Salmon, G (2000) *E-moderating: The key to teaching and learning on-line*, Kogan Page, London

Slavin, R E (1994) Student teams–achievement divisions, in *Handbook of Cooperative Learning*, ed S Sharan, pp 3–19, Greenwood Press, Westport, CT

Smith, P J (2000) Preparedness for flexible delivery among vocational learners, *Distance Education*, **21** (1), pp 29–48

Smith, P J (2001) Enhancing flexible business training through computer-mediated communication, *Industrial and Commercial Training*, **33** (4), pp 120–25

Smith, P J and Sadler-Smith, E (2001) Towards a strategic use of computer-mediated communication to support flexible learning in the workplace. Paper presented at the 15th Biennial Form of the Open and Distance Learning Association of Australia, September, Sydney

Smith, P J and Smith, S N (1999) Differences between Chinese and Australian students: some implications for distance educators, *Distance Education*, **20** (1), pp 64–80

Smith, P J and Smith, S N (2002) Supporting Chinese distance learners through computer-mediated communication: revisiting Salmon's model, in *Computer Support for Collaborative Learning: Foundations for a CSCL community*, ed G Stahl, pp 611–12, Lawrence Erlbaum, Hillsdale, NJ

Stacey, E (1996) Becoming flexible and virtual: the impact of technology on traditional university teaching and learning, in *The Changing University*, eds L Hewson and S Toohey, pp 44–48, University of NSW, Sydney

Stacey, E (1998) Learning collaboratively in a CMC environment, in *Teleteaching 98: Distance Learning, Training and Education, Proceedings of the XV IFIP World Computer Congress*, ed G Davies, pp 951–60, Vienna and Budapest

Stacey, E (1999) Collaborative learning in an online environment, *Journal of Distance Education*, **14** (2), pp 14–33

Stacey, E (2001) Quality participation online: establishing social presence, *Research in Distance Education* (No 5) Deakin University, Geelong

Stacey, E, Evans, T, Smith, P and Rice, M (2001) An evaluative case study of online learning: evaluating and researching online courses at Deakin University, Australia, in *Proceedings of International Conference Telecommunications for Education and Training,* eds H Sponberg, Z Lustigova and S Zelanda, pp 227–33, Charles University, Prague

von Glasersfeld, E (1987) Learning as a constructive activity, in *Problems of Representation in the Teaching and Learning of Mathematics,* ed C Janvier, pp 3–18, Lawrence Erlbaum, Hillsdale, NJ

Vygotsky, L S (1978) *Mind in Society: The development of higher psychological processes,* Harvard University Press, Cambridge, MA

Walther, J B (1996) Computer-mediated communication: impersonal, interpersonal, and hyperpersonal interaction, *Communication Research,* **23** (1), pp 3–41

Chapter 12

Collaboration and community through simulation/role-play

Karen Murphy and Yakut Gazi

Introduction

As Web use in higher education increases, so does the need to provide learners with authentic learning experiences for developing critical thinking skills for participation in an increasingly complex telecommunications-oriented culture. Official US reports have found 'a relative paucity of true, original research dedicated to explaining or predicting phenomena related to distance learning' (Institute for Higher Education Policy, 1999, p 30) and called for research on how people learn in the Internet age, how new tools support and assess learning gains, and what kinds of organizational structures support these gains (Web-Based Education Commission, 2000).

Garrison (2000) described the need for 'sustained real two-way communication' (p 13) to be at the core of the educational experience, using methods and technologies that incorporate a collaborative approach to the learning transaction in distance education. Instructors have increasingly incorporated learning transactions in their courses by involving learners in threaded discussions, with the result that learners can create their own democratic public culture as deliberators. According to

Romiszowski (1997), the most effective types of teaching-learning practices are 'experiential exercises followed by interpersonal interaction in small groups. . . with facilitators to guide the group towards useful conclusions' (p 33).

Problems related to providing socialization support for e-learners focus primarily on instructors' inability to incorporate experiential learning activities that will foster interaction and collaboration among learners. Instructors may lack the knowledge of how to implement such activities, they may be hesitant to try such innovative practices at a distance, or they may not have the necessary administrative or technological support. In the case of Web-based scenarios, instructors may lack sufficient technical skills and time for acquiring those skills (Naidu *et al*, 2000). Instructors need to know how to design their own experiential learning activities or adapt existing activities and provide scaffolding that will help learners to structure their own learning. One experiential activity that may be used effectively in e-learning contexts is simulation/role-play.

The goals for this chapter are to a) identify the characteristics of simulation/role-plays that foster collaborative learning environments and development of e-learning communities; and b) contribute to an understanding of how to design and implement simulation/role-plays to provide socialization support for e-learners. By encouraging socialization and interaction among students through such experiential activities as simulation/role-play, instructors can foster collaboration and community building in e-learning environments.

Review of the literature

Three compatible trends in the Internet age are constructivism, development of a sense of community, and experiential activities. The constructivist paradigm is the approach that most closely approximates Dewey's (1938) call for active learning. Learning environments involving experiential activities that provide for interaction and collaboration may lead to the development of communities of practice (Lave and Wenger, 1991).

Constructivism

Constructivism is the worldview that recognizes learning as the process of constructing meaning about, or making sense of, our experiences (Vygotsky, 1978). Learning constructively, particularly in the social constructivist paradigm, requires an environment situated in 'coherent, meaningful, and purposeful activities' (Brown *et al*, 1989, p 34) designed to support collaboration, personal autonomy and active learning. Collaborative learning refers to activities in which small groups of people work together to accomplish shared goals to create meaning, explore a topic, or improve skills online (Harasim *et al*, 1995). The shift in roles from the instructor as a content expert to a facilitator of learning has been accompanied by a shift from teacher-centred to learner-centred instruction (Gunawardena, 1992).

Development of community

Through collaboration and interaction students may enhance their learning through the development of a community. As Osterman (2000) described, a community exists when its members experience a sense of belonging or personal relatedness, which is important to students not only for their academic achievement but also for their social and psychological well being. Communities of learners and practice are social organizations in which knowledge, values, identities and goals are shared (Jonassen, 1999) and have mechanisms for sharing what is learnt (Bielaczyc and Collins, 1999). Lave and Wenger (1991) proposed that when learners participate fully in the socially situated practices of a community, learning is a process of becoming part of a community of practice.

Experiential activities

Self-directed and real-life experiences include interactive activities such as small-group discussions, simulation games, project-based work, and collaborative problem-solving activities to solve educational problems (Romiszowski and Mason, 1996). For example, small-group discussions have dominated the online literature (Harasim *et al,* 1995), whereas examples of simulation games used in e-learning environments appear less frequently (Reader and Joinson, 1999), and the guidance available for educators to develop simulations for delivery by the Web is still rare (Cote and Jarvey, 1997). Project-based work online is gaining increased attention as a type of problem-solving activity (Collis, 1997). Finally, collaborative problem-solving activities in traditional and distance courses include online tutorials between partners in classes in two countries (Cifuentes and Shih, 2001) and research activities among classes in universities throughout the world (Murphy *et al,* 1995).

Simulation/role-play activities

The terms simulation, game, role-play, simulation-game, role-play simulation and role-playing games are used interchangeably in the literature (Tompkins, 1998).

A simulation game is a replication of real-life experience involving at least two players who operate under explicitly set rules for achieving a predetermined goal in a certain period of time. A simulation is a broad concept that typically includes an element of role-play (Tompkins). Simulations imitate real-life situations, whereas in role-playing the participant represents some character type known in everyday life. Simulations usually involve students in decision making, communicating and negotiating with others. Independent of the terminology used, these techniques provide the students with 'either a highly simplified reproduction of part of a real or imaginary world or a structured system that incorporates the material to be learned' (van Ments, 1999, p 3).

Simulations

Examples of simulations of natural phenomena in computerized environments for enhancing learning are numerous (McDonagh, 1999) and have proved to be effective in increasing students' learning gains (Geban *et al,* 1992). Computerized simulations, especially in science, where students are given the chance to explore and transform the concept or task, can replace real-life experimentation or help carry out experiments or demonstrations such as the Interactive Frog Dissection (Kinzie, 1994) that would otherwise be impossible due to cost, perceived danger or damage, or time constraints. In computer simulations, a physical object can be displayed on the computer screen, which allows students to manipulate the object to learn more about it. Additionally, a student may input an action; the computer reacts and provides feedback on the consequences of the action. Students can also experience different roles, such as social worker, parent, child and teacher through software programs that simulate the experiences of people in social work (Cote and Jarvey, 1997).

Role-play

Role-play is the particular type of simulation concentrating attention on the interaction of people (van Ments, 1999). In this type of simulation, functions performed by different people under a variety of circumstances are analysed. The idea of role-play is asking people to imagine that they are either themselves or other people in certain situations and then imitate those people's behaviour under the given circumstances. By doing so, they learn about the people, or situation, or both, through testing out their possible patterns of behaviour or examining the interacting behaviour of the group (van Ments). Role-plays are advantageous in terms of enabling students to express feelings easily, empathize with others and understand their motivations. Such student-centred activities as simulations/role-plays are significant in that the group can control content and pace of the activity.

Online simulation/role-play

Simulation and role-play are an integral part of online environments such as MOOs and MUDs. In these environments the participants are encouraged to perform a role, and the definition and expectations of these roles differ from one environment to another. MOO role-plays may pose a threat to community relationships, especially when the use of nicknames or anonymous participation is encouraged (Wellman and Gulia, 1999) or when competition rather than collaboration is emphasized. A basic difference between role-playing in MOOs and in e-learning environments is that the latter focus primarily on achieving learning outcomes through a structured path and creating a community of learners through collabora- tion. Simulations have been used frequently in computer-assisted instruction (Cote and Jarvey, 1997), and role-plays are employed commonly in MOOs (Turkle, 1998). More recently, however, both simulations and role-plays are used in e-learning environments and even developed by instructors using role-play simulation generators (Naidu *et al*, 2000). We present Mythica, a scenario-based simulation/ role-play activity in e-learning courses, to add to this research literature.

Simulation/role-play in e-learning environments: Mythica

This chapter's focus is on how to incorporate and integrate simulation/role-play activities into online courses to provide socialization support for university students. Two models were used in pursuing our goals: Jonassen's (1999) model for designing constructivist learning environments, and Cifuentes *et al's* (1997) model of computer conferencing design considerations. Jonassen's constructivist learning environments model focuses on the problem, question, or project that learners attempt to solve or resolve, with the aid of various interpretive and intellectual supports. In this model, the learning activities (exploration, articulation and reflection) are achieved with the instructional activities of modelling, coaching and scaffolding (see Figure 12.1).

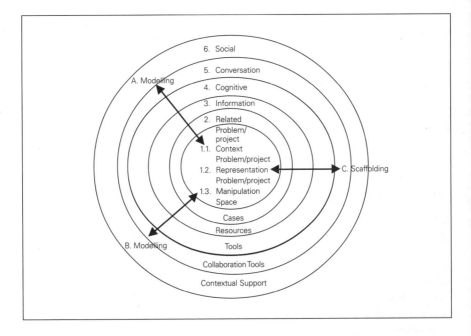

Figure 12.1   *From 'Designing Constructivist Learning Environments' (p. 218) by D. Jonassen, in* Instructional Design Theories and Models: A New Paradigm of Instructional Theory, *Vol. 2, by C. M. Reigeluth (Ed.), 1999, Mahwah, NJ: Erlbaum, Adapted with permission.*

The Cifuentes *et al* model situates the Jonassen model in an e-learning environment by presenting an interaction of key computer conferencing design considerations. In the Cifuentes model (see Figure 12.2) the all-encompassing requirement is adequate technological preparation, which surrounds the other design considerations: two administrative design issues (grading system and grouping), and three instructional design considerations (collaboration, relevance and learner control). We selected these two models because together they include key issues in a constructivist approach to integrating simulation/role-play activities into online courses.

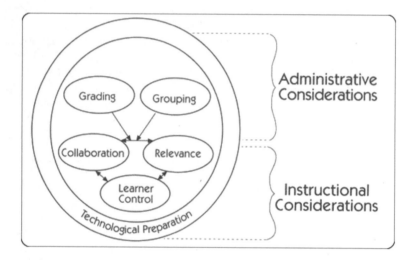

Figure 12.2 *From 'Design Consideration for Computer Conferences' by L. Cifuentes, K. L. Murphy, R. Segur, and S. Kodali, 1997,* Journal of Research on Computing in Education, *30, p. 197. Adapted with permission. Copyright © 1997, ISTE (International Society for Technology in Education), 800.336.5191 (US & Canada) or 541.302.3777 (Int'l), iste@iste.org, www.iste.org. All rights reserved.*

We describe the design and development of a simulation/role-play called 'Mythica' in a graduate course designed to provide a thorough overview of the history, theory, research and practice of educational technology at Texas A&M University. In each of four 14-week semester-long offerings of the course, students accessed the Web site to obtain course information and contribute to threaded discussions about occupations in the field, and they used FirstClass® computer conference software to post their assignments and communicate with their classmates and instructor.

The course was designed for students to engage in constructivist learning through a combination of independent and collaborative activities. The single collaborative activity was for each student to co-facilitate one activity and participate in the other activities, which were based on learning objectives and both required and supplementary readings. The first three activities were threaded discussions and the final activity was the simulation/role-play Mythica (Murphy, Moran and Weems, 2000). Mythica was the final activity because of the culminating nature of its content, which also gave students practice facilitating and participating in three previous discussions. The facilitator groups were formed at the beginning of each semester after students were asked to rank their first three choices. The instructor then organized the facilitating groups by taking into consideration the students' rankings as well as learner characteristics including country of origin, gender and e-learning experience. The students' challenge for the simulation/role-play was to develop a proposal for teaching English to the citizens of Mythica, a mythical oil-producing country comprised of 18 islands and inhabited by people accustomed to learning by rote memorization. The guiding questions to the short Mythica scenario are:

- Who is your target audience?
- What are your instructional goals and objectives?
- What instructional strategies and methods will you use?
- What delivery modes will you use?
- How will you provide for various forms of interaction (students with content, teachers, other students, and technology)?
- How will you evaluate the students' achievement and the program itself?
- How will you provide for the gradual transfer of ownership?

We analysed Mythica FirstClass conferences and evaluations in each course offering and included ideas from a case study of project-based learning (Murphy and Gazi, 2001). Through these analyses, we illustrate how a simple scenario-based simulation/role-play can act as a pivotal force that incorporates the instructor role and student roles – students-as-facilitators and students-as-participants – within the technology infrastructure of a computer conference. Figure 12.3 presents our model for integrating a simulation/role-play into an e-learning environment. The next sections describe the elements of the figure as exemplified by Mythica.

Nature of the activity

Project-based learning activities in online settings are intended to provide an active, engaging and dynamic setting for small groups of learners to collaborate in solving a problem and developing a product (Collis, 1997). Murphy and Gazi (2001) identified three characteristics of project-based learning activities that produce positive learning outcomes among e-learners: authentic activities, collaborative work and communication via telecommunications, and opportunities for knowledge enhancement and skill building. The nature of the Mythica simulation/role-play activity offers e-learners active participation and application of knowledge to a simulated real world experience. The learning objectives for the Mythica activity facilitated active learning of content: the students used the readings to meet the challenge presented in the scenario, so that the content became 'a means to an end,

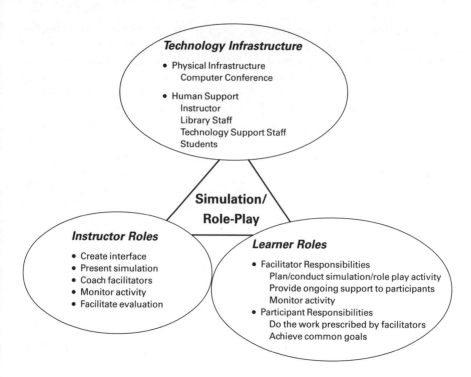

Figure 12.3   *Model for integrating a simulation/role-play into an e-learning course*

not an end in itself' (Oliver, 1999, p 244). In student evaluations, Mythica facilitators commented on the activity's effectiveness in encouraging active learning and covering the content in an entertaining and informative manner, and participants reflected that the activities encouraged active learning, made them feel involved, and covered the objectives effectively (Murphy, Moran and Weems, 2000), as corroborated by a student: 'I can see where the assignments are designed to build on each other. Mythica tied them all together in a practical scenario' (p 3). The simulation evolved into a simulation/role-play when facilitators asked participants to adopt such roles as instructional designer or technology transition team coordinator to develop a successful proposal for Mythica.

Technology infrastructure

An institution's technology infrastructure centres on the physical infrastructure but also requires human support, including technology and educational technology support staff, instructional design staff, and subject experts (Bates, 2000). Similarly, Evans and Nation (2000) charged that we 'give attention to the provision of adequate infrastructure, and the skilled humans to support it, as well as supporting thoroughly collaborative efforts in developing the new pedagogies' (p 172).

The physical infrastructure of each course included the FirstClass server software, and interactive videoconferencing for one course offering that used videoconferences in alternating sessions about half the time. Researchers recommend establishing 'boundaries around a protected space' in which to work and communicate (Palloff and Pratt, 1999, p 61). FirstClass provided such a safe place through a complex mix of email, chat rooms, threaded discussions, file attachments and dedicated workspaces for collaborative editing of text files.

Mythica's human infrastructure consisted of a variety of personnel in addition to the instructor. At the beginning of each semester, the instructor provided an orientation and training session, while library staff provided a seminar on accessing resources online. The technology support staff included computer support personnel for all courses and videoconference staff for one course. In addition, graduate assistants were hired occasionally as instructional designers or teaching assistants. Finally, students with FirstClass experience acted as peer tutors to novices, helping them complete lab exercises. In one course offering, students at both videoconference sites took turns as technology facilitators, thereby enabling the activity facilitators to focus on content.

Roles of instructor and of students

The instructor, the students-as-facilitators, and the students-as-participants adopted specific roles and used a variety of instructional and learning strategies to conduct the Mythica activity. Each role is integral to the overall success of the simulation/role-play activity and builds on the technology infrastructure.

The *instructor* provided modelling, scaffolding and coaching (Jonassen, 1999). She modelled appropriate conferencing behaviours at the beginning of the semester by facilitating a threaded discussion and giving immediate feedback to contributors. Scaffolding included organizing the readings; presenting the scenario, questions, and learning objectives; and creating private FirstClass conferences and collaborative documents. The instructor's coaching role involved distributing facilitation by dividing the task into component parts and assigning different parts to different people, followed by urging the Mythica facilitators to observe the process of previous activity facilitators. Throughout, the instructor monitored the facilitator discussions, interjecting both substantive comments (eg, 'Maybe Group Y (and Group X) need reminders about CAI (computer-assisted instruction) for tutorials, drill and practice, simulations') and supportive comments (eg, 'You have such fantastic ideas! Keep 'em rolling!'). Coaching also included both meeting with the facilitators in a real-time chat just before they opened their activity and monitoring the daily progress of the activity.

The *students-as-facilitators* created group-learning contracts, which provided an agreement of their responsibilities (Murphy, Mahoney and Harvell, 2000). Mythica facilitators were responsible for presenting the simulation/role-play and the related questions to the participants. Depending on the number of participants, the facilitators formed the activity groups. The facilitators acted as 'intelligent novices' (Brown *et al*, 1993, p 190) by providing similar scaffolding to the participants

(Murphy, Mahoney and Harvell, 2000). They used collaborative documents to develop their plans and create outlines and documents, taking care to be 'very detailed in the writing of the procedures for the activity. . . look(ing) at every detail of the process from the perspective of the participants'. The facilitators' coaching activities included replying, weaving responses and sending private email to individual participants to encourage them to participate by 'more than just post(ing) a response'. In contrast to the other activity facilitators, Mythica facilitators used varied instructional strategies to increase collaboration and reduce competition among participants by increasing conflict between the participants and such external constraints as time limits and creativity (Thiagarajan, 1998). Facilitators' key instructional strategies for modelling, coaching and scaffolding included the following:

- work together diligently and regularly, adapting to each other's schedules;
- build upon previous groups' experiences and knowledge gained in earlier activities;
- create a role-play environment;
- provide immediate feedback to participants with ancillary information and by asking pointed questions.

The *students-as-participants* were responsible for following the instructions of the students–as–facilitators in answering the scenario questions, which helped them develop their group Mythica proposals. This procedure, as described by one participant, involved substantial time to prepare for the activity: 'I have to read and organize the thoughts in the books, then answer the questions and observe the discussion among all participants and facilitators. The best stance of a participant is always to be ready to answer and give feedback.' The participants responded in threaded discussions or collaborative documents, as defined by the facilitators, to help their team members refine their replies. In general, they recognized the value of trying to understand each other as they worked toward common goals. For example, one student concluded, 'I listened to the others and saw the difference and similarities among us. Sometimes I needed to compromise. . . and sometimes I needed to stick to my opinions. Whatever I did was to show I am a responsible and collaborative person to work with others for the goals of successfully finishing the project.'

The Mythica simulation/role-play generally fostered a sense of community among the students. Both facilitators and participants developed communities of practice that resulted from the instructor's role as a facilitator of learning and corresponding focus on learner-centred instruction (Gunawardena, 1992). The group-learning contracts guided the facilitators in developing a community as they established common behaviour guidelines and communication protocols, identified member roles and developed contingency plans. An element of fun often accompanied the facilitators' activity planning, as shown in the following excerpt from a chat:

Facilitator A: Bye guys – It's been fun!
Facilitator B: Hoooooooowl!!!!!
Facilitator A: We shall conquer the Mythicans
Facilitator C: Charge-e-e-e-e-eeeeeeeeeee

As a result of the facilitators' collaboration and scaffolding, the participants often experienced belonging (Osterman, 2000) and were able to 'cross a threshold from feeling like outsiders to feeling like insiders' (Wegerif, 1998) in their simulation/ role play.

Recommendations

This chapter aimed to present simulation/role-play as a scenario-based experiential activity to create a collaborative learning environment and a sense of community among e-learners. Based on the Jonassen (1999) and Cifuentes *et al* (1997) models, we described a collaborative learning environment for both students-as-facilitators and students-as-participants. Some Mythica facilitators motivated the participants by giving them more control over their learning, as suggested by Cifuentes *et al*, through such activities as role-playing and having the groups post their own final proposals in FirstClass. As a conversation or collaboration tool, FirstClass afforded the capability of exploration, articulation and reflection recommended by Jonassen but did not provide for alternative discourse structures such as argumentation and problem-solving (Jonassen and Remidez, 2002). How can we write or adapt simple scenarios into simulation/role-plays and design them in elegant ways that both foster socialization and allow for divergent thinking, as Smith and Stacey suggest in this section of the book? We recommend several design considerations for instructors/designers to enhance collaboration and community through simulation/ role-play activities in e-learning:

● conduct simulation/role-play activities first in a face-to-face mode to build confidence;
● schedule simulation/role-play activities for a greater length of time than other activities and for later in the semester, after students participate in less complex activities;
● form appropriately sized student groups of facilitators (three to four) and participants (seven to nine);
● provide implicit and explicit scaffolding that includes guidelines for time- and task-management;
● adopt the role of coach, giving control to student activity facilitators to encourage collaboration rather than competition.

A future possibility is to use melded information and communications technologies to deliver simulation/role-play, such as Web video instead of a text-based environment. With the advent of technologies of digital content production and dissemination and efforts to resolve bandwidth problems, experiential activities such as simulation/role-play can be enhanced to resemble real-life experiences more closely. Tools that could be used currently include Tegrity® (http://www.3com.com/solutions/en_US/solutionslab/alliance_tegrity.html) and Virage® (http://www.virage.com/), which enable the creation, management and distribution of digital media. Universal design and equity issues surrounding the use of multimedia products are gaining importance, with efforts underway to address them. As professionals tackle bandwidth issues, these and more sophisticated tools will be accessible to broader audiences, creating richer experiential activities in e-learning.

Further research can provide insight to instructors and designers in adapting experiential activities, designing a course infrastructure, and preparing students to facilitate the activity. Continuing investigation of strategies used by instructors, students-as-facilitators and students-as-participants will shed light on the productivity of e-learning experiences and environments. Communication patterns among facilitators and among participants as groups can be examined from a discourse analytic point of view to reveal the speech acts, conversational patterns and even the power structures, to have a better understanding of group dynamics and paths leading to success.

References

Bates, A W (2000) *Managing Technological Change: Strategies for college and university leaders,* Jossey-Bass, San Francisco, CA

Bielaczyc, K and Collins, A (1999) Learning communities in classrooms: a reconceptualization of educational practice, in *Instructional Design Theories and Models: A new paradigm of instructional theory,* ed C M Reigeluth, Vol 2, pp 188–228, Lawrence Erlbaum, Mahwah, NJ

Brown, A L, Ash, D, Rutherford, M, Nakagawa, K, Gordon, A and Campione, J C (1993) Distributed expertise in the classroom, in *Distributed Cognitions: Psychological and educational considerations,* ed G Salomon, Cambridge University Press, Cambridge

Brown, J S, Collins, A and Duguid, P (1989) Situated cognition and the culture of learning, *Educational Researcher,* **18** (1), pp 32–42

Cifuentes, L and Shih, Y-D (2001) Teaching and learning online: a collaboration between US and Taiwanese students, *Journal of Research on Computing in Education,* **33,** pp 456–74

Cifuentes, L, Murphy, K L, Segur, R and Kodali, S (1997) Design considerations for computer conferences, *Journal of Research on Computing in Education,* **30,** pp 172–95

Collis, B (1997) Supporting project-based collaborative learning via a World Wide Web environment, in *Web-based Instruction,* ed B Khan, pp 213–19, Educational Technology, Englewood Cliffs, NJ

Cote, D and Jarvey, D (1997) The development of an instructional simulation on the World Wide Web. Accessed 28 May 2001, from: http://home.istar.ca/~djcote/projects/paper.htm

Dewey, J (1938) *Experience and Education,* Macmillan, New York

Evans, T and Nation, D (2000) Understanding changes to university teaching, in *Changing University Teaching: Reflections on creating educational technologies,* eds T Evans and D Nation, pp 160–75, Kogan Page, London

Garrison, R (2000) Theoretical challenges for distance education in the 21st century: a shift from structural to transactional issues. Accessed 28 May 2001, from: http://www.irrodl.org/content/v1.1/randy.pdf

Geban, Ö, Askar, P and Özkan, I (1992) Effects of computer simulations and problem-solving approaches on high school students, *Journal of Educational Research,* **86** (1), pp 5–10

Gunawardena, C N (1992) Changing faculty roles for audiographics and online teaching, *The American Journal of Distance Education,* **6** (3), pp 58–71

Harasim, L, Hiltz, S R, Teles, L and Turoff, M (1995) *Learning Networks: A field guide to teaching and learning online,* Massachusetts Institute of Technology, Cambridge, MA

Institute for Higher Education Policy (1999) *What's the Difference? A review of contemporary research on the effectiveness of distance learning in higher education.* Report commissioned by the American Federation of Teachers and the National Education Association, Washington, DC. Accessed 3 November 2000, from http://www.ihep.com

Jonassen, D (1999) Designing constructivist learning environments, in *Instructional Design Theories and Models: A new paradigm of instructional theory,* ed C M Reigeluth, Vol 2, pp 215–39, Lawrence Erlbaum, Mahwah, NJ

Jonassen, D and Remidez, H (2002) Mapping alternative discourse structures onto computer conferences, in *Proceedings of CSCL 2002, Computer support for collaborative learning: Foundations for a CSCL community,* ed G Stahl, pp 237–44, Lawrence Erlbaum, Hillsdale, NJ

Kinzie, M (1994) The interactive frog dissection: an on-line tutorial. Accessed 3 November 2000, from http://curry.edschool.virginia.edu/go/frog/

Lave, J and Wenger, E (1991) *Situated Learning: Legitimate peripheral participation,* Cambridge University Press, Cambridge

McDonagh, M (1999) Update: references to recent articles, in *Simulation and Gaming Research Yearbook: Simulation and games for strategy and policy planning,* eds D Saunders and J Severn, Vol 7, pp 271–8, Kogan Page, London

Murphy, K L and Gazi, Y (2001) Role plays, panel discussions, and simulations: project-based learning in a web-based course, *Educational Media International,* **38** (4), pp 261–270

Murphy, K L, Mahoney, S E and Harvell, T J (2000) Role of contracts in enhancing community building in web courses, *Educational Technology and Society,* **3** (3), pp 409–21. Accessed 3 September 2000, from http://ifets.ieee.org/periodical/vol_3_2000/e03.html

Murphy, K L, Moran, J A and Weems, M (2000) Mythica: case study analysis via the web. Paper presented at the annual convention of the Association for Educational Communications and Technology, October, Denver, CO

Murphy, K, Cochenour, J, Rezabek, L, Dean, A F, Gibson, C, Gunawardena, C, Hessmiller, R and Yakimovicz, A (1995) Computer-mediated communications in a collaborative learning environment: the Globaled 93 project, in *17th World Conference for Distance Education: One world many voices,* ed D Sewart, Vol 2, pp 407–10, Open University, Milton Keynes

Naidu, S, Ip, A and Linser, R (2000) Dynamic goal-based role-play simulation on the web: a case study, *Educational Technology and Society,* 3 (3), pp 409–21. Accessed 9 March 2001, from http://ifets.ieee.org/periodical/vol_3_2000/b05html

Oliver, R (1999) Exploring strategies for online teaching and learning, *Distance Education,* 20 (2), pp 240–54

Osterman, K F (2000) Students' need for belonging in the school community, *Review of Educational Research,* 7 (3), pp 323–67

Palloff, R M and Pratt, K (1999) *Building Learning Communities in Cyberspace: Effective strategies for the online classroom,* Jossey-Bass, San Francisco, CA

Reader, W and Joinson, A (1999) Promoting student discussion using simulated seminars on the Internet, in *Simulation and Gaming Research Yearbook: Simulation and games for strategy and policy planning,* eds D Saunders and J Severn, Vol 7, pp 139–49, Kogan Page, London

Romiszowski, A J (1997) Web-based distance learning and teaching: revolutionary invention or reaction to necessity?, in *Web-based Instruction,* ed B H Khan, pp 25–37, Educational Technology, Englewood Cliffs, NJ

Romiszowski, A J and Mason, R (1996) Computer-mediated communication, in *The Handbook of Research for Educational Communications and Technology,* ed D H Jonassen, pp 438–56, Simon and Schuster Macmillan, New York

Thiagarajan, S (1998) The secrets of successful facilitators. Accessed 12 March 2002, from http://www.thiagi.com/article–secrets.html

Tompkins, P K (1998) Role playing/simulation, *The Internet TESL Journal,* 4 (8). Accessed 28 June 2001, from http://iteslj.org/Techniques/Tompkins–Role Playing.html

Turkle, S (1998) All MOOs are educational: the experience of 'Walking through the self', in *High Wired: On design, use, and theory of educational MOOs,* eds C Haynes, and J R Holmevik, *pp* ix–xix, University of Michigan, Ann Arbor

van Ments, M (1999) *The Effective Use of Role-play: Practical techniques for improving learning,* Kogan Page, London

Vygotsky, L S (1978) *Mind in Society: The development of higher psychological processes,* Harvard University Press, Cambridge, MA

Web-Based Education Commission (2000) *The Power of the Internet for Learning: Moving from promise to practice,* report of the Web–Based Education Commission to the President and the Congress of the United States. Accessed 20 January 2001, from http://www.ed.gov/offices/AC/WBEC/FinalReport/

Wegerif, R (1998) The social dimension of asynchronous learning networks, *Journal of Asynchronous Learning Networks,* 2 (1). Accessed 28 June 2001, from http://www.aln.org/alnweb/journal/vol2_issue1/wegerif.htm

Wellman, B and Gulia, M (1999) Virtual communities as communities: net surfers don't ride alone, in *Communities in Cyberspace,* eds M A Smith and P Kollock, pp 167–94, Routledge, New York

Part 4

Assessment of learning outcomes

Chapter 13

Broadening assessment strategies with information technology

Catherine McLoughlin

Traditional and Web-based assessment compared

Educators can be in no doubt of the demands of society for lifelong capable learners who are able to perform cognitive and metacognitive tasks and demonstrate competencies such as problem solving, critical thinking, questioning, searching for information, making judgements and evaluating information (Oliver and McLoughlin, 2001). The illustration of a continuum of assessment types in Figure 13.1 represents the changing nature of assessment, showing a transition from a focus on testing to a focus on learning and transfer of understanding.

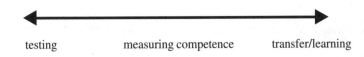

testing   measuring competence   transfer/learning

Figure 13.1   *The continuum of assessment types*

The traditional approach to assessment was largely a form of objective testing, which valued students' capacity to memorize facts and then recall them during a test situation. Testing was concerned with measuring a range of cognitive skills, though many of these tests relied on quantifiable approaches rather than qualitative displays of skills and knowledge. Magone *et al* (1994) called this the 'one right answer mentality'.

Another form of assessment depicted in the continuum is the measurement of competencies, or what is called 'sequestered problem solving' (Schwartz *et al,* 2000). In these contexts students are asked to solve problems in isolation and without the resources that are typically available in the real world such as texts, Web-resources and peers. Often these tests of aptitude are single shot, and summative rather than formative. In contrast, assessment that supports learning and knowledge transfer provides the basis for future learning and continuing motivation to learn. This approach is sometimes called the 'alternative assessment movement', as it is concerned with authentic performance (Cumming and Maxwell, 1999). Both testing and measuring competence as forms of assessment have been critiqued as being controlling, limiting and contrary to student-centred teaching and learning. Morgan and O'Reilly (1999) add the following criticisms of traditional assessment practices:

- a lack of variety and autonomy and student choice;
- lack of applied work-based and project-based learning;
- overuse of summative forms of assessment;
- limited use of peer and self-assessment strategies.

Other indicators of the need to rethink online assessment have come from Bull and McKenna (2000) who argue that 'the development and integration of computer-aided assessment has been done in an ad hoc manner'. In a similar vein, Angelo (1999) maintains that we need a more compelling vision of assessment, research-based guidelines for learner-centred assessment, and a new mental model of assessment. While computer-assisted assessment is rapidly gaining ground as a convenient and cost-effective means of assessing learning outcomes, there is a need to adopt more holistic models of learning that focus on processes rather than outcomes. Later in this chapter innovative forms of assessment are proposed that capitalize on networked learning, opportunities for self and peer assessment and the creation of authentic learning environments that enable learning to be monitored and assessed in both formative and summative ways.

Pedagogical models of online assessment

The changing focus of pedagogy that has been achieved through online learning and networked technologies is readily evident in the forums for collaboration and interaction among distributed learners (Coomey and Stephenson, 2001). As increasing numbers of students go online, one of the major challenges is how to reengineer courses, increase flexibility and quality and assess students online (Collis and Moonen, 2001). Looking at the array of computer-based tools available, it is possible to identify several theoretical frameworks and pedagogical models that drive online assessment. Educators and instructional designers need to know how these frameworks can guide the design of online assessment tasks, and how elements of each are relevant in designing formative and summative assessment tasks. Below, some frameworks are identified that can be useful starting points for assessment. These look at assessment from the varying perspectives of learning outcomes, resource-based learning, process-based learning and authentic assessment. In the final analysis this section will propose an holistic model for online assessment that synthesizes elements from all approaches.

Learning outcomes and assessment

In planning learning and assessment tasks, one view is that designers must have a clear notion of intended learning outcomes. Examples of desired learning outcomes cited by Ramsden (1992) are comprehension of key concepts and ways of understanding in a discipline, and the development of abilities to integrate theoretical and practical knowledge in professional applications. There are a number of schemes that describe a range of learning objectives and break down learning objectives into component parts or hierarchies (Bloom,1956; Gagne *et al*, 1992). Of these the most popular has been Bloom's taxonomy, which has been applied by several researchers in creating computer-based tasks to assess various kinds of performance (Dalgarno, 1998; King and Duke-Williams, 2001). In a recent update of Bloom's taxonomy, six levels of objectives remain linked to performance in understanding, applying, synthesizing and applying knowledge (Anderson *et al*, 2000). For test generation, this taxonomy is likely to remain a useful starting point for designing assessment, but lacks reference to processes of learning and the context of assessment.

Resource-based assessment

Web-based and distance learning are based on the notion that learners can access a wide range of resources, often not prescribed by the teacher in order to pursue their own learning goals (Oliver and McLoughlin, 1999). Often resource-based learning assumes that students have a repertoire of learning skills and strategies, such as information management, search strategies and information literacy skills. This means that learning and support of skills must be balanced with the assessment of students' performance. Assessment in resource-based learning contexts needs to ensure that learners are given sufficient feedback on how they approach tasks, and provide well-structured tasks that enable students to develop a sense of how well they are coping with these demands (MacDonald *et al*, 1999). The implications of resource-based learning are that assessment tasks need to be flexible, reveal the nature of students' prior knowledge, address misconceptions and misunderstandings and ensure that appropriate and timely feedback is given.

Authentic assessment

In order to reflect the complexity of learning, it is now recognized that assessment should reflect more than a single aspect of performance, or overemphasize cognitive outcomes (Bennett *et al*, 2000). Frameworks that challenge one-dimensional views of student performance recognize that assessment tasks need to reflect a number of core components of performance and competence ie, functional skills, cognitive abilities, personal skills and values/professional capabilities (Cheetham and Chivers, 1996). This expanded view of assessment is also referred to as authentic, performance-based assessment, the main components of which are depicted in Figure 13.2. Each of these elements needs further elaboration.

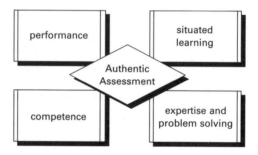

Figure 13.2   *Authentic, performance-based assessment*

Performance

This aspect of authentic assessment focuses on the need to ensure that performance is observed and measured through actual demonstration or execution of a task or real-life performance (Wiggins, 1998). In addition, the performance should encompass the whole task and not just part of it. In a case study presented later in this chapter, Web-based learning is shown to have the capacity to support the principles of authentic assessment and whole task performance.

Competence

Competence-based performance is the second dimension of authentic assessment, because of its link to real world contexts. However, the literature often uses the terms *authentic* and performance *assessment* interchangeably. According to Baker and O'Neill (1994, p 15) 'Performance-based assessment may also emphasize authenticity, that is the task is intended to be inherently valuable to student.' Reeves and Okey (1996) propose that the distinction surrounds the degree of authenticity in the context in which the performance is conducted. It is now recognized that multimedia and Web-based learning environments provide settings and conditions that support active demonstrations of competence (Herrington and Herrington, 1998).

Expertise and problem solving

The third dimension of authentic performance recognizes complexity and expert performance, and the need to assess higher order cognition (Newman and Archbald, 1992). Examples of technology-supported assessment include the use of anchored environments where students engage in complex scenarios that require problem-solving skills (Harper *et al,* 2000).

Situated learning

This dimension recognizes that context affects what is learnt and assessed, and that the context of assessment should match as closely as possible the context of learning and performance. However, as learners are also expected to be able to transfer learning from one context to another, there are degrees of situatedness. In a study of the use of multimedia authoring, McFarlane *et al* (2000) showed that assessment tasks based on multimedia authoring enabled students to make their conceptual and procedural thinking explicit, and enabled meaningful judgements about their cognitive achievements.

Figure 13.3 presents an extension of the four aspects of assessment depicted above, with the integration of performance, authenticity, competence, situated learning and problem solving. The dimensions are an adaptation of those developed by Reeves (2000), who proposed a number of core principles that can be applied to the design of constructivist online environments. These principles have been adapted to provide specific parameters depicted in Figure 13.3 to guide the design of online assessment tasks utilizing communications technologies.

Practitioners and theorists are in agreement that computer-based and online forms of assessment need to be reviewed in order to ensure that tasks are diverse and capable of offering multiple measures of cognition, skill, performance and higher order cognition (Reeves, 2000; Thelwall, 2000). The next section provides examples of online assessment that meet these principles and that allow for diagnosis, monitoring and demonstration of competence and that broaden the range of competencies that can be assessed.

Examples of online assessment that support multiple indicators of performance

There is a huge array of online resources, tools and software now available for online assessment. Table 13.1 presents a summary of these, showing that summative, formative and diagnostic approaches are possible in computer-based environments.

In the next section, examples are provided of assessment types that showcase learner achievement in a range of skills. These assessment tasks include:

Explanation of dimensions

Task-oriented: Assessment items must resemble actual learning tasks.

Challenging: Assessment tasks should require application of concepts to new domains and problems.

Authentic: Tasks and problems should be real rather than contrived.

Responsive: Tasks should enable the provision of feedback to improve performance.

Reflective: Tasks should enable learners to develop metacognitive skills.

Goal-oriented: Students should perceive that the goals of assessment are congruent with desired learning outcomes.

Multiple indicators: Assessment should provide multiple indicators of performance.

Self-regulatory: Tasks should foster self-direction rather than dependence on teacher-transmitted knowledge.

Social negotiation: Tasks should be embedded in contexts that offer social construction of understanding.

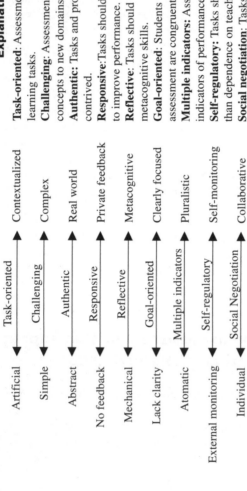

Artificial	← Task-oriented →	Contextualized
Simple	← Challenging →	Complex
Abstract	← Authentic →	Real world
No feedback	← Responsive →	Private feedback
Mechanical	← Reflective →	Metacognitive
Lack clarity	← Goal-oriented →	Clearly focused
Atomatic	← Multiple indicators →	Pluralistic
External monitoring	← Self-regulatory →	Self-monitoring
Individual	← Social Negotiation →	Collaborative

Figure 13.3 *Pedagogical framework for online assessment adapted from Reeves & Reeves (1997)*

Table 13.1   *Examples of online and computer-based assessment strategies*★

Assessment task	Type of assessment	Example of skills assessed
Bulletin board tasks	Formative	Interpersonal skills, collaboration, peer review and evaluation, interpersonal skills
Electronic journal	Diagnostic, formative	Reflection
Drag and drop items	Summative	Recall and application of concepts
Mini–test	Summative	Synthesis and application of concepts
Multiple choice	Formative and summative	Depends on types of questions
Multiple response	Formative and summative	Comprehension, analysis and synthesis
Open access random tests	Formative, diagnostic and summative	Comprehension, analysis, synthesis, review of concepts
Practice test	Diagnostic	Self-directed learning
Peer assessment	Formative and summative	Collaboration, reflection, metacognition
Pretest	Diagnostic	Depends on questions
Portfolio	Formative and summative	Lifelong learning, self-direction, metacognition, project management
Quiz	Formative and summative	A range of cognitive skills depending on the questions asked
Question bank final quiz	Summative	A range of cognitive skills depending on the questions asked
Revision quiz	Formative	A range of cognitive skills depending on the questions asked
Reflective log	Formative	Metacognition, self-evaluation, self-monitoring
Self-assessment	Formative	Self-evaluation, self-monitoring
Short answer	Formative, summative	Application and transfer of knowledge
Simulation and role play	Formative and summative	Higher order thinking

★Examples of tools and assessment practices involving these examples can be found in Brown *et al* (1999) and on the CAA website at: http://www.lboro.ac.uk/service/ltd/flicaa/conf2001/

- digital portfolios;
- networked peer assessment;
- problem solving online.

Taking into account the principles for alternative assessment mentioned earlier, several examples can be provided that demonstrate how assessment practices enable a range of learning outcomes and competencies to be fostered, scaffolded and assessed online.

Example 1: Networked peer assessment

The assessment task described here is taken from a course of study in which adult learners and professionals seek to develop their skills in multimedia design, in a tertiary degree programme. The framework used in the course to promote the learning process is shown in Figure 13.4. It is focused on the promotion of independent learning using a listserv and online resources, peer support and collaboration, which in turn promote the development of professional skills and process knowledge. Also, as part of an authentic learning task, students share their knowledge with their industry partners, and work in teams to create multimedia products that meet industry specifications. The task involves the creation of a Web site or the design of an e-commerce business product to meet industry needs. This is the real world task that students engage in and it is also a formative assessment task. Students work in teams to prepare a project plan, a project specification and an actual product that meets industry standards. Three sets of assessment criteria are used in the assessment process: those provided by peers who work in teams to provide feedback on project design; those provided by team members themselves (self-assessment) and those provided by the tutor, seeking alignment with course objectives.

The technology provides the medium for display of the product, but also supports process skills, communication and asynchronous discussion of assessment criteria. The social scaffolding of learning takes place on the listserv, which provides scope for learners to:

- negotiate projects with industry from initial stage to completion;
- discuss and share ideas through asynchronous conferencing;
- review and discuss criteria for self and peer assessment;
- engage in peer review of draft project plans;
- elicit feedback from industry partners on the quality of the product.

The online environment supports the social and cognitive aspects of assessment and makes the process transparent, formative and integrative. Real life problems are essentially multidimensional, and this assessment task provides learners with multiple criteria that can be applied to create a worthwhile product. Additionally the skills to work effectively in a team are crucial within this environment and

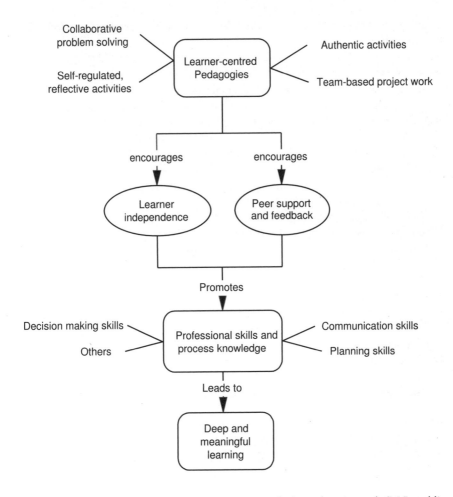

Figure 13.4 *Student assessment process in a networked peer learning task (McLoughlin and Luca, 2001)*

therefore the assessment of both group and individual efforts are part of the assessment system.

Example 2: Problem solving online

Recent research in assessment shows that teachers are beginning to develop more purposeful environments to assess higher order thinking skills and to gather both qualitative and quantitative data as supporting evidence (Kendle and Northcote, 2000). Web-based assessment enables peer and group assessment and, by allowing students to work together, helps them communicate and share ideas. Oliver and McLoughlin (2001) provide an example of a Web-based system with the infra-structure for a learning activity whereby learners are organized into small groups, within their larger class cohort. The Web-based system provides the following functionalities:

- a series of weekly problems are presented online and each week students work and collaborate in the Web-based environment to create a group solution;
- once a group has posted its solution, it can view the solutions of other groups;
- each group is required to read the solutions of the others and to select the best solutions for commentary (a form of peer assessment);
  - the class tutors add their marks to provide an overall mark for each group solution;
  - the best solutions from each workshop are displayed and students can review these;
  - the system maintains a record of the marks obtained by each group and shows this in graphical form for each problem;
  - at the end of the course, the system provides the marks for each student across the range of problems solved.

This activity has been demonstrated to provide many learning opportunities and advantages. These include the following:

- Students find the problem-solving activities extremely motivating.
- The activities enable on and off-campus learners to be part of the same learning environment.
- Learners can support each other through activities in the shared learning spaces.
- The activities encourage and support the development of inquiry skills in using the Web for evaluation of information.
- Students develop generic skills in forming arguments and creating logical answers as they seek to provide solutions to the problems presented online.

There is sound theoretical support for this form of online assessment environment (Segers and Dochy, 2001). Several recent studies affirm that online problem-solving tasks provide effective support for learning:

- A problem-based learning environment encourages learners to reflect on their ideas and strategies and to articulate their views (McLoughlin and Luca, 2001; Oliver and McLoughlin, 2001).
- Students learn from the communication and interaction with their peers in the problem-solving process (eg, Jonassen et al, 1999).
- The scope for communication and collaboration provides for meaningful interactions and purposeful engagement in the learning process (McConnell, 2000).

Example 3: Using online portfolios

As stated previously, the goals of the contemporary curriculum are now oriented towards more complex curricular objectives and more complex performances, and so it is essential that assessment practices enable students to demonstrate skills, knowledge and competencies in diverse and meaningful ways, and to mirror professional practice (McLoughlin and Luca, 2001). One of the most powerful means of supporting a range of skills through online assessment is to allow students to create an online portfolio. Many institutions have now constructed electronic portfolio systems on the Web as a means of supporting and monitoring assessment process skills and enabling students to create an electronic file of learning resources and personally meaningful reflections on study experiences. Mostert and Knoetze (2001) for example, offered students specially designed shells and templates from which to construct their electronic portfolios. Students maintain the portfolio online and it can be accessed by tutors who can provide feedback, or put on display for other students for peer review (Chang, 2001). Some examples of the types of content that students can submit in the portfolio are:

- daily notes on learning progress;
- learning notes gained from texts and conferences;
- self-reflections on learning processes;
- peer evaluations of work;
- questions about areas needing attention;
- special projects and achievements.

The development of a portfolio is a dynamic process that is integrated with both formative and summative assessment processes. One of its strengths is that it gives students greater control and ownership of the learning process while providing scope for self and peer assessment and the showcasing of a broad range of achievements.

Overcoming the disadvantages of traditional assessment

Computer-based assessment may suffer an 'image problem' as some assume it is capable only of summative testing using multiple-choice tests derived from item banks. Increasingly, computer-based assessment is enabling innovative approaches to formative assessment that 'close the gap between actual and desired levels of performance' (Sheingold and Frederiksen, 1994). A number of factors have already been cited concerning the potential value of networked learning environments and computer-based assessment. Current software development and the interactive capabilities of the Web enable the creation of procedural, conceptual, cognitive and collaborative assessment tasks and support student expression of prior knowledge, experience and learning in personally meaningful ways.

The future of online assessment

Already, in terms of pedagogy, implementation and administration, computer-delivered assessment is outstripping conventional forms of assessment and, in the words of Bennett (2001) is 'reinventing assessment'. What is the evidence for this? Certainly, online assessment is capable of greater flexibility, cost-effectiveness and time saving. It has been these attributes that have made it appealing in an age of competitive higher education funding and resource constraints. Current online designs can support group and individual feedback, self-testing by students, flexibility and the diagnosis of misconceptions so that early intervention can be planned. The added benefit of computer-based assessment is its motivational and self-regulatory nature. By allowing students to test their own knowledge and understanding, they can decide when, where and how often to take a test, ensuring preparedness for learning.

In terms of pedagogy, the underpinnings of online assessment are solidly constructivist and have the capacity to offer multiple indicators of student performance. Current demands of employers and universities are for graduates with cognitive and social competencies such as critical thinking, team skills, communication and problem solving. Since the goals of learning are aimed towards achievement of specific competencies, assessment practices must also generate opportunities for students to interpret, analyse and evaluate arguments. Online assessment affords the tools, media and transparency to meet these demands.

In summary, the communicative and collaborative attributes of online environments and new software for designing tests, quiz items and a range of tasks that can be created exemplify a reinvention of traditional pedagogy and an holistic approach to learning. First, the integration of learning and assessment is possible in these environments by offering learners multiple avenues to demonstrate achievement, offer feedback and develop both the processes and outcomes of learning. Second, online settings for learning provide access to resources, peers and a range of authentic tasks within a social context where discussion and critical analysis are central. In new assessment approaches, what is most important is to extend, foster and showcase the competencies required for real-life practice. Trends in assessment have moved from a culture of testing and standardized tests to a culture of learning. In this chapter, examples have been provided of learner-centred tasks that capitalize on the social and interactive capabilities of the Web to provide levers for rethinking assessment and creating multiple indicators of learning achievement.

References

Anderson, L W, Krathwohl, D R and Bloom, B S (2001) *Taxonomy for Learning, Teaching and Assessing: A revision of Bloom's taxonomy of educational objectives,* Longman, London

Angelo, T (1999) Doing assessment as if learning matters most, *AAHE Bulletin,* May, Accessed 15 February 2002, from http://www.aahe.org/Bulletin/angelomay99 htm

Baker, E L and O'Neill, H F (1994) Performance assessment and equity: a view from the USA, *Assessment in Education,* **1,** pp 11–26

Bennett, N, Dunne, E and Carrre, C (2000) *Skills Development in Higher Education and Employment,* The Society for Research into Higher Education and Training and Open University Press, Buckingham

Bennett, R E (2001) How the Internet will help large-scale assessment reinvent itself, *Educational Policy Analysis Archives,* **9** (5).Accessed 17 April 2002, from http://epaaasuedu/epaa/v9n5html

Bloom, B S (1956) *Taxonomy of Educational Objectives: The cognitive domain* (Handbook 1), David McKay, New York

Brown, S, Race, P and Bull, J (1999) *Computer-assisted Assessment in Higher Education,* Kogan Page, London

Bull, J and McKenna, C (2000) Computer assisted assessment center update, *Proceedings of the 4th International Conference on Computer Assisted Assessment.* Accessed 17 April 2002, from http://www.lboro.ac.uk/service/ltd/flicaa/conf2000/pdfs/jbullpdf

Chang, C (2001) Construction and evaluation of a web-based learning portfolio system: an electronic assessment tool, *Innovations in Education and Teaching International,* **38** (2), pp 144–55

Cheetham, G and Chivers, G (1996) Towards a holistic model of professional competence, *Journal of European Industrial Training,* **20** (5), pp 20–30

Collis, B and Moonen, J (2001) *Flexible Learning in a Digital World,* Kogan Page, London

Coomey, M and Stephenson, J (2001) Online learning: it's all about dialogue, involvement, support and control according to the research, *Teaching and Learning Online,* pp 37–52, Kogan Page, London

Cumming, J J and Maxwell, G S (1999) Contextualizing authentic assessment, *Assessment in Education: Principles, Policy and Practice,* **6,** pp 177–94

Dalgarno, B (1998) Choosing learner activities for specific learning outcomes: a tool for computer assisted learning, *EDTEch 98 proceedings.* Accessed 17 April 2002, from http://cleomurdoch.edu.au/gen/aset/confs/edtech98/pubs/articles/abcd/dalgarnohtml

Gagne, R M, Briggs, L J and Wagner, W W (1992) *Principles of Instructional Design,* Harcourt, Brace, Janovich, Orlando, FL

Harper, B, Hedberg, J, Corderoy, B and Wright, R (2000) Employing cognitive tools within interactive multimedia applications, in *Computers as Cognitive Tools,* ed S P Lajoie, pp 227–46, Lawrence Erlbaum, London

Herrington, J and Herrington, T (1998) Authentic assessment and multimedia: how university students respond to a model of authentic assessment, *Higher Education Research and Development,* **17** (3), pp 305–21

Jonassen, D, Prevish, T, Christy, D and Stravrulaki, E (1999) Learning to solve problems on the Web: aggregate planning in a business management course, *Distance Education,* **20** (1), pp 49–57

Kendle, A and Northcote, M (2000) The struggle for balance in the use of quantitative and qualitative online assessment tasks, in *Learning to Choose,*

Choosing to Learn, eds R Sims, M O'Reilly and S Sawkins, Coffs Harbour. Accessed 17 April 2002, from http://www.ascilite.org.au/conferences/coffs00/

King, T and Duke-Williams, E (2001) Using computer aided assessment to test higher level learning outcomes, *Proceedings of the 4th International Conference on Computer Assisted Assessment.* Accessed 2 March 2002, from http://www.lboro.ac.uk/service/ltd/flicaa/conf2001/indexhtml

MacDonald, J, Mason, R and Heap, N (1999) Refining assessment for resource-based learning, *Assessment in Higher Education,* **24** (3), pp 345–54

Magone, M E, Cai, J, Silver, E A and Wang, N (1994) Validating the cognitive complexity and content quality of a mathematics performance assessment, *International Journal of Educational Research,* **21** pp 317–340

McConnell, D (2000) Examining collaborative assessment processes in networked lifelong learning, *Journal of Computer Assisted Learning,* **15** (2), pp 232–43

McFarlane, A, Williams, J M and Bonnett, M (2000) Assessment and multimedia authoring: a tool for externalising understanding, *Journal of Computer Assisted Learning,* **16** (3), pp 201–12

McLoughlin, C and Luca, J (2000) Networked learners: online tasks to foster team communicative skills, in *Making the Critical Connection: Communication skills in university education,* ed C Beasly, pp 99–108, Edith Cowan University, Perth

McLoughlin, C and Luca, J (2001). Lifelong learning, workbased learning and partnerships for learning in research and development in higher education, **24**, pp 97–110, NCP Printing, University of Newcastle.

Morgan, C and O'Reilly, M (1999) *Assessing Open and Distance Learners,* Kogan Page, London

Mostert, E and Knoetze, J G (2001) Implementing an electronic portfolio assessment strategy: Multiple pathways for diverse learners. *Proceedings of the 4th International Conference on Computer Assisted Assessment.* Accessed 17 April 2002, from http://www.lboro.ac.uk/service/ltd/flicaa/conf2001/indexhtml

Newman, F M and Archbald, D A (1992) The nature of authentic academic achievement, in *Towards a New Science of Educational Testing and Achievement,* eds H Berlak, F M Newman, E Adams, D A Archbald and T Burgess, pp 70–83, State University of New York Press, Albany, NY

Oliver, R and McLoughlin, C (1999) Curriculum and learning-resource issues arising from the use of web-based course support systems, *International Journal of Educational Telecommunications,* **5** (4), pp 419–38

Oliver, R and McLoughlin, C (2001) Exploring the practice and development of generic skills through web-based learning, *Journal of Educational Multimedia and Hypermedia,* **10** (3), pp 307–25

Ramsden, P (1992) *Learning to Teach in Higher Education,* Routledge, London

Reeves, T C (2000) Alternative assessment approaches for online learning environments in higher education, *Journal of Educational Computing Research,* **23** (1), pp 101–11

Reeves, T and Okey, J R (1996) Alternative assessment for constructivist learning environments, in *Constructivist Learning Environments: Case studies in instructional design,* ed B G Wilson, pp 191–202, Educational Technology Publications, Englewood Cliffs, NJ

Reeves, T and Reeves, P (1997) Effective dimensions of interactive learning on the World Wide Web, in *Web-based Instruction,* ed B Khan, pp 59–66, Educational Technology Publications, Englewood Cliffs, NJ

Schwartz, D L, Biswas, G, Bransford, J D, Bhuva, B, Balac, T and Brophy, S (2000) Computer tools that link assessment and instruction: investigating what makes electricity hard to learn, in *Computers as Cognitive Tools: No more walls,* ed S P Lajoie, pp 273–307, Lawrence Erlbaum, Englewood Cliffs, NJ

Segers, M and Dochy, F (2001) New assessment forms and problem-based learning: the value added of students' perspective, *Studies in Higher Education,* **26** (1), pp 328–43

Sheingold, K and Frederiksen, J (1994) Using technology to support innovative assessment, in *Technology and Education Reform,* ed B Means, Jossey-Bass, San Francisco CA

Thelwall, M (2000) Computer-based assessment: a versatile educational tool, *Computers and Education,* **34** (2), pp 37–49

Wiggins, G P (1998) *Educative Assessment,* Jossey-Bass, San Francisco CA

Chapter 14

Applying assessment principles and expanding the focus of assessment to enhance learning online

Alex Radloff and Barbara de la Harpe

Introduction

There is often a gap between what universities espouse as the outcomes of successful university study and what is actually taught and learned. More often than not, the emphasis is on discipline-related content knowledge (eg facts, procedures and principles) rather than on other aspects of learning such as skills and attitudes that underpin lifelong learning, as well as the factors involved in the learning process itself (Biggs, 1999; Hativa and Goodyear, 2002). This content knowledge emphasis is often reflected in the types of assessment tasks students are set, regardless of the mode of instruction. It is not surprising that in most courses content knowledge is the main focus of assessment since many academics regard themselves as content experts and may find their role as teachers challenging. As Sutherland (1996, p 91) points out:

(t)he reasons that faculty find it difficult to assess non-content outcomes are the same as the reasons they find it difficult to consider using new teaching approaches. Faculty are experts in their field of study. They have spent their professional lives developing skill and confidence in their abilities as chemists, sociologists, rhetoricians, and art historians. Their training and focus has been on content, and few have been supervised or mentored in teaching and evaluating students.

Moreover, the assessment tasks that are set may not always be informed by sound assessment principles and practices.

The new educational technologies can be a trigger for reconsidering what and how we assess. For academics engaged in online course development, as is the case when developing courses for any mode, it means that they need to understand and apply the principles of effective assessment when designing learning environments online.

In this chapter, we explore the role of assessment in learning based on current theory and research and present the case for expanding assessment to encompass more than content knowledge. We provide examples of assessment tools and tasks that can be used in online courses to assess content as well as process learning outcomes and how students develop as learners. Our aim is to encourage developers to include in online courses assessment tasks that expand and enhance learning outcomes.

The role of assessment in learning

Assessment plays a crucial role in what and how students learn and what and how teachers teach (Biggs, 1999; Dochy, 2001). Indeed, as has been pointed out by many researchers, assessment drives the curriculum. Both students and teachers pay attention to those aspects of a course that are assessed and may ignore those that are not, irrespective of the stated learning objectives for the course. Assessment sends messages about what is important and valued in a course (Sambell *et al*, 1999) and students will respond accordingly (Brown *et al*, 1997; Scouller, 1998).

Principles of effective assessment

Assessment is most likely to enhance online learning when the design of assessment tasks is informed by principles of effective assessment. These principles have been well documented in a number of publications including, among others, the American Association for Higher Education Assessment Forum's nine principles of good practice for assessing student learning, an assessment manifesto (Brown *et al*, 1996), the code of practice for assessment developed by the British Quality Assurance Agency for Higher Education (Race, 2001, pp 33–34) and seven steps to fair assessment (Suskie, 2000). The following assessment principles are particularly pertinent to enhancing learning:

- aligning assessment with learning objectives and learning activities;
- using a range of assessment tasks;
- developing and communicating assessment criteria;
- using both formative and summative assessment;
- including peer and self-assessment; and
- providing prompt and constructive feedback.

Assessment needs to be carefully aligned with the learning objectives and learning activities, since assessment influences the learning approach that students adopt (Biggs, 1999). If assessment tasks focus on content knowledge only and not on understanding and skills or on the process of learning, even though these latter may be included in the learning objectives, students will focus on what is being assessed, namely, recall of content. Aligning assessment with learning objectives and learning activities is a prerequisite for the design of effective online courses.

Different assessment tasks are suited for assessing different learning outcomes and each type of assessment task has its strengths and weaknesses (Brown *et al*, 1997; Race, 2001; Radloff and Wright, 2000). For example, short-answer tests tend to focus on knowledge, are easy to mark and are perceived as 'objective', while essays tend to focus on understanding, are more difficult to mark and are perceived as 'subjective'. Moreover, students need opportunities to demonstrate their learning in ways that are compatible with their strengths as learners (Biggs, 1999). In online courses, wherever possible, assessment should include a range of tasks to take into account the breadth of learning outcomes and students' diverse talents and ways of knowing.

Whatever form the assessment takes, students benefit from knowing what their performance will be judged on and the standard required to meet different levels of achievement. Having clearly articulated criteria and standards also increases the reliability of marking and facilitates the provision of targeted feedback that gives students information about what they have done well and helps them focus on areas that need improvement. Involving students in identifying the assessment criteria can help them better understand the purpose of the assessment task and how they can prepare for it (Race, 1995). This is especially important in online courses when self and peer assessment of learning is used.

Both formative and summative assessments are important for learning (Nightingale *et al*, 1996). Formative assessment provides information about progress in learning, while summative assessment provides information about the learning outcomes as a result of a learning activity. The same assessment task may provide either formative or summative assessment information depending at which point in learning it is used. Formative assessment is particularly helpful in shaping student behaviour and in providing feedback to the teacher about the effectiveness of different learning tasks for achieving the desired learning outcomes. Formative assessment is especially valuable when learning is done online because of the importance of regular feedback for pacing learning and staying on task.

Peer and self-assessment have the advantage of involving students in the assessment process in ways that support their own learning as well as their development as learners (Topping, 1998). Having the opportunity to review and comment on others' work can help students clarify their thinking and understanding as well as gauge their efforts against the standard of work being produced by other students. It can also enhance collaboration and effective group work (Brown *et al,* 1997; Hinett and Thomas, 1999). Furthermore, experience with peer and self-assessment can help students develop the skills and confidence they will need for lifelong learning. When well planned and implemented, self and peer assessment can be as reliable as single or double marking and can encourage and reinforce peer interaction and collaboration (Brown *et al,* 1997). These aspects of learning are particularly challenging to achieve in online courses.

Providing prompt and constructive feedback is a key factor in supporting learning and maintaining student effort. As Boud (1991, p 29) points out:

> one of the most valuable contributions anyone can make to another person's learning is constructive feedback. Whether as a student or as a teacher each one of us has the capacity to provide useful information to other people which will help them to learn more effectively.

To be most effective, feedback needs to be timely, clear, specific, meaningful to the learner and realistic in terms of the overall learning objectives. Ensuring that students receive regular feedback is particularly important in online courses where there may be few opportunities for more informal types of feedback that occur in campus-based courses.

Applying these assessment principles consistently in online courses will increase student engagement in learning, improve the quality of their learning outcomes and enhance their satisfaction with the learning experience.

Expanding the focus of assessment

Much assessment is used in ways that fail to provide appropriate feedback about important aspects of learning and learning outcomes other than content knowledge and thus contribute little to the development of students as effective learners. The traditional view of teaching and learning tends to focus on assessment of content knowledge and on academic achievement as the main outcome of learning, that is, the products of learning rather than the how and why of student learning, in other words, the motivational, affective, cognitive and metacognitive factors in learning (McKeachie *et al,* 1986). This is so, despite the considerable evidence that these factors have a major influence on the quality of learning and on learning outcomes (see de la Harpe, 1998, for a summary of the literature; de la Harpe and Radloff, 2001).

Motivational factors include student interest and involvement in learning such as beliefs in the importance and value of different learning activities and confidence in being able to achieve learning goals. Affective factors include student emotional reactions – both positive and negative – to learning, that is, feelings associated with learning. Cognitive factors focus on how students learn, remember and understand and include problem solving, thinking and the use of a variety of learning strategies such as rehearsal, elaboration and organization. Metacognitive factors include student knowledge of the learning process and of themselves as learners as well as control of the learning process through planning, monitoring, evaluating and adapting learning.

Both students and teachers generally have little knowledge of how these factors influence learning and learning outcomes. As a result, students are disadvantaged as learners since, as Cross (1998, p 7) notes:

> (m)ostly, students get grades that tell them how they have done relative to their classmates. That information is not useful feedback on their progress as learners, nor does it do anything to help students develop skills for self-assessment.

Teachers too may be disadvantaged in that they rarely seek feedback from students about students' progress as learners or about whether and how students are becoming effective learners – information that can inform their teaching practice. When teachers do seek feedback, they tend to ask students to comment on a narrow range of teaching activities rather than on how students are learning (Powney and Hall, 1998).

As a result, neither students nor teachers are able to make informed decisions about learning or teaching despite the fact that if 'the improvement of learning is the priority for the twenty-first century, teachers and students need to be able to use the results of their assessment to improve their own performance' (Cross, 1998, p 7). This is encouraged when assessment is expanded to include not only a focus on students' content knowledge but also on how they are developing as learners in terms of motivation, affect, cognition and metacognition.

Examples of assessment tools and tasks

There are a variety of assessment tools and tasks that can be used to expand assessment to include motivational, affective, cognitive and metacognitive aspects of learning. These can take the form of questionnaires and surveys, interviews, writing tasks and teacher constructed techniques. One or more of these tools can be used as an integral part of a course in any discipline and many if not all can be designed for use online. How some of these can be used as part of an online course is described below using three examples. The examples focus on assessing one or more of the following aspects of learning:

- motivational aspects such as interest in and attitude to learning, level of confidence as learners and expectations of the outcomes of learning;
- affective aspects such as feelings about the learning task and self as learner as well as managing both positive and negative feelings;
- cognitive aspects such as use of learning strategies like memorization, note-making, summarizing, identifying main ideas and categorizing information, as well as time-management, use of resources and help-seeking; and
- metacognitive aspects such as awareness and knowledge of the learning process, the learning environment and the self as learner, as well as planning, monitoring, evaluating and adapting learning.

Assessing motivational, cognitive and metacognitive aspects

One way of assessing student motivation for learning and the cognitive and metacognitive strategies they are using to learn and how these may change as a result of learning experiences, is to ask them to complete the Motivated Learning Strategies Questionnaire (MSLQ).

The MSLQ (Pintrich *et al*, 1991) is a standardized 81-item Likert-type self-report questionnaire designed to measure students' motivational orientations and learning strategy use. It consists of two sections – Motivation and Learning. The Motivation section includes items such as 'The most satisfying thing for me in this course is trying to understand the content as thoroughly as possible', 'It is my own fault if I don't learn the material in this course' and 'I have an uneasy, upset feeling when I take an exam'. The Learning Strategies section includes items such as 'When I study the readings for this course I outline the material to help me organize my thoughts', 'Before I study new material thoroughly I often skim it to see how it is organized' and 'Even when course materials are dull and uninteresting, I manage to keep working until I finish'. The full MSLQ takes approximately 20 to 30 minutes to complete. A quick MSLQ version focusing on metacognitive factors is available at http://www.ulc.arizona.edu/cgi-bin/MSLQ.exe?option=generatetest.

Students can be required to complete the MSLQ at the start of an online course and again at the end of the course or after they have completed a mid-course assessment task. They can then be asked to analyse their responses and write a self-reflective commentary on what changes they will make to how they learn. Marks are allocated for the quality of students' self-reflective commentary.

An example of how the MSLQ has been integrated into the course: Cognition, Human Learning and Motivation, offered by Dr Marilla Svinicki at the University of Texas is available at http://www.utexas.edu/academic/cte/staff/svinicki/svinicki.html.

Assessing affective aspects

A way to assess how students in an online course feel about learning, the learning and assessment tasks and themselves as learners, and about the impact of these feelings on their performance, is to ask students to complete the Zuckerman Affect Adjective Checklist (AACL).

The AACL (Docking and Thornton, 1979; Zuckerman, 1960) is a self-report instrument consisting of 21 key adjectives embedded in a total of 60 adjectives with various affective connotations, arranged in alphabetical order (see Table 14.1). Respondents select the words that describe how they are feeling about a particular situation. The AACL takes about two minutes to complete and is easy to use.

Table 14.1 *Sixty adjectives showing the 21 embedded key words on the Zuckerman Affect Adjective Checklist (AACL)*

absorbed	afraid (+)	aimless	ambitious	annoyed
aware	bored	calm (-)	careless	cautious
challenged	cheerful (-)	cheated	comfortable	confused
contented (-)	creative	curious	dedicated	desperate (+)
disappointed	efficient	entertained	excited	fearful (+)
fortunate	frightened (+)	happy (-)	hopeless	impatient
incapable	inspired	interested	joyful (-)	lazy
loving (-)	miserable	misplaced	nervous (+)	organized
overloaded	panicky (+)	pleasant (-)	pleased	productive
pushed	refreshed	regretful	rewarded	satisfied
secure (-)	serious	shaky (+)	steady(-)	tense (+)
terrified (+)	thoughtful (-)	upset (+)	weary	worried (+)

To help students to become more aware of the relationship between their feelings and learning online, they can be asked to complete the AACL a number of times during the course. Students then submit a commentary about their feelings and how these may have changed, and what impact they had on their performance. Students share their commentaries in discussion groups online and discuss strategies for managing feelings. The most frequently mentioned strategies can be collated and posted as a resource for the whole class.

An example of how the AACL has been integrated into an online course: Teaching and Learning Online developed by Fox, Herrmann, de la Harpe and Radloff from Curtin University of Technology is available at http://www.curtin.edu.au/teaching/.

Assessing cognitive and metacognitive aspects

A way to assess how students are developing as learners, how they go about learning and their understanding of the learning process, in other words, cognitive and metacognitive aspects of learning, is to ask students to keep a learning portfolio or log in which they describe their learning and reflect on their learning experiences (Alderman *et al,* 1993; Hartley, 1998; Melograno, 1994). Students may create such a portfolio electronically and make it available to other students and/or the instructor to provide commentary and feedback on.

An example of how a learning portfolio has been integrated into online courses on Natural Resource Management offered by Dick Richardson and Patricia Richardson at the University of Texas, Austin is available at http://www.esb.utexas.edu/drnrm/classtopics/general/OLR.htm, accessed 8 July 2002.

An example of the use of learning logs in the course: Information Technology and Society offered by Dr David Newman at Queen's University, Belfast, is available at http://www.qub.ac.uk/mgt/itsoc/proj/learnlog.html, accessed 8 July 2002.

These examples show how, with some adaptation of existing assessment tasks and a degree of creative thinking, assessment can be expanded to include a focus on content as well as on the skill and will involved in learning.

Other assessment tools

There are other assessment tools that can be used to expand the focus of assessment along the lines already described; some of these are listed in Table 14.2. For a more in depth discussion of these, see de la Harpe and Radloff (2000). These tools can be incorporated into online courses as an integral part of assessment in the context of whatever is being learned using the principles of effective assessment already described.

Table 14.2 *Tools for assessing aspects of learning*

Aspect	Tool	Reference
Motivational and/or Cognitive and/or Metacognitive	Learning and Study Strategy Inventory (LASSI)	Weinstein *et al* (1988)
	Study Process Questionnaire (SPQ)	Biggs (1987)
	Classroom Assessment Techniques (CATs)	Angelo and Cross (1993)
Cognitive and Metacognitive	Self-Regulated Learning Interview Schedule (SRLIS)	Zimmerman and Martinez-Pons (1986)
	Learning statements	Boulton-Lewis *et al* (1996)
Metacognitive	Metacognitive Awareness Inventory (MAI)	Schraw and Dennison (1994)
	Perceived Self Efficacy for Writing Scale (PSEWS)	Zimmerman and Bandura (1994)
Affective	State-Trait Anxiety Inventory (STAI)	Spielberger (1983)

A number of these tools are available on the web making their use in assessment tasks in online courses easy. These include:

- the Study Process Questionnaire (SPQ) (http://www.geocities.com/gprss_edu/spq.htm);
- the Learning and Study Strategy Inventory (LASSI) (http://www.hhpub lishing.com/Assmlnst.html);
- examples of Classroom Assessment Techniques (CATs) (http://www.psu.edu/celt/CATs.html; http://www.siue.edu/~deder/assess/catmain.html).

Conclusion and recommendations

In this chapter we have provided an overview of the role that assessment plays in learning and described key principles of effective assessment. We have presented a case for expanding assessment to include a focus on motivational, affective cognitive and metacognitive aspects of learning in addition to content knowledge. We have offered some examples of ways in which this can be done as part of regular assessment in online courses to provide feedback to students and teachers that can inform both learning and teaching practices.

The challenge for course developers is to move beyond the traditional view of teaching and learning with its emphasis on assessment of content knowledge when designing assessment for online courses. Moving online provides an opportunity to apply what we know about effective assessment rather than simply to replicate outdated assessment practices. Using the principles of effective assessment and expanding assessment to encompass both content and process learning outcomes will enhance the quality of learning online to the benefit of both learners and teachers.

References

Alderman, M K, Klein, R, Seeley, S K and Sanders, M (1993) Metacognitive self-portraits: pre-service teachers as learners, *Reading Research and Instruction,* **32** (2), pp 38–54

Angelo, T A and Cross, K P (1993) *Classroom Assessment Techniques: A handbook for college teachers* (2nd ed), Jossey-Bass, San Francisco CA

Biggs, J (1987) *Student Approaches to Learning and Studying,* ACER, Hawthorn, Victoria

Biggs, J (1999) *Teaching for Quality Learning at University,* SRHE and Open University Press, Buckingham

Boud, D (1991) *Implementing Student Self-assessment,* HERDSA Green Guide No 5, HERDSA, Campbelltown, NSW

Boulton-Lewis, G M, Wilss, L and Mutch, S (1996) Teachers as adult learners: their knowledge of their own learning and implications for teaching, *Higher Education,* **32,** pp 89–106

Brown, G, Bull, J and Pendlebury, M (1997) *Assessing Student Learning in Higher Education*, Routledge, London

Brown, S, Race, P and Smith, B (1996) An assessment manifesto, in *500 Tips on Assessment*, Kogan Page, London. Accessed 3 March 2002, from http://wwwlguacuk/deliberations/assessment/manifesthtml

Cross, K P (1998) Classroom research: implementing the scholarship of teaching, in *Classroom Assessment and Research: An update on uses, approaches, and research findings*, ed T Angelo, pp 5–12, Jossey-Bass, San Francisco CA

de la Harpe, B (1998) Design, implementation and evaluation of an in-context learning support program for first year education students and its impact on educational outcomes. Unpublished doctoral dissertation, Curtin University of Technology, Perth

de la Harpe, B and Radloff, A (2000) Informed teachers and students: the importance of assessing the characteristics needed for lifelong learning, *Studies in Continuing Education*, **22** (2), pp 169–82

de la Harpe, B and Radloff, A (2001) The value of assessing learning strategies for effective learning: strengthening the partnership between learners and teachers. Paper presented at the HERDSA International Conference, July, Newcastle, NSW

Dochy, F (2001) A new assessment era: different needs, new challenges, *Research Dialogue in Learning and Instruction*, **2,** pp 11–20

Docking, R A and Thornton, J A (1979) Anxiety and the school experience. Paper presented at the annual conference of the Australian Association for Research in Education, November, Melbourne

Hartley, J (1998) *Learning and Studying: A research perspective,* Routledge, London

Hativa, N and Goodyear, P (2002) Research on teacher thinking, beliefs and knowledge in higher education: foundations, status and prospects, in *Teacher Thinking, Beliefs and Knowledge in Higher Education*, eds N Hativa and P Goodyear, pp 335–59, Kluwer Academic, Dodrecht

Hinett, K and Thomas, J (eds) (1999) *Staff Guide to Self and Peer Assessment,* Oxford Centre for Staff and Learning Development, Oxford

McKeachie, W J, Pintrich, P R, Lin, Y and Smith, D A F (1986) *Teaching and Learning in the College Classroom: A review of the research literature,* Technical Rep No 86-B-0010, National Centre for Research to Improve Postsecondary Teaching and Learning, University of Michigan

Melograno, V J (1994) Portfolio assessment: documenting authentic student learning, *The Journal of Physical Education, Recreation and Dance*, **65** (8), pp 50–60

Nightingale, P, Te Wiata, I, Toohey, S, Ryan, G, Hughes, C and Magin, D (1996) *Assessing Learning in Universities,* University of New South Wales Press, Sydney, NSW

Pintrich, P R, Smith, D A, Garcia, T and McKeachie, W J (1991) *A Manual for the Use of the Motivated Strategies for Learning Questionnaire (MSLQ),* National Center for Research to Improve Postsecondary Teaching and Learning, University of Michigan, Ann Arbor, MI

Powney, J and Hall, S (1998) *Closing the Loop: The impact of student feedback on students' subsequent learning*, SCRE Rep No 90, The Scottish Council for Research in Education, Edinburgh

Race, P (1995) The art of assessing, *New Academic*, **5** (3). Accessed 3 March 2002, from http://wwwlguacuk/deliberations/assessment/artof_contenthtml

Race, P (2001) *The Lecturer's Toolkit: A practical guide to learning, teaching and assessment*, 2nd edn, Kogan Page, London

Radloff, A and Wright, L (2000) Assessing student learning, *Professional Development Online*, Curtin University of Technology. Accessed 3 March 2002, from http://ceacurtineduau/pdo/tandlhtml

Sambell, K, Sambell, A and Sexton, G (1999) Student perceptions of the learning benefits of computer-assisted assessment: a case study in electronic engineering, in *Computer-assisted Assessment in Higher Education*, eds S Brown, P Race and J Bull, pp 179–91, Kogan Page, London

Schraw, G and Dennison, R S (1994) Assessing metacognitive awareness, *Contemporary Educational Psychology*, **19,** pp 460–75

Scouller, K (1998) The influence of assessment method on students' learning approaches: Multiple choice question examination versus assignment essays, *Higher Education*, **35,** pp 453–72

Spielberger, C D (1983) *Manual for the State-Trait Anxiety Inventory*, Consulting Psychologists Press, Palo Alto, CA

Suskie, L (2000) Fair assessment practices: giving students equitable opportunities to demonstrate learning, *AAHE Bulletin*, May. Accessed 3 March 2002, from http://wwwaaheorg/bulletin/may2html

Sutherland, T E (1996) Emerging issues in the discussion of active learning, in *Using Active Learning in College Classes: A range of options for faculty*, eds T E Sutherland and C C Bonwell, Jossey-Bass, San Francisco CA

Topping, K (1998) Peer assessment between students in colleges and universities, *Review of Educational Research*, **68** (3), pp 249–76

Weinstein, C E, Zimmerman, S A and Palmer, D R (1988) Assessing learning strategies: the design and development of the LASSI, in *Learning and Study Strategies: Issues in assessment, instruction, and evaluation*, eds C E Weinstein, E T Goetz and P A Alexander, pp 25–40, Academic Press, San Diego, CA

Zimmerman, B J and Bandura, A (1994) Impact of self-regulatory influences on writing course attainment, *American Educational Research Journal*, **31** (4), pp 845–62

Zimmerman, B J and Martinez-Pons, M (1986) Development of a structured interview for assessing student use of self-regulated learning strategies, *American Educational Research Journal*, **23,** pp 614–28

Zuckerman, M (1960) The development of an affect adjective checklist for the measurement of anxiety, *Journal of Consulting Psychology*, **24,** pp 457–62

Chapter 15

The use of online assessment in stimulating a deeper approach to learning

Carol Johnston

Introduction

Teaching in the higher education sector has moved away from the information transfer mode of the past towards a student-centred learning focus. A key factor facilitating this move towards student-centred learning has been the development of electronic learning technologies that have increased the range of tools now available to academics in their teaching. There has also been a renewed interest in how to use assessment effectively to achieve desired learning objectives. Assessment is a powerful tool in determining the type of learning, skills and outcomes that we wish our graduates to achieve. Whether we like it or not our students are driven rather more by grades and assessment than an intrinsic love of learning. Indeed Boud (1990) finds that assessment more than any other factor determines whether students will take a deep or surface approach to their studies. It seems therefore that the harnessing of this powerful motivational tool to achieve learning outcomes that are important in high quality learning environments is a productive avenue to explore.

Perceptions of appropriate assessment are related to the objectives that particular stakeholders have in the higher education environment. Employers want students to graduate with good communication, teamwork, collaboration, problem solving, critical thinking, and computer/technology skills. They also want them to possess the ability to learn independently, to adapt to changing circumstances, to navigate knowledge resources, to deal with ambiguity and uncertainty, to engage in self-directed, lifelong learning and to continually identify gaps in their own knowledge. Academics are likely to see their teaching objectives in terms of the development of intellectual independence. In times of budget constraints, university administrator objectives relate to ensuring that resources are used efficiently and effectively and that changes in teaching practice including assessment do not result in a rise in costs. Students meanwhile are concerned about career options and they therefore value assessment that will assist in the development of skills likely to impress employers. Electronic online learning technologies offer a range of new strategies to address stakeholder objectives.

When assessment is used as a tool in achieving these objectives a number of issues arise in the higher education context. This context is one where there is a new recognition of the importance of generic skills, where the expectations of students are changing and where there is a diverse cultural and socio-economic mix. Among the issues to be addressed is the provision of rich and timely feedback on student work, issues associated with plagiarism as well as the challenge associated with the effective use of new electronic learning technologies themselves.

This chapter focuses on how assessment and specifically online assessment can be used to influence the approach to learning that is most likely to achieve the objectives of the various stakeholders in higher education. Factors to consider in designing online assessment strategies are discussed and an example of an online assessment system is described.

Purpose of assessment

There are several reasons for assessing students. First, assessment can provide students with a valuable form of feedback on their progress in understanding the subject. This form of assessment is formative in the sense that it contributes to the formation of knowledge and skills both in the student and in the teacher in that it can inform future practice. Secondly, assessment is needed in order to grade students so that they can receive some sort of accreditation for passing the subject or course at a particular standard. This summative form of assessment typically takes place at the end of a learning process, often in the form of an examination, and the results are final. There is little feedback in this instance. Thirdly, assessment can influence the approaches that students take to their study and can provide the motivation that leads to the achievement of key learning outcomes. For assessment to be effective in influencing study behaviour and providing a source of motivation, Zeidner (1992) argues that it needs to relate to appropriate study behaviour, to provide extensive coverage of the course, to occur frequently and be clearly related to the course goals. He also notes that most students and teachers do not see assessment in this light. They both consider it primarily as an optimal indicator of student achievement rather than a means of enhancing motivation or shaping classroom behaviour. This third purpose of assessment provides the principle focus of this chapter.

Approaches to learning

The influence of assessment on student approaches to and perceptions of learning is well documented (Entwistle, 1987; Entwistle and Ramsden, 1983; Laurillard, 1984; Ramsden,1984). Educators over the past two decades have been interested in using assessment as one avenue through which to stimulate the type of learning most likely to achieve the objectives of the various stakeholders in higher education (Entwistle, 1987; Entwistle and Ramsden, 1983; Säljö, 1981; Watkins, 1982).

This type of learning was first identified by Marton and Säljö (1976) in their seminal work that distinguished between deep and surface approaches to learning. Students who use a deep approach are personally involved in the learning task and seek to obtain some underlying meaning. A deep approach is where the student attempts to understand and relates new ideas to previous knowledge, to experience and to conclusions. The student attempts to comprehend the material rather than replicate it. Such students are likely to read extensively around a given topic, to discuss the topic and ultimately to achieve higher grades on assessment tasks than students who use a surface approach (Biggs, 1987, 1989). These students are independent learners who are in control of their own learning.

A surface approach to learning on the other hand is where the student has a reproductive conception of learning. Here the student's intention is to complete set tasks and to memorize information; the student does not reflect on the material to be learnt and focuses on discrete elements without integration. Students will commit unrelated facts to their short-term memory but are unlikely to be able to establish meaning or relationships between or within given tasks.

Ramsden (1985) notes that the approaches to learning are not necessarily mutually exclusive. Students may adopt different approaches according to the task, the course or the teaching context. In this sense, teachers have a direct and powerful impact on the learning outcomes of their students. Similarly, a desire to understand at a deeper level will not, of itself, necessarily give rise to this outcome as students differ in terms of their cognitive development (Perry, 1970), their perceptions of the course or task itself (Meyer *et al*, 1990), previous experience which they bring to the task (Entwistle and Ramsden, 1983) and their perceptions of the assessment demands of the subject.

Kember (1991) investigated how students could be encouraged to develop a deep approach to learning and how teachers could also be encouraged to adopt instructional strategies that would foster this deep approach. He observed that there was widespread support for a deep approach by lecturers and teachers and this was frequently noted as a goal of education. However, the difference between the espoused goals and the reality was marked in so far as there was little evidence that the goals were being achieved (Biggs, 1987; Gow and Kember, 1990). Surface level thinking and the transmission of factual knowledge occupied more time than the fostering of deeper critical level thinking. Disturbingly, several studies (Biggs, 1987; Gow and Kember, 1990; Johnston *et al*, 2000; Norton *et al*, 2001) have demonstrated that a deeper approach to learning in higher education actually declines as students move through the course.

Ramsden (1992, p 67) suggests, 'the methods we use to assess students are one of the most critical of all influences on their learning' (see also for review, Marton *et al*, 1984). The amount and type of assessment that students are asked to undertake will influence their approach to learning. If they are assessed too much and if the thinking skills that are assessed are of a lower order, students will respond by adopting a surface approach to learning in preparing for such assessment tasks. It is appropriate to ask therefore how the curriculum, the setting and the assessment could be changed to increase the likelihood that students will adopt a deep approach to study and how electronic learning technologies can be used to facilitate this.

Assessment to stimulate deep approaches to learning

The assessment of student learning begins with an aligned curriculum and clear educational objectives (see Figure 15.1). Educational objectives should drive not only 'what' we choose to assess but also 'how' we do so. Where questions about educational objectives and goals are ignored, assessment can become an exercise in measuring what is easy, rather than a process of improving the achievement of those elements of the curriculum that we see as important. It follows that it is important to develop clearly stated subject-learning outcomes for each assessment task that are drawn from the subject objectives and are shared with students, so they know what is expected of them.

Learning approaches vary with the tasks set for assessment. Factors that are seen as fostering a surface approach to learning are unrealistic workloads, over-assessment, assessment only in the form of an examination, assessment that assesses only lower order thinking skills, and inappropriate feedback. Feedback on an individual's performance is important because it facilitates learning and should lead to an improvement in performance through increasing motivation. However, improvements in performance will only be attained if the feedback is specific, timely, accurate and realistic in terms of what is achievable and is expressed in such a way that encourages students to reflect on their performance if necessary (Boud, 1995; Brown and Pendlebury, 1992). Nevertheless, it is important that students do not rely solely on feedback from academics but evolve into effective responsible and autonomous learners through the development of self-assessment (self-evaluation) skills (Baume, 1994). Such skills should help students to become realistic

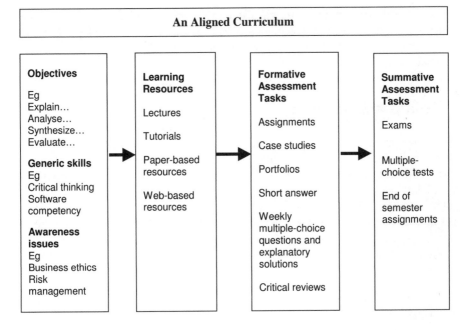

Figure 15.1   *An aligned curriculum*

judges of their own performance and better able to monitor their own learning and skills development (Boud, 1995).

There are several design strategies in relation to assessment and feedback that can stimulate deeper approaches to learning. While in the early stages of the subject it may be tempting to use grades as an incentive, prompt return of assignments plus consistent standards throughout the process are more likely to be effective than grade inflation or grade deprivation. Comments on student work should be brief and well focused, clear, specific, personal and honest. Electronic learning technologies allow the compilation of a database of typical comments for each assessment task that can be quickly cut and pasted into a paragraph for inclusion at the end of the piece. Provision of models of appropriate responses after the submission date allows students to compare their answers with the model. This is an active form of feedback that requires students to reflect on their own learning. Publication of student work on the Intranet is appropriate for the same reason. In addition, it is possible to get students to comment on other students' work. Formative computer assisted assessment can allow students to be automatically directed through feedback to follow up references and resources. Students find it stressful having several deadlines close together so it is advisable to timetable assessment so that it is not concentrated in any particular week. And finally, variety in forms of assessment is desirable.

In short, assessment that is likely to stimulate deep approaches to learning will be 'aligned' with the subject objectives, varied and require active student participation in all learning tasks; there will also be rich and extensive feedback strategies in place. Electronic learning technologies have an important role to play in fostering a deep approach to learning and a case where this was used effectively is discussed in the next section.

Online assessment

In this section, one example of using online assessment to stimulate desired approaches to learning and key skills is reported. This example was undertaken at the University of Melbourne in the Faculty of Economics and Commerce. Critical and Analytical Learning in Macroeconomics (CALM) was implemented in the Department of Economics. The subject, Introductory Macroeconomics, has over 1,200 first-year students. The CALM system aims to encourage positive attitudes towards macroeconomics, deeper approaches to learning and confidence in critical thinking skills. The project's design is based on the assumption that the achievement of these aims is more likely when students reflect on their own learning, where the stimulus for learning is real world problems and issues, and where assessment rewards the ability to analyse, synthesize and critically evaluate complex material.

In the first week of the semester, all students are enrolled in the Introductory Macroeconomics tutorial programme. This consists of a 'face-to-face' Collaborative Problem Solving (CPS) tutorial and a secure online interactive Web page that allows access only to those members of the same CPS tutorial (see Johnston *et al,* 2000 for a discussion and evaluation of CPS tutorials). It is through this tutorial-based Web page that students interact with the CALM system and the assessment that they undertake through the semester; see Figure 15.2.

The CALM system uses an 'issues-based' approach to assignment work. Students are presented with background information relating to a particular event drawn from contemporary experience. Where possible, the event is something that has occurred in the very recent past (sometimes in the same week as when the assignment is made available to students) and is amenable to analysis using the theoretical tools developed in the lecture and tutorial programme and in the set text. The aim is to encourage students to see the practical usefulness of their subject material and to equip them to make more sense of current economic events. Three macroeconomic issues are posted to an 'Issues' page over the course of the semester; one at week two, one around week five and one at week eight. These issues are designed to draw on current economic events and in 2000 involved in the first instance a discussion and application of the criteria used to rank countries' macroeconomic performance. The second CALM issue related to a rationalization of an apparent contradiction in two newspaper articles published on the same day, one reporting on Australia's high rate of economic growth, the other reporting on a major slump in Australia's housing construction industry. The third issue required an explanation of why the value of the Australian dollar against the US dollar fell immediately after the release of National Accounts figures confirming Australia's high rate of economic growth. Students are asked to respond to each issue. This

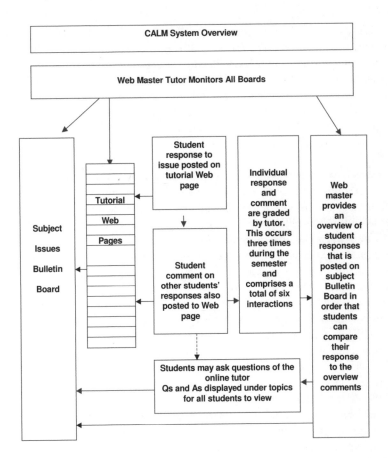

Figure 15.2 *CALM system overview*

requires the student to apply the economic theory developed in lectures and CPS tutorials to the issue. All responses are electronically submitted to the CALM 'Responses' page.

Students can edit and change their own responses up to the submission date. After this date, all students in their respective tutorials can view all of the responses derived from that tutorial. Student identification is removed when responses appear on the responses page to allow for privacy concerns. The display of the tutorial members' responses provides students with useful feedback on the standard of their own work in relation to others in the tutorial and also allows them to see the range of possible responses to the same issue.

The next stage in the process is designed to develop reflective and critical thinking skills in students. Students read the responses posted by their tutorial group and then select and reserve *one* response on which to comment critically. Students are provided with a list of criteria on which to base their comment and a sample generic critical comment on which to model their work. Following final submission, all responses and comments are available for all CALM tutorial members to view. This process is repeated for each of the three issues, meaning that students submit a total of six pieces of work during the semester (three responses and three comments) at intervals of around two weeks.

At the end of each issue, responses and comments are assessed and results posted to the student's individual CALM page so that students have a record of how well they are performing. The first issue carries relatively less weight than the other two in the overall assessment of the subject to allow students to become familiar with the system.

Feedback to students is provided in a number of forms. Students receive a mark on their response and comment; are able to view other students work in their own tutorial; can view model responses and comments provided by the lecturer; are provided with the online tutor's overview report at the end of each issue; and can obtain individual personal comment from the tutor who has assessed their work. The learner is expected to take an active role in the feedback process through self-reflection and comparison with others work and the model responses.

An online tutor is available to all students through CALM. Students can ask questions at any time and, typically, these are answered within a 24-hour period. The questions and answers are posted to a CALM bulletin board for all students to see. This allows all students to have access to the information, not just the student who posed the question. Questions are identified by topic so that students can refer to the bulletin board when they are revising for examinations or completing an assignment. The online tutor can post messages to individual students as well as to all students enrolled in the subject.

CALM builds on studies which show that an individual student's achievement is consistently and positively related to the level of help that the student gives to others (Palinscar and Brown, 1984; Slavin, 1990). The CALM system provides the opportunity to interact in a structured way with peers through reading other students' work and commenting upon it. This process compels students to externalize their thoughts and make their ideas explicit. Enhanced understanding results because students must think about the material and develop and structure explanations. Other benefits of students interacting directly with their peers about their learning include improved communication skills, increased individual self-confidence and new levels of openness to ideas. Strategies for active learning of this kind have been widely documented (see, for example, Meyer and Jones, 1993).

The online critique of others' work allows for physical anonymity, which is a great equalizer. Shy or reclusive learners have more opportunity to 'speak' out and are sure class members will hear them. Harasim (1990) argues that online educational interactions, being revisable, archival and retrievable, augment the users' control over the substance and process of the interactions. This learner-centeredness combined with active participation in an interactive collaborative written environment lays the groundwork for deep learning to occur through construction, revision and sharing of knowledge.

Importantly, in relation to the approach taken in the CALM project, Levin and Thurston (1996) report that there is a positive 'audience effect' of publishing on the Intranet for others. Students make a greater effort to produce polished essays and assignments if these are to be Intranet published. The asynchronous nature of online interactions allows students time to reflect on a topic before completing an online task. More generally the advantages of online delivery of elements of subjects are the increased interaction between students and students and staff in terms of both the quantity and intensity of the interaction; better access to group knowledge and support; a more democratic environment where students respond to content rather than to personalities; convenience of access; and, for many, increased motivation (Harasim *et al*, 1997; Laurillard, 1993).

Much has been gained from using the CALM system. Students' confidence in their abilities, both computer and Internet related, and in relation to their facility for critical and analytical thinking, showed significant improvement. Student attitudes to macroeconomics were more positive and given that the subject is compulsory, this result is particularly satisfying. The evidence we have is that the CALM system is an effective way in which to assist students to learn and in which to foster the skills that are required of graduates (Johnston and Olekalns, 2002).

Conclusion

Provided the technology is stable and reliable, linking assessment to it indicates to students that this is an integral and important part of their course. The CALM experience has indicated several key areas that need to be carefully considered when implementing this type of programme:

1. First and foremost is the issue of security. Students must be confident that their work is not available to others before the due date and that when it is submitted online it has been submitted safely and not 'lost in the ether'.
2. A great deal of student anxiety can be eliminated using sample questions and modelling answers, or providing examples of excellent previous students' work.
3. It is necessary to give clear instructions in a variety of formats to ensure that all students have access to them.
4. Confusion can be reduced where there is a limitation of unnecessary choice in relation to how to accomplish computer-related tasks. For example, while there are a number of ways to copy and paste, one simple way should be all that is included in instructions to students.
5. The key infrastructure issues of bandwidth and server capacity need to be considered in the design stage.
6. While the large majority of students at the University of Melbourne are computer literate, 2 to 4 per cent require considerable assistance. This is relatively easy when student numbers are small but in large subjects (>500 students) this can become a problem. The online assessment system must cater for all levels of student expertise.
7. Finally, disaster recovery strategies need to be in place at the outset to address unforeseen events like a server crashing. System breakdowns are frustrating and can have wide-reaching consequences.

Several advantages of using a system like CALM for online assessment have been confirmed:

- Feedback can be provided early and is richer than the mere provision of marks on an individual's work.
- The student becomes an active participant in obtaining feedback through reflection on their own work and the work of others.
- Students report that given the greater volume of part-time work they appreciate the flexibility of being able to submit assessment tasks from home.
- International students report improved communication between students and between students and staff, and staff report observing a higher quality of work published on the Intranet.
- Student attitudes to subjects where online assessment has been implemented have been improved in part because the assessment tasks are framed within current context and issues.
- There is evidence that confidence in critical thinking is improved.
- Finally, there has been less copying or plagiarism as file sizes, key words and phrases can be tracked.

The adoption of electronic learning technologies in teaching practice requires significant reflection in relation to all aspects of subject design and in this sense provides a number of worthwhile challenges to academic staff. Where staff in the faculty have taken up the challenge they have found the experience to be cost-effective in terms of time and effort, after the initial set-up costs, and rewarding in terms of changes in student attitudes, learning and skill development.

References

Baume, D (1994) *Developing Learner Autonomy* (SEDA paper No 84), SEDA, Birmingham

Biggs, J (1987) *Student Approaches to Learning and Studying,* Australian Council for Education Research, Melbourne

Biggs, J (1989) Approaches to the enhancement of tertiary teaching, *Higher Education Research and Development,* **8** (1), pp 7–25

Boud, D (1990) Assessment and the promotion of academic values, *Studies in Higher Education,* **15** (1), pp 101–10

Boud, D (1995) *Enhancing Learning through Self-assessment,* Kogan Page, London

Brown, G and Pendlebury, M (1992) *Assessing Active Learning: Effective learning and teaching in higher education* (Module 11), CVCP, Sheffield

Entwistle, N (1987) *Understanding Classroom Learning,* Hodder and Stoughton, London

Entwistle, N and Ramsden, P (1983) *Understanding Student Learning,* Croom Helm, Beckenham

Gow, L and Kember, D (1990) Does higher education promote independent learning?, *Higher Education,* **19** (3), pp 307–22

Harasim, L (1990) *Online Education: Perspectives on a new environment,* Praeger, New York

Harasim, L, Hiltz, S, Teles, L and Turoff, M (1997) *Learning Networks: A field guide to teaching and learning online,* The MIT Press, Cambridge, MA

Johnston, C and Olekalns, N (2002) Enriching the learning experience: a CALM Approach, *Studies in Higher Education,* **27** (1), pp 103–19

Johnston, C, James, R, Lye, J and McDonald, I (2000) An evaluation of the introduction of collaborative problem solving for learning economics, *Journal of Economic Education,* **31** (1), pp 13–29

Kember, D (1991) Instructional design for independent learning, *Instructional Science,* **20** (4), pp 289–310

Laurillard, D (1984) Learning from problem solving, in *The Experience of Learning,* eds F Marton, D Hounsell and D Entwistle, Scottish Academic Press, Edinburgh

Laurillard, D (1993) *Rethinking University Teaching: A framework for the effective use of educational technologies,* Routledge, London

Levin, J and Thurston, C (1996) Research summary: educational electronic networks, *Educational Leadership,* **54** (3), pp 46–50

Marton, F and Säljö, R (1976) On qualitative differences in learning: 1. Outcomes and process, *British Journal of Educational Psychology,* **46,** pp 4–11

Marton, F, Hounsell, D and Entwistle, D (eds) (1984) *The Experience of Learning,* Scottish Academic Press, Edinburgh

Meyer, C and Jones, T B (1993) *Promoting Active Learning: Strategies for the college classroom,* Jossey-Bass, San Francisco CA

Meyer, J H F, Parsons, P and Dunne, T T (1990) Individual study orchestrations and their association with learning outcome, *Higher Education,* **20** (1), pp 67–89

Norton, L, Tilley, A, Newstead, S and Franklyn-Stokes, A (2001) The pressures of assessment in undergraduate courses and their effect on student behaviors, *Assessment and Evaluation in Higher Education,* **26** (3), pp 269–84

Palinscar, A and Brown, A (1984) Reciprocal teaching of comprehension-fostering and comprehension-monitoring activities, *Cognition and Instruction,* **2,** pp 117–75

Perry, W G (1970) *Forms of Intellectual and Ethical Development in the College Years,* Holt Rhinehart and Winston, New York

Ramsden, P (1984) The context of learning in academic departments, in *The Experience of Learning,* eds F Marton, D Hounsell and N Entwistle, pp 193–216, Scottish Academic Press, Edinburgh

Ramsden, P (1985) Student learning research: retrospect and prospect, *Higher Education Research and Development,* **4** (1), pp 51–69

Ramsden, P (1992) *Learning to Learn in Higher Education,* Routledge, London

Säljö, R (1981) Learning approach and outcome: some empirical observations, *Instructional Science,* **10** (1), pp 47–65

Slavin, R (1990) Research on cooperative learning: consensus and controversy, *Educational Leadership,* **48,** Dec/Jan, pp 52–54

Watkins, D (1982) Identifying the study process dimensions of Australian university students, *Australian Journal of Education,* **26** (1), pp 76–85

Zeidner, M (1992) Key facets of classroom grading: a comparison of teacher and student perspectives, *Contemporary Educational Psychology,* **17** (3), pp 224–43

Chapter 16

Cognitive apprenticeship learning – ensuring far transfer of knowledge through computer-based assessment

Ashok Patel, Kinshuk and David Russell

Introduction

Stiggins (1999) recommended fundamental rethinking on assessment as the long tradition of attempting to incorporate assessment into school improvement equations have focused almost totally on the use of standardized tests. He found little emphasis on assessment in the preparation or professional development of teachers and concurred with several authors (eg, Calfee and Masuda, 1997; Farr and Griffin, 1973; McMillan, 2001) that teachers and administrators needed to grasp the assessment concepts, principles, techniques and procedures. Graue (1993) noted that the teacher-made emulations of standardized tests presented a barrier in implementing more constructivist instructional approaches and that the temporal and philosophical distance between assessment and instruction gradually led to assessment constraining and ultimately narrowing the scope of instruction –

deskilling both the teachers and students. Since the student performance reported on official documents is a product of assessment, the assessment strategy strongly influences learning activities and could undermine the objectives of a teaching and learning system (Patel *et al*, 1999).

Wiggins (1998) recognized that the nature of assessment influenced what was learnt and affected the degree of student engagement in the learning process. He used the term 'educative assessment' to describe techniques and issues that should be considered when designing and using assessments, for instance degree of engagement and problem-based tasks; nature of feedback and how it was delivered; forms of assessment and how students prepared for them. He favoured authentic assessment – with feedback and opportunities for further improvement rather than a simplistic mechanism to audit learning. The two distinct aspects of assessment, first as a mechanism of self-testing and learning and second as a measure of knowledge and skills acquired, are referred to as the formative and summative aspects of assessment. The former helps the students in their learning activities by providing opportunities for self-testing and removing misconceptions. The latter attempts to periodically sum up the skills and knowledge gained with the purpose of assessing learner performance. The complete learning experience, therefore, involves frequent loop-backs between concept acquisition, formative assessment and to a lesser degree, summative assessment.

Computers can be gainfully harnessed for both types of assessments and provide a powerful learning environment, especially when the learning is based around formative assessment supported by immediate and dynamic feedback. This chapter briefly looks at the traditional and emergent perspectives shaping assessment and discusses the relationships between concept acquisition, formative assessment and summative assessment in the design and implementation of 'Byzantium' Intelligent Tutoring Tools (ITT) and the Intelligent Assessment provided by the accompanying 'Byzantium Marker'. These computer-based resources were produced under the Teaching and Learning Technology Programme (TLTP) of the Higher Education Funding Councils of the UK and have been independently evaluated at a Scottish university in a study covering three years (Stoner and Harvey, 1999).

Assessments: theoretical models, types and role in knowledge acquisition

The traditional perspective of assessment is based on the old theories of instruction and still exerts dominant influence on current practice. Its key notions were social efficiency coupled with heredity-based theories of individual differences and scientific management connected with behaviourist learning theories. The psychological theories, in turn, employed scientific measurement of ability and achievement. The social efficiency movement was based on the belief that scientific methods could solve the problems of industrialized and urban society and the principles of scientific management, originally intended for maximizing industrial efficiency, could equally be applied for educational purpose (Kleibard, 1995). Precise measurement standards ensured that each skill was mastered at the desired level and scientific measures of ability could be used to determine who was best suited for different vocational careers.

The behavioural model (eg Gagne, 1965; Hull, 1943; Skinner, 1954) viewed learning as an accumulation of stimulus–response associations. The underlying assumptions of this model are:

- learning is the accumulation of atomized bits of knowledge;
- the learning process is tightly sequential and hierarchical;
- knowledge transfer is limited and each objective must be taught explicitly;
- tests should be used frequently to ensure mastery before proceeding to the next objective;
- tests equate to learning;
- motivation is based on positive reinforcement of many small steps.

The cognitive revolution reintroduced the concept of mind amidst these mechanistic theories of learning. Learning is now seen as an active process of mental construction. Cognitive theory also suggested that existing knowledge structures and beliefs enable or impede new learning; that intelligence involves awareness about when and how to use skills, and that *expertise* is acquired in the form of a systematic and coherent way of thinking and representing problems, not just a collection of vast amounts of information. This constructivist model requires that the perception of assessment must change. It should better represent important thinking and problem solving skills of each domain of learning as well as be connected to contexts of application. In order for assessment to play a more useful role in helping students learn, it needs to be moved to the centre of the learning process.

Knowing what a student is able to do independently and extending the boundaries of that knowledge with expert guidance, is integral to Vygotsky's (1978) notion of the 'zone of proximal development'. Dynamic assessment that enables feedback and guidance specifically targets gaps in knowledge and provides scaffolding towards further learning. Genuine understanding is closely linked to the ability to transfer knowledge and apply it to new situations. Research studies show that learning is more likely to transfer if students have the opportunity to practise with a variety of applications (Bransford, 1979).

The preceding discussion can provide valuable insight for successful harnessing of Information and Communication Technology (ICT) into the curriculum. Norman (1986), while discussing human–computer interaction, introduced the notions of 'gulf of execution' and 'gulf of evaluation'. We believe that these notions aptly apply to the learning of any new concept. Initially, the concept has to be grasped in the context of its utility or application. Any gap in this understanding represents a gulf of execution as the deficiency curtails efficient application of the conceptual knowledge. Such a gap may be bridged through active engagement with drill and practice sessions or simulations. Once the concept has been understood, it requires deeper reflection, most probably within a larger context, to *truly* understand it. Thus situations that present the concept in different contexts and enable deeper reflection help in bridging the gulf of evaluation.

The diagram in Figure 16.1 captures these relationships between different types of learning and different types of assessment (based on Patel *et al*, 1999). The upper half represents the *know-how* aspect of knowledge, indicating efficient execution of learnt rules and relationships and this type of knowledge is gained readily from active learning. The lower half represents the *know-why* aspect of knowledge, indicating a deeper level of understanding that is obtained through reflection. A learner initially experiences a shortfall between the knowledge possessed and that required to execute a given task and this gulf of execution needs to be bridged through practice employing some form of formative assessment providing feedback on missing knowledge and misconceptions. To reduce the cognitive load, the formative assessment initially needs to be based on identical or very similar representation structures to those that were used for learning activities. In the next phase, formative assessment should employ alternative representation structures to enable differential emphasis on constituents and to provide richer contextual information, with a view to deepen the understanding of the causal and contextual factors. The diagram seeks to highlight the fact that formative assessment serves as a vital continuation to initial learning of new concepts, affording powerful opportunities for active engagement as well as reflection.

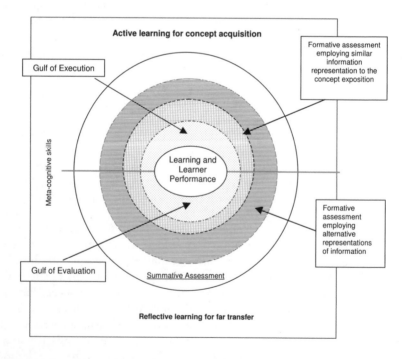

Figure 16.1   *Nature of learning and types of assessment*

The formative assessment is particularly important from the point of convincing the learners that they have learnt and now know something. Jensen (2000) noted that slow, discouraged, or low motivation learners do not usually possess strong self-convincing strategies and may either self-convince too easily without adequate knowledge of the subject matter or only self-convince with much difficulty due to low self-esteem or self-confidence. Adequate formative assessment opportunities are beneficial to both types of slow learners. Bright learners, on the other hand, possess more accurate self-convincing skills and their self-confidence and knowledge acquisition mutually raise each other to higher levels. However, lumbering them with excessive amounts of formative assessments creates boredom. Computer-based formative assessments, with large data banks or random generating capability, are ideal as they can cater for both the slow and bright learners to their satisfaction.

Scheduled periodic summative assessments prompt the easy self-convincers to put in some more formative assessment effort. It should be noted, however, that with inappropriate summative assessments, there is hardly any inducement to work through a series of formative assessments covering application and reflection, thus encouraging deficient learning. The benefit of keeping meta-cognitive skills in view is that it can increase the effectiveness of learning. Bjork (1994) observed that in general, compared to distributing practice sessions on a given task over time, massing practice or study sessions on the to-be-learnt procedures or information produces better short-term performance or recall of that procedure or information, but markedly inferior long-term performance or recall.

The following section briefly reviews phases of skill acquisition and how this knowledge can guide the design of cognitive apprenticeship based tutoring systems that are built mainly around formative assessment.

Phases of skill acquisition and the cognitive apprenticeship framework

VanLehn (1996) has discussed a framework for reviewing cognitive skill acquisition and suggested that Fitts' well-known categorization of the three phases of motor skill acquisition (early, intermediate and late) also applies to cognitive skill acquisition.

In the *early phase*, dominated by reading, discussing and other general information acquiring activities, the student is attempting to understand the domain concepts without yet trying to apply the acquired knowledge. The primary focus is on studying the expository instructional material.

The *intermediate phase* begins when the student turns his or her attention to solving problems. In most cases the attempt is made after observing and following the solution steps for a few problems that have already been solved. Though the student may refer back to the expository material, the primary focus at this stage is on solving problems. At the end of this phase, the student can solve problems without conceptual errors though he or she may still commit unintended errors or slips (Norman, 1988). The slips are generally indicative of the lack of attention arising from the increasing confidence of the student. Such slips may remain uncorrected as the student may not have adequately developed a sense of judgement about the overall solution and does not feel that something isn't right!

During the *late phase*, the students improve in accuracy and speed through practice as the procedures carried out for solving the problem are fully grasped and internalized.

The three-phase distinction, though an idealization because the boundaries between the phases are not precise, is nevertheless useful as it indicates that learning resources for cognitive skill acquisition in any domain may usefully be categorized into three types. The first category is the *expository material* that may contain hyperlinks to facilitate movement between hierarchically, semantically or laterally connected notions. The second category consists of *formative assessment* material with immediate and dynamic feedback at each step. The immediate feedback ensures that the student's error is corrected as soon as it occurs and there is no danger of rehearsing an incorrect conception. The dynamic nature of feedback ensures that the immediate feedback is provided for each sub-goal. The student is thus assured of better interactivity with the learning resource and is freed from the cognitive load of being concerned about a chain of sub-goals at this stage of learning. The final category is based on *summative assessment* to enable free application of knowledge gained by the student, allowing any slips and errors. A delayed feedback after completion of one or more summative problems may then be provided for the student to inspect.

A practical application of this categorization can be found in the Byzantium Intelligent Tutoring Tools (ITT). The first screen in all the ITTs offers a menu shown in Figure 16.2. The student selects *Basic Concepts* for expository material, *Interactive Mode* for formative assessment and *Assignment Mode* for summative assessment. The fourth option, *View Marked Work* is selected for inspection of marked assignments and provides feedback on the attempted solution for each assignment problem.

While the foregoing discussion is based on the phases of cognitive skill acquisition as idealized distinct categories, the continuum between the early and intermediate phase is perhaps better captured in the functionality oriented cognitive apprenticeship framework suggested by Collins *et al* (1989). The framework requires that the following functionality should be present in a tutoring system:

● The students can study task–solving patterns of experts to develop their own cognitive model of the domain (*modelling*). The ITTs provide a Basic Concepts mode presenting textual/graphical explanations and solved examples. The same material is also available through the Help button in the interactive learning mode.

● The students can solve tasks on their own by consulting a tutorial component (*coaching*). The ITTs offer qualitatively better coaching through interactive guidance and dynamic feedback while a student is attempting to solve a problem.

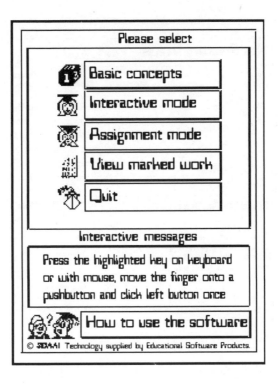

Figure 16.2 *Byzantium ITT main menu*

● The tutoring activity of the system is gradually reduced with the student's improving performances and problem solving (*fading*). The ITTs provide help *by exception* and the tutoring activity is triggered by an illegal or incorrect attempt. With the improvement in performance there is less tutoring intervention.

With well-designed learning resources employing granular interface, it is possible to learn from simpler interactions. The learning tasks are decomposed into smaller components at varying levels of granularity with the perspective shift enabled through the user interface as briefly explained below (for more details see Patel and Kinshuk, 1997). There is no need for the system to engage in complex inferencing about user knowledge as the system can provide a simple correct/incorrect feedback at a coarser grain size. Where necessary, the system can advise the student to use a fine-grained interface for more detailed interaction, as shown under *Interactive Messages* in Figure 16.3.

The figure shows a problem space in the Capital Investment Appraisal ITT. The proposed investment can be evaluated using one or more of four techniques, three of which can be selected initially by appropriate pushbuttons on the left-hand side pane. The student is given some project data to evaluate. In the shown example,

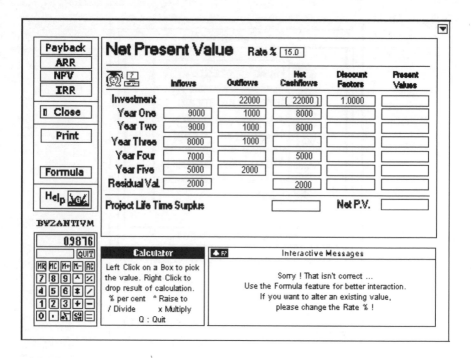

Figure 16.3 *Net present value screen in the Capital Investment Appraisal ITT*

the student is using NPV or the Net Present Value technique and is attempting the discount factor for end of Year 1. The value of the discount factor attempted by the student was incorrect so the interactive message advised the use of Formula feature. The feature employs a fine-grained interface, shown in Figure 16.4, called up using the Formula pushbutton.

The ITTs have Just-in-time scaffolding and Built-in fading, as demonstrated by the following attributes:

1. The system does not force a student to use a rigid sequence of data entry or a particular pathway to the overall solution. The expert model records its own pathway to the solution; however, the system recognizes all the valid pathways and alters its guidance in line with the student actions.
2. The system offers scaffolding only when the student demonstrates a need for it through an erroneous action. This support is based on a branch construct, either repeatedly informing the students about non-feasibility of their action and suggesting an intermediate step as explained in item 3 or offering a graded feedback as explained in items 4 to 6.
3. If the attempted value cannot be obtained directly from the available information on the screen, the system suggests that the student first attempts an intermediate step. However, if the student has performed some mental

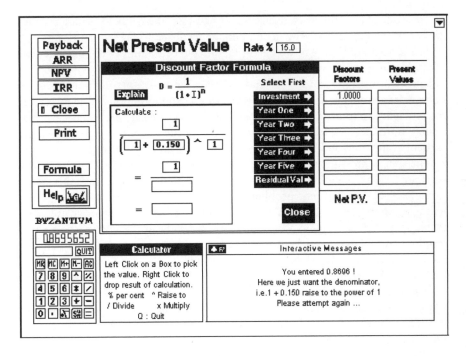

Figure 16.4   *Fine-grained Discount Factor pop-up interface*

operations and attempted a correct value, the system does not insist that the intermediate step be carried out first.

4. If the attempted value is incorrect at the first attempt, the system merely notifies that it was incorrect and allows re-examination.

5. On the second incorrect attempt, the system advises the correct relationship to use. This, the second level of feedback, is the workhorse of intermediate phase of cognitive skill acquisition as it indicates misconceptions and helps in getting rid of them with the immediate feedback.

6. On the third incorrect attempt, the system shows the calculation using the actual data. This level of feedback has been observed only at the initial stage of the intermediate phase as the student is still grasping the various domain concepts by placing them in relation to each other.

In the Interactive mode, the student has to initiate some action before the system offers any guidance. The feedback's purpose is to spur the students' own self-explanations by pointing out the correct action. At any stage of interactive learning, the students can refer back to the expository material by using the Help pushbutton. This allows the students to navigate back and forth between the work they are doing and the textual explanations and solved examples provided in the expository material. The system requires greater engagement by the students while giving them greater control over the learning actions. It harnesses the natural learning capabilities of an intelligent being by giving enough feedback to prevent an impasse.

The system holds the knowledge of the inter-relationships of the variables and is capable of generating practice problems. It randomly selects some variables as independent variables and assigns random values within the programmer-specified bounds. It then applies its knowledge to derive an expert solution before presenting the problem to a student. Towards the end of the Intermediate phase, a teacher may wish to introduce problems in a narrative form for the student to experience more authentic situations and interpret the data provided in a free form.

The system provides an 'enter your own' problem data option. However, some variables have a fixed value in the interactive mode to prevent misuse of this option for solving the assignment problems with interactive guidance. The problem narration, therefore, needs to be designed around these fixed values. It still offers ample scope for variation and in return for this handicap, the system offers a rich scope of summative assessment that can be computer marked. The Byzantium assessment system is described in Patel *et al* (1998).

The combination of ITT and Byzantium Marker is capable of identifying and giving partial score for 'incorrect interpretation but application of correct method', just like a human tutor marking the work. The computerized marking enables a very fast turnaround. The advantages of frequent summative testing are three-fold. First, it motivates the students to be more attentive to and put adequate effort into the interactive learning. Secondly, such increased attention shortens the intermediate phase of skill acquisition; and finally there is a greater amount of and more frequent feedback to support the late phase of skill acquisition. The learning path consists of transition through observation, interactive learning, simple testing, learning and testing involving multiple contexts and/or interpretation of text narrative. The ITT architecture also provides a customization facility for creating appropriate templates by specifying various parameters. The templates can then be used for the purpose of both the structured and non-structured problems.

The implementation of cognitive apprenticeship in the Byzantium tutors has been successful, as demonstrated by the findings of an independent evaluation briefly discussed in the next section.

Feedback from an independent evaluation

Stoner and Harvey (1999) carried out an independent evaluation at the University of Glasgow, involving Byzantium and another widely used package called Understand Management Accounting, distributed by EQL International. Stoner's (2002) observations about the two packages were that the latter was a fairly traditional computer-based learning software that presented core material as text and graphics, followed by examples. The lessons were interspersed with questions and tasks requiring student interaction and the formative feedback was basic but broadly encouraging in nature. In comparison, Byzantium provided practice in numerical management accounting by generating random variations on standard example questions and by providing the tools to complete them, requiring students to work out answers from base data towards solution values, or vice versa, or in both directions. He found that Byzantium emulated a range of question types, including incomplete records, typically used to enhance the understanding of accounting techniques. In addition to the two packages, student opinions were also obtained on lectures, textbooks, tutorials and workshops.

In their study, involving a three-year comparison of examination performance and feedback from focus groups, Stoner and Harvey found the results to indicate that students' performance had improved significantly over the period since learning technology materials were introduced and that this improvement appeared to be mainly reflected in the students' ability to complete numeric questions. The student feedback focus groups' comments, while comparing Byzantium to the EQL package and to the textbooks, were:

> Prefer Byzantium because EQL package waffles on about what you already know and provides no incentives to pay attention to what it says. Byzantium offers instant feedback, is more involving and you can do as many questions as you like.
>
> Byzantium was useful because you could go over bits you were unsure about. It was better than a book because it was interactive. With the interactive questions you tend to pay more attention than you would to a book.

Of the two tutoring systems, 71 per cent of students showed a preference for Byzantium material while 8 per cent indicated no particular preference. In relation to Byzantium, 92 per cent of the students liked being able to repeatedly try random questions, and 84 per cent reported an improvement in confidence in their ability to perform accounting calculations, and 69 per cent indicated that they liked to be able to make mistakes in private. The students wanted more tutoring systems like Byzantium for other topics and were positive about Computer Aided Learning (CAL) in general, observing that it was good to use CAL if the tutoring software was good.

The way forward

The cognitive apprenticeship based approach to designing learning software for introductory accounting has been successfully validated through the Byzantium ITTs. An important observation in the Stoner and Harvey study was that the student performance was affected by the quality of integration of the learning resource in the curriculum. The implementing teacher is therefore a very important partner in the process. Following Pareto's rule it may be safe to say that a well-designed tutoring system is likely, on average, to satisfy 80 per cent of any teacher's requirement. However, it is the remaining 20 per cent that most probably represents the individual idiosyncrasies that differentiate one teacher from another and therefore likely to be emphasized by the implementing teacher. One way to encourage wider use of various learning resources is to enable the implementing teacher to contribute through configuring the learning space, incrementally adding and restructuring where necessary, the scope and functionality of various learning components.

The standardized Web browser and communications capability of the Internet provides a powerful technology to achieve this. While this platform provides a much better scope for presenting expository material, two other powerful enhancements possible to the Byzantium ITTs are mentioned below.

Extending the ITT methodology on to the Internet

The success of the stand-alone ITTs has opened the way to create Intelligent Tutoring Applications (ITAs) over the Web employing the same underlying model. The Web permits various tutoring modules to be created, held and accessed in a structured manner across vast distances, provided there are suitable authoring tools that assist in elicitation or modification of knowledge rules and a modular software architecture is adopted that not only separates the knowledge base, expert model, student model and the tutoring module, but also separates the interface manager from the data about various controls on the interface and their contents. Such a modular structure enables data-driven software applications and ensures greater ease in incremental development and modification – in most cases, just by altering the data about the interface controls. With the appropriate structuring parameters, the ITAs created or incrementally modified by different teachers build up to a large inventory of accessible knowledge that can be utilized by all the teachers in various configurations of single or multiple ITAs to create hyper-ITS, a flexible intelligent tutoring system.

As an example, consider the Capital Investment Appraisal (CIA) ITT discussed earlier. It is geared towards learning the application of four different appraisal techniques with a view to accepting or rejecting an investment proposal. Since the ITT is coded in Visual C++, it is very difficult to make any significant modifications and each modification requires the services of a software engineer. However, when it is converted into a Web-based ITA as discussed above and authoring tools are made available, different teachers may harness it in different hyper-ITSs.

One such possible implementation may be for ranking investment proposals in order of priority by creating a higher-level interface for storing and ranking the appraisal results and linking it to multiple instances of the CIA ITA. As a further refinement, a teacher may add modifications to take into account the decision maker's attitude to risk. Another possible implementation is to combine the CIA ITA with an ITA for learning probabilistic outcomes and expected values, so that uncertainty of future cash flows may be reflected through optimistic, most likely and pessimistic probable cash flows. A third possible implementation, obviously, is to link the two implementations above to rank multiple proposals with probable cash flows. Through incremental modifications made by different teachers, this approach provides the ability to rapidly and relatively easily build up a large inventory of different ITAs and their combination into hyper-ITS systems.

Improving diagnostics through process modelling

Though Byzantium ITTs employ an overlay model and provide feedback by comparing the student and expert models, they use a very powerful interface feature in the integrated calculator to enable detailed process modelling. The calculator allows picking values and dropping results by using the left and right mouse click respectively. Monitoring user interactions with the integrated calculator provides the system with a window into the learner's mental processes. While improved diagnostics based on process modelling may have limited value for interactive learning (carried out with immediate and dynamic feedback so there is no scope for making a series of mistakes), it can offer much better delayed feedback in case of the computer-marked summative assessments.

Conclusion

Computer-based assessment has come a long way but we are still at an early threshold of the appearance of serious and substantial applications. Byzantium ITTs have now been used in real learning environment for more than five years and at many institutions of higher and further education. What Byzantium has achieved is exciting and though substantial work will be needed to create the hyper-ITS infrastructure, the potential demonstrated so far is breathtaking!

References

Bjork, R A (1994) Memory and metamemory considerations in the training of human beings, in *Metacognition: Knowing about knowing,* eds J Metcalfe and P Shimamura, pp 185–206, The MIT Press, Cambridge, MA

Bransford, J D (1979) *Human Cognition: Learning, understanding, and remembering,* Wadsworth, Belmont, CA

Calfee, R C and Masuda, W V (1997) Classroom assessment as inquiry, in *Handbook of Classroom Assessment: Learning, adjustment and achievement,* ed G D Phye, Academic Press, New York

Collins, A, Brown, J S and Newman, S E (1989) Cognitive apprenticeship: teaching the crafts of reading, writing and mathematics. in *Knowing, Learning and Instruction,* ed L B Resnick, pp 453–94, Lawrence Erlbaum, Hillsdale, NJ

Farr, R and Griffin, M (1973) Measurement gaps in teacher education, *Journal of Educational Measurement,* **7** (1), pp 19–28

Gagne, R M (1965) *The Conditions of Learning,* Rinehard and Winston, New York

Graue, M E (1993) Integrating theory and practice through instructional assessment, *Educational Assessment,* **1,** pp 293–309

Hull, C L (1943) *Principles of Behavior: An introduction to behavior theory,* Appleton-Century, New York

Jensen, E (2000) Curriculum with the brain in mind, *Brain-based Learning,* pp 210–11, The Brain Store, San Diego, CA

Kleibard, H M (1995) *The Struggle for the American Curriculum: 1893–1958*, Routledge, New York

McMillan, J H (2001) *Essential Assessment Concepts for Teachers and Administrators*, Corwin, Thousand Oaks, CA

Norman, D A (1986) Cognitive engineering, in *User Centered System Design: New perspectives on human-computer interaction*, eds D A Norman and S W Draper, pp 31–61, Lawrence Erlbaum, Hillsdale NJ

Norman, D A (1988) To err is human, *The Psychology of Everyday Things*, pp 105–40, Perseus Books Group, USA

Patel, A and Kinshuk (1997) Granular interface design: decomposing learning tasks and enhancing tutoring interaction, in *Advances in Human Factors/Ergonomics Design of Computing Systems: Social and ergonomic considerations*, eds M J Smith, G Salvendy and R J Koubek, pp 161–4, Elsevier Science, Amsterdam

Patel, A, Kinshuk, and Russell, D (1998) A computer-based intelligent assessment system for numeric disciplines, *Information Services and Use*, **18** (1–2), pp 53–63

Patel, A, Russell, D and Kinshuk (1999) Assessment in a cognitive apprenticeship-based learning environment: potential and pitfalls, in *Computer-aided Assessment in Higher Education*, eds S Brown, P Race and J Bull, pp 139–47, Kogan Page, London

Skinner, B F (1954) The science of learning and the art of teaching, *Harvard Educational Review*, **24,** pp 86–97

Stiggins, R (1999) *Assessment, student confidence and school success.* Accessed February 2002, from http://www.pdkintl.org/kappan/k9911sti.htm

Stoner, G (2002) Using learning technology resources in teaching management accounting, in *BEST Stories: Business Education Support Team, Learning and Teaching Support Network UK*, eds D Hawkridge and A Forrester. Accessed March 2002, from http://www.business.ltsn.ac.uk

Stoner, G and Harvey, J (1999) Integrating learning technology in a foundation level management accounting course: an e(in)volving evaluation. Paper presented at the CTI-AFM annual conference, April, Brighton, UK

VanLehn, K (1996) Cognitive skill acquisition, *Annual Review of Psychology*, **42,** pp 513–39

Vygotsky, L S (1978) *Mind in Society: The development of higher psychological processes*, Harvard University Press, Cambridge, MA

Wiggins, G (1998) *Educative Assessment: Designing assessments to inform and improve student performance*, Jossey-Bass, San Francisco CA

Part 5

Providing feedback

Chapter 17

A feedback model and successful e-learning

Yiping Lou, Helena Dedic and Steven Rosenfield

Introduction

This chapter discusses feedback as part of a model of self-regulating systems in learning and teaching, and illustrates how elaborate and effective feedback can be provided in e-learning environments. From the constructivist perspective, learners construct new knowledge by cognitively elaborating new information and by reconciling data gained through their own observation and experimentation, as well as through feedback from teachers, with previously held views. Similarly, teachers can also be thought of as course designers who function as self-regulating systems. They construct new task and feedback structures in a process that involves elaboration and experiments, as well as reconciliation of previously held views with information they gather from data provided by learners' actions and performance.

The word 'feedback' is often used loosely. In this chapter, feedback is defined as an informational message sent by one element of a system to another element, with the expectation that the receiving element will use this message to modulate its performance. For example, a heating system in a house consists of thermostats, a control switch and a heat source. The thermostats compare room temperature to a predetermined desired temperature, and then send messages to the switch telling it to either turn the heat source on or off (Doig, 2000). Such a system can only be functional if: appropriate messages are sent to the switch (the thermostat is not placed near a draughty window causing incorrect signals to be sent); messages are correctly interpreted by the switch (a newly installed digital switch would find messages sent by an old analog thermostat incomprehensible); the heat source itself is capable of responding effectively to the situation (a weak heat source in a very large and draughty house will not keep the house warm no matter how many accurate messages are sent to the switch by the thermostat).

Similarly, when considering the situation in which feedback is to be used to effectively promote meaningful learning, several conditions must be met: appropriate corrective messages need to be sent to learners; the messages themselves need to be interpretable by learners; and learners need to possess prerequisite prior knowledge, motivation and strategies to respond effectively to the feedback they receive. In particular, learners depend on the instructional setting to provide both the tasks from which they can draw data, and the feedback structures that allow them to gauge their performance (Pintrich *et al*, 1993). In turn, the teachers who create these same tasks and feedback structures need feedback from the learners regarding their effectiveness. Thus, effective teaching depends on teachers being sent appropriate messages; their ability to interpret those messages; and having appropriate skills to respond to them effectively.

In this chapter we will first review the feedback literature, concentrating on feedback design issues such as type, timing and sources of feedback in both face-to-face and computer-mediated instructional settings. The computer-mediated instructional settings mentioned in this chapter refer to face-to-face course designs in which simulations are available to students via the Web and/or in which students and teachers use computer-mediated communication (CMC) outside of the classroom. We will then focus on the differences inherent in the learning environment when shifting from a face-to-face setting to a technology-enhanced environment, and the impact such differences have on both task and feedback structures. Illustrations of the nature of such differences as well as examples of effective task and feedback strategies in such contexts will be drawn from science classes using Web-based computer simulations and social science classes using CMC.

Type of feedback and its impact on learning

Research on feedback has accumulated a wealth of information concerning the impact of feedback upon student learning. Several meta-analyses and narrative reviews have synthesized this research, and indicated that there is a significant positive effect on student achievement of providing feedback versus not doing so, but the effects of elaborate feedback with explanations are generally significantly larger than simple feedback (Azevedo and Bernard, 1995; Bangert-Drowns *et al*, 1991).

An essential part of learning in both the sciences and social sciences is the development by each student of an understanding of the cycle often called 'the scientific method' (observations, leading to a belief about some structure governing a particular phenomenon, testing of that belief through additional observations, and either formation of new beliefs or further generalization of the old beliefs). Computer-mediated instruction in science and mathematics increasingly makes use of simulations, which provide learners with visual feedback enabling them to travel through this cycle of discovery (Papert, 1980). In physics, visual feedback without elaboration was found to be less effective than visual feedback with elaboration (Rieber *et al*, 1996). These authors speculate that learners, while interacting with a simulation, might be focusing on successful completion of the activity, as opposed to reflecting on the underlying physics principles.

Timing of feedback

In many reviews and studies 'timing' refers to the time interval between the learner's response to a stimulus (ie, question) and the feedback provided. The research focus was often on the comparison between immediate and delayed feedback, with more positive effects usually found for immediate than delayed feedback in applied classroom research (Kulik and Kulik, 1988) and computer-based instruction (Azevedo and Bernard, 1995).

Another aspect of feedback timing that is rarely studied but perhaps is more important is the provision of feedback during learning activities (Butler and Winne, 1995). The instructional setting may be such that learners obtain feedback during the initial stages of the learning process, while they are still grappling with newly introduced concepts. On the other hand, feedback may be delivered during a later stage of concept development, when learners are testing their understanding. Feedback may be most effective if it guides cognitive activities, during which knowledge is accreted, tuned and restructured (Rumelhart and Norman, 1978).

Sources of feedback

Feedback sources can be classified as external or internal (Butler and Winne, 1995). Research on feedback has primarily focused on external feedback as provided by a teacher, either directly or via a computer. This literature overlooks another possible source of external feedback, from peers. Although small-group cooperative learning has generally been accepted as an effective learning strategy (eg, Abrami *et al*, 1995; Lou *et al*, 1996; Lou *et al*, 2001), instructors rarely integrate formal student-to-student feedback into the instructional design for the following reasons (Latham, 1997): instructors are unsure that students are capable of providing effective feedback without proper training; even in cooperative settings, competitive students may choose not to give quality feedback to peers; students may possess bias toward peers of different races or genders; and some students may not appreciate the need for and rewards of peer feedback.

Internal feedback, on the other hand, is feedback generated by the learner during his or her own cognitive process of monitoring (Butler and Winne, 1995). Self-regulating learners monitor their own academic performance, affect and learning strategies. They rely on their internal feedback to guide appropriate corrective action if their goals are not being met. They seek external feedback when they cannot resolve problems on their own. Such students are more likely to respond to feedback from teachers by taking corrective measures, provided they can appropriately interpret that feedback. Amongst students who score low on self-regulation, however, feedback from a teacher may fail to elicit a corrective response for a number of reasons, such as improper interpretation of the feedback or lack of appropriate corrective strategies. A new model of self-regulation emerges that includes learners' responses to both internal (traditionally part of self-regulation literature) and external (traditionally part of feedback literature) feedback (Butler and Winne, 1995).

A model of effective feedback

We have revised and expanded Butler and Winne's (1995) model of self-regulation to create a new model of effective feedback (see Figure 17.1). Our model views learners as active self-regulators who seek feedback and then respond to it. Teachers, as course designers, form another self-regulating system that initiates changes based on feedback gathered from learners' actions and performance. Peers who offer constructive criticism form another self-regulating system that interacts with that of the learner.

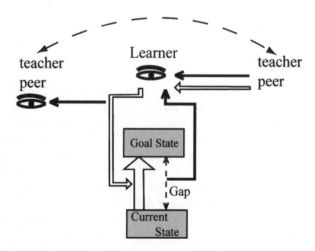

Figure 17.1 *A model of effective feedback in e-learning*

In the model, learning/teaching involves simultaneous feedback loops, one that is centred on the learner and another (completed by the dashed line) that is centred on the teacher/peer. Solid arrows indicate feedback, while hollow arrows represent corrective actions in response to feedback. Note that a teacher/peer's corrective action is at the same time external feedback from the point of view of the learner. To portray this duality we use both solid and hollow arrows flowing from the teacher/peer to the learner. Two important factors that influence whether feedback provided will help to close the gap between the current state and goal state of desired performance are: 1) a clear picture of the goal state, and 2) the ability of the learner to carry out the corrective action.

While this model describes both face-to-face and computer-mediated learning, there are vital differences in the type, timing and sources of feedback used in these learning settings. For example, in face-to-face classrooms, feedback to individual learners during the learning process tends to be short and simple due to time constraints. More elaborate feedback may be provided to the whole class targeting a mythical 'average student'. Public feedback aimed at an 'average student' discourages and bores high-ability students while it confuses less adept ones. However, when elaborate feedback is one-on-one, between teacher and an individual student, only the student involved in the interaction benefits.

In the computer-mediated environment individual feedback no longer needs to be private, nor need public feedback be targeted at the 'average student'. For example, with discussion boards public feedback provided by the teacher to an individual student can benefit other students with similar misconceptions. This knowledge motivates teachers to provide more elaborate feedback, which leads to higher performance standards in the class.

On the other hand, teaching and learning in the face-to-face settings have the advantage of synchronous verbal and non-verbal communication. In face-to-face settings, a good instructor is constantly 'reading' the class and modifying instruction to maintain student involvement. In computer-mediated settings this type of information is absent and new ways of 'reading' involvement must be used.

Using two very different computer-mediated settings, we will draw lessons concerning interlocked loops of a learner and a teacher; and then interlocked loops of a learner and peers.

Feedback and Web-based simulations

Interactive simulations are now frequently used in computer-mediated instruction in calculus and physics courses. In general, the intention is to allow learners to rapidly generate many 'instances' of a particular phenomenon. Learners are expected to discover a pattern or rule that explains the phenomenon (hypothesize), and then to verify their hypothesis by interpreting visual (graphical) feedback.

For example, students may be asked to observe a tangent line as it moves left to right along a graph of a function. Having observed the animation, students are then asked to make predictions about the graph of the derivative of the given function (values of the slopes of the tangent lines). Then, by simply changing an index value, the simulation adds a dynamic plot of the graph of the derivative function matching the movement of the tangent line. The resulting graph of the derivative function then confirms or negates student predictions (http://sun4.vaniercollege.qc.ca/calsim). After students have repeated this process with different functions, each time appropriately interpreting the visual feedback provided by the simulation, many discover the relationship between a function and its derivative. If the discovery is made, then students have gained meaningful understanding of not only this particular relationship, but also of a more general mathematical thought process.

In face-to-face classrooms the teacher can explain such a relationship, but not expect students to discover it in this deeper manner. On the other hand, the teacher obtains feedback from both classroom discussion and non-verbal messages students send, aiding him or her in assessing how meaningful an understanding of the concept students have. In response to such feedback the teacher can modify instruction immediately. In a computer-mediated environment, where students interact with a computer simulation, the teacher does not get this same feedback.

Thus, on the surface it appears that the use of simulations, with visual feedback, enhances student understanding at the expense of feedback for the teacher. However, the situation is not that simple. The use of simulations to facilitate learning complex concepts imposes demands on learners that they have not encountered previously in face-to-face settings. Some students may lack even basic computer skills that are necessary for learning in a computer-mediated environment. While the number of such students is rapidly decreasing, any such students may find that this context hinders rather than facilitates learning. In addition, many students may have developed a rigid method of monitoring their own understanding in a subject and thus may not value feedback that is delivered through the computer interface (Dedic *et al,* 2001).

Often the ability of students to interpret complex visual (graphical) messages is limited. In our work we found two ways of helping students to make sense of such feedback: deliver visual messages in stages, with initial messages being visually simple and gradually adding layers of complexity; and augment visual feedback with elaborative textual feedback (Alalouf *et al,* 2002). Adding elaborative textual feedback to visual feedback improves student learning. However, how such feedback is delivered changes how students use simulations. We tried elaborative feedback as text placed immediately after simulations. Unfortunately, given such easy access to textual explanations, most students decided to forgo experimentation altogether and instead just read the text to learn what they could have, and ideally should have, discovered visually through the simulations.

Those annoying 'pop-up' advertisements seen on all too many Web pages suggested another possible mechanism for delivering elaborative feedback. While students were working with simulations, questions were made to pop-up on their screens, an impromptu quiz if you will. Student responses were evaluated and verbal feedback provided by the computer. Pop-up feedback screens can be triggered in a number of ways: length of time the student has spent on the simulation page; tied to a particular activity on the simulation page; or under student control, as a button. Our experiments with the timer indicate a number of shortcomings to this method: some students move frequently between the simulation page and other textual materials, thus continually restarting the timer, and hence either never see the pop-up or experience it repeatedly; some students move through a simulation page so rapidly that they never experience the pop-up; some students work so slowly that the pop-up arrives prematurely for them (Alalouf *et al*, 2002). Our experimental results show that high achievers decode complex visual feedback, requiring only that the complexity be layered, while low achievers require the layering of complexity as well as elaborative textual feedback. Furthermore, we found that student achievement, when using all of these techniques simultaneously, is superior to student achievement in a traditional face-to-face instructional setting (Dedic and Rosenfield, 2002).

Another difficulty with visual feedback is that students need to translate visual information into appropriate mathematical vocabulary. Pop-up quiz questions that modelled such translation proved to be particularly helpful in aiding students to formulate an appropriate mental model of the concept they were experimenting with. We have also found that it is important to structure simulations and their use so that underlying patterns are more likely to be visible. For example, if the objective of a simulation is to discover that there is a linear relationship between two variables, then the independent variable should only be allowed to vary in an organized fashion. Thus, in a simulation of a spring-mass system, if the student is to discover how the period of oscillation depends on the mass, the simulation should allow only integral multiples of an original mass.

Providing feedback to teachers is a problem in computer-mediated environments for two reasons: the teacher does not obtain such information directly from students, and modifications to the environment require preparation time, resulting in a delay in teachers' responses to any feedback that is obtained. We found that both students' answers to pop-up quizzes and access to log files of student activity can generate the feedback that teachers need; however both of these means for obtaining feedback must be built into the environment (eg Winne, 1989). In fact our research demonstrates that students' answers on pop-up quizzes correlate with achievement after the activity, thus feedback in the form of answers to pop-up quizzes allow us to predict how students are developing conceptual understanding. Further, access to log files allows teachers to trace students' activities during use of simulations. While teachers routinely assess student motivation, metacognition and/ or prior knowledge in face-to-face settings, further research will be required to determine whether teachers can draw analogous feedback from log file data.

The section above discussed, in a science class setting, the changes wrought on both the learner and the teacher feedback loops by the use of interactive simulations. In the section below, we discuss a social science class setting, where discussion plays a larger role in the course and CMC offers new possibilities to learner, teacher and peer feedback loops.

Feedback and Web-based discussion boards

CMC tools such as Web-based discussion boards are increasingly being used in distance education courses or as a supplement to traditional face-to-face classroom teaching and learning, especially in social science courses. One common usage of a discussion board is to enable group or class discussions on topics and issues related to the course. The asynchronous communication provides students with opportunities to reflect and respond to each other thoughtfully. A considerable amount of research has shown that learners can benefit from these discussions through cognitive elaboration and sharing of different perspectives, prior experiences and distributed cognition when learners are actively engaged (see the chapter by Sims in this book for a more detailed discussion).

Another effective use of a discussion board is for teachers to provide public and elaborate feedback to either an individual student, or the whole class, so as to benefit more students. For example, in class or group discussions, the instructor can monitor the discussion and provide feedback when misconceptions arise. In our social science classes, we also used discussion boards to provide detailed feedback on each individual or group project and to encourage all students to read each others' work as well as the instructor's feedback as a way of not only learning from each other but also developing a better perception of the desired learning goals.

A less often used method of providing feedback, using CMC, is structured feedback between and among students working on different projects. Few studies have been conducted to document how such peer feedback can be structured successfully due to the concern that learners are unable to provide each other with quality feedback (Latham, 1997). In the examples below, we describe two courses, one graduate course in instructional design and one undergraduate course in educational technology integration, where peer feedback was successfully designed and implemented using group space on Blackboard (2000), an online course builder.

Most of the participants in the graduate course were in-service teachers. During the course, students worked in small groups on a semester-long instructional design project. Initially, each group used their own online group space to post project work and to exchange ideas amongst the group members, in addition to the face-to-face class meetings. To encourage cross-group collaborative learning, group areas were open and accessible to all members of the class, and students could ask questions and make suggestions to any group that they visited. The students generally found this cross-group collaboration helpful. However, as the semester progressed and the amount of interaction increased, most students found it hard to follow all other projects online. To alleviate this problem, while continuing to encourage collaborative learning, each group was assigned a specific group that they were to follow and provide feedback to. Student course evaluation data, as well as comments in students' journals, indicated that they liked the more focused approach.

Most of the students in the undergraduate course were pre-service teachers. During the course students worked on a number of short projects to learn to use various technology tools and to design technology-enhanced lesson activities for their current or future students. A few strategies were used to provide guidance, modelling and scaffolding so as to effectively implement peer feedback in this class. One strategy employed was for the instructor to provide detailed individualized feedback for each project online during the early part of the course. The instructor's feedback served students as a model of how to provide constructive feedback.

A second guidance strategy used was the provision of an evaluation rubric. The rubric was given to the students before the start of their projects. They first used it as a guideline in developing their own work, and later used it as a checklist when evaluating other students' work. This strategy was found to be effective for short and less complex projects.

Another guidance strategy was developed and implemented for complex design projects. The students would first evaluate some outside resources as a group and then the whole class shared group responses and developed a common understanding of the characteristics of good work. The results of the class discussion were then compiled into an evaluation rubric, both as a guideline for project development and as a tool for evaluating the work of other students.

As indicated in the midterm and end of course evaluations, students responded very positively to peer feedback. With percentages ranging between 71 and 93, the students liked the peer feedback experience; felt that their projects improved as a result of the feedback they received; thought that evaluating work of other groups or students provided them with multiple perspectives as to how projects could be done; and stated that by helping them to see the strengths and limitations of other students' work, their own work had improved.

The findings in the two courses indicate that, if appropriate structures and guidance are provided, peer feedback during project-based learning can be beneficial to both the provider and the receiver of the feedback. Peer feedback places students in the position of providing feedback, not just receiving it. This promotes student meta-cognitive and critical thinking skills, and helps students to develop multiple perspectives, thereby increasing achievement motivation and improving self-regulation in learning.

Conclusion

At the core of this chapter lies our model of feedback that involves interlocked feedback loops, portraying learners and teachers/peers as actors who provide and receive feedback. The model is based on constructivist learning theory and self-regulated learning. It emphasizes the importance of gathering learners' process and performance data and providing feedback during the learning activities so that learners will be guided effectively toward achieving their desired learning goals.

Our findings on feedback in science and social science classes indicate that e-learning settings offer the opportunity to enhance feedback during the learning process so that student learning outcomes and affect are improved. However, it is important to note that effective feedback structures are not automatically a part of interactive simulations, CMC or other e-learning settings, and that teachers must actively design them in and recursively continue to refine them through experimentation.

References

Abrami, P C, Chambers, B, Poulsen, C, De Simone, C, d'Apollonia, S and Howden, J (1995) *Classroom Connections: Understanding and using cooperative learning,* Harcourt-Brace, Toronto

Alalouf, E, Klasa, J, Dedic, H and Rosenfield, S (2002) Conceptual understanding versus algorithmic computation in calculus: Strawman or real conflict. Paper presented at the annual meeting of the Association de la Recherche Collegial, Quebec, Canada

Azevedo, R and Bernard, R M (1995) A meta-analysis of the effects of feedback in computer-based instruction, *Journal of Educational Computing Research,* **13** (2), pp 111–27

Bangert-Drowns, R L, Kulik, J A and Morgan, M T (1991) The instructional effect of feedback in test-like events, *Review of Educational Research,* **61**, pp 213–38

Blackboard, Inc (2000) *Blackboard, version 5,* Computer software, Blackboard, Washington, DC

Butler, D L and Winne, P H (1995) Feedback and self-regulated learning: a theoretical synthesis, *Review of Educational Research,* **65**, pp 245–81

Dedic, H and Rosenfield, S (2002) The impact of interactive Web-based materials on student conceptual understanding in differential calculus. Paper presented at the annual meeting of the American Educational Research Association, New Orleans, LA

Dedic, H, Rosenfield, S, Cooper, M and Fuchs, M (2001) Do I really hafta? WebCAL: a look at the use of livemath software in Web-based materials that provide interactive engagement in a collaborative learning environment for differential calculus, *Educational Research and Evaluation,* **7** (2–3), pp 285–312

Doig, S M (2000) *Developing an Understanding of the Role of Feedback in Education.* Accessed 28 February 2002, from http://www.tedi.uq.edu.au/conferences/ A_conf/titles.html

Kulik, J A and Kulik, C L C (1988) Timing of feedback and verbal learning, *Review of Educational Research,* **58**, pp 79–97

Latham, A S (1997) Learning through feedback, *Educational Leadership,* **54**, pp 86–87

Lou, Y, Abrami, P C and d'Apollonia, S (2001) Small group and individual learning with technology: a meta-analysis, *Review of Educational Research,* **71**, pp 449–521

Lou, Y, Abrami, P C, Spence, J C, Poulsen, C, Chambers, B and d'Apollonia, S (1996) Within-class grouping: a meta-analysis, *Review of Educational Research,* **66**, pp 423–58

Papert, S (1980) *Mindstorms: Children, computers and powerful ideas,* Basic Books, New York

Pintrich, P R, Marx, R W and Boyle, R A (1993) Beyond cold conceptual change: the role of motivational beliefs and classroom contextual factors in the process of conceptual change, *Review of Educational Research,* **63**, pp 167–99

Rieber, L P, Tzeng, S, Tribble, K and Chu, G (1996) Feedback and elaboration within a computer-based simulation: a dual coding perspective, *Proceedings of Selected Research and Development Presentations,* 1996 National Convention of the Association for Educational Communications and Technology, Indianapolis, IN

Rumelhart, D and Norman, D (1978) Accretion, tuning and restructuring: three modes of learning, in *Semantic Factors in Cognition,* eds J W Cotton and R Klatzky, Lawrence Erlbaum, Hillsdale, NJ

Winne, P H (1989) Theories of instruction and of intelligence for designing artificially intelligent tutoring systems, *Educational Psychologist,* **24**, pp 229–59

Chapter 18

Interactivity and feedback as determinants of engagement and meaning in e-learning environments

Rod Sims

Introduction

This chapter examines the ways in which feedback plays a critical role within e-learning environments in terms of participant engagement and the construction of meaning. It emphasizes that the effectiveness of communication between course participants largely depends on the dynamics between learner, computer, other humans, information resources and/or learning objects – all of which contribute to the interactive and collaborative experience. Within this computer-mediated context therefore, the participant's interactivity is critical to success, and the means by which feedback is conceptualized, structured and activated by each player within the e-learning environment is the foundation for that interactivity, enabling communication and subsequent engagement.

Whether students are on campus and using online resources and communication, or remote and totally dependent on computer-mediation for access to other participants and content material, e-learning environments are prolific. However, implementing e-learning environments without embracing the necessary educational rationale and good practice is problematic (Brennan *et al,* 2001; Sims, 2001a). Similarly, anecdotal data from my own teaching environment suggest that teachers are confronting different and complex workloads and that students are not necessarily equipped with the skills and competencies to take advantage of e-learning features. While providing the potential for collaborative communities, e-learning environments continue to require significant effort to achieve their educational potential.

The first section of this chapter highlights the importance of feedback and agreed understandings of its role in educational and e-learning processes. The second section focuses on strategies for both teachers and learners to enhance their e-learning experience by constructing feedback that is consistent with current understandings of the learner-computer interface, encapsulated by the term 'interactivity'. These strategies are contextualized by examining options for maximizing the effectiveness of feedback within the range of interactive encounters afforded through e-learning and explained within a classification of specific features for feedback within online environments. Selected illustrations of these environments are presented, focusing on the common asynchronous threaded discussions enabled by popular learning management systems. Through this analysis, feedback is constructed as a major factor contributing to individual learning as well as the overall success of e-learning applications.

The importance of feedback

A critical aspect of e-learning is the extent to which participants gain value from communication and collaborative activities, the two-way process between participants and/or content items. If neither the teacher nor the learner receives appropriate feedback relevant to their contribution, the generation of meaning and engagement within that environment will be diminished. This applies both to contributions made by other persons and from the content associated with discrete learning objects.

As illustrated in Figure 18.1, a participant within an e-learning network is making both proactive or self-initiated requests and reactive responses. The solid lines represent the communication and feedback links between the participant and the environment, while the dotted lines highlight other interactions taking place within the e-learning community. Unless appropriate and timely feedback is provided within that environment, the learning activity may be impeded, resulting in compromised communication and diminished meaning being derived from the exchange (Sims, 2001b).

The importance of feedback to all computer-based learning environments is widely acknowledged: 'Feedback should be positive. It should avoid negative statements, sarcasm, and should never demean the learner. Feedback should be corrective. It should provide the learner with information to improve future performance' (Alessi and Trollip, 2001, p 115).

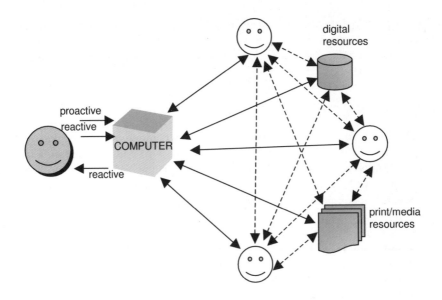

Figure 18.1   *Participant view of e-learning environment*

But feedback can be more than positive and corrective. Laurillard (1993, p 61) argues forcibly that 'action without feedback is completely unproductive for a learner. . . feedback has to be meaningful' and Wlodkowski (1999, p 244) states that 'feedback is information that learners receive about the quality of their work. . . (it) is probably the most powerful process that teachers and other learners can regularly use to affect a learner's performance'. Feedback must therefore be value-added, enhancing not just confirming an action. Laurillard (1993) differentiates these as *intrinsic*, where feedback is a natural consequence of an action, and *extrinsic*, where feedback is an external comment to a situation, with information embedded within the feedback leading to correction and adaptation of performance.

How then does this relate to the egalitarian world of e-learning, where all learners and teachers can be conceived as equal participants in the learning process? Palloff and Pratt (1999, p 123) conclude that 'an important element that should be built into an online course is the expectation that students will provide constructive and extensive feedback to each other' but caution that 'the ability to give meaningful feedback, which helps others think about the work they have produced, is not a naturally acquired skill'. When working in an e-learning environment, participants interact and receive feedback both intrinsically, from operation of the computer equipment and information displayed on the interface, and extrinsically, from the information embedded within resources accessed and communications received. While it is essential to know that operations have been successfully completed (intrinsic feedback), the critical element is the meaning that is derived from extrinsic feedback directly related to the learning outcomes. Using feedback successfully not only involves constructing a response but also ensuring that all participants are enabled with the competencies to interpret ongoing feedback consistent with the characteristics of the learning environment (enabled through the interface) and the anticipated communication process (described by the learning strategy).

Communication

Feedback therefore is the essence of all educational communication, and will define the quality of the overall interaction. By focusing on communication, a more comprehensive understanding of the interactive dynamic will emerge and assist in the creation of prescriptions and guidelines for e-learning. One particular facet of understanding communication is the various influences that affect the construction of meaning:

> Meanings are not to be found or understood exclusively in terms of acts of communication, but are produced within specific cultural contexts. Moreover, communication can be understood as the practice of producing meanings. Communication practices refer to the ways in which systems of meaning are negotiated by participants in a culture and culture can be understood as the totality of communication practices and systems of meaning. (Schirato and Yell, 1996, p 1)

The importance for e-learning is therefore to emphasize the recipients and the meanings they will place on information received, which in turn are based on their particular cultural, gendered and social background and experiences. Equally important is to recognize that e-learning communities are likely to establish their own set of meanings and culture, impacting on the way in which the content is understood. This is significant, as different cohorts of participants may interpret learning activities in different ways. Consequently we must continue to explore ways in which individual learners can gain value by applying their own meanings and interpretations to the exchanges. Re-emphasizing the learners in the overall process, and how they might wish to deal with and interpret the content, remains a critical component in coming to understand better the value that can be obtained from creating educational environments where learners interact and communicate through computers.

Participants as actors

One means by which learners can gain more recognition in the broad educational environment is to cast them in specific roles, such as information gatherer, consolidator or peer assessor, which addresses the potential of e-learning environments to embrace the concepts of actors, theatres and narrative (Laurel, 1991). This option is supported by more recent studies, which have found that where narrative is evident a better learning experience was provided (Plowman, 1996) and that without a context or narrative, the overall understanding of the learning environment can be compromised (Sims, 2001b). For e-learning specifically, the actor analogy has been expressed in terms of tones and voices (Collison *et al*, 2000). The reconstruction of the participant's role in e-learning is therefore a critical factor in making it work effectively, and casting the participant as actor may enhance the way feedback is presented and interpreted (Hedberg and Sims, 2001; Sims, 1999).

If the interactions are constructed and modelled as a play, what role will the learner take – one of audience or actor – and if the latter, what form of actor: improviser, performer or understudy? How these roles are selected and understood will both affect and determine the quality of the dialogue and therefore influence the value of feedback to the participants.

Maximizing the benefits of feedback

Based on the importance and interplay of intrinsic and extrinsic feedback, the link between communication and meaning as well as the role participants might take, the following discussion follows two interrelated threads. The first addresses interactions within e-learning environments and the second presents a set of strategies by which engagement and meaning will result from interactions within e-learning environments. It is only by understanding the relationship between interactivity across an e-learning environment and its impact on effective feedback that the full benefits of collaborative learning will be realized.

E-learning and interactivity

The value of interactivity comes from the extent to which participants in the learning process are able to manipulate the learning environment to meet their own particular needs (Aldrich *et al*, 1998; Sims, 2000). Although these studies focused on computer-mediated learning with content resources, the outcomes have a direct impact on e-learning through four discrete elements of interaction and the associated role that feedback plays in supporting communication to enhance engagement and meaning. These elements are derived from the work of Wagner (1994), Anderson and Garrison (1998) and Sims *et al* (2001), who articulated and elaborated the learner:interface, learner:content, learner:teacher and learner:learner interactions. For this discussion, to reinforce the collaborative nature of e-learning, the teacher and learner roles have been collapsed to that of *participant*, although clearly there are specific and unique roles for the teacher and the learner within the broad range of e-learning, as represented in the interactions shown in Figure 18.2.

Participant:interface

Any e-learning context requires participants to access and interpret the visual presentation of content, implement the actions necessary to navigate through that

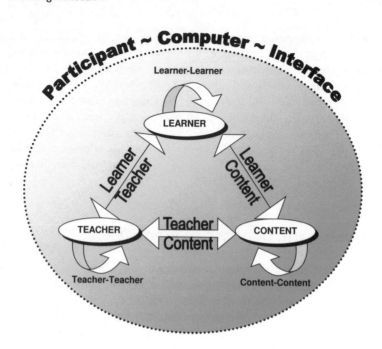

Figure 18.2 *Elements of interactivity with e-learning environments*

content and complete transactions integral to the learning process. The participant must also be able to interpret the communication framework presented by the system and establish an appropriate mental model of that environment in order to play the role necessary to achieve their goals. As described by Hedberg and Sims (2001), ensuring participants have the competencies to work with the interface, and that the interface itself can adapt to their level of ability, is an essential aspect of successful negotiation of the interface, and the ways in which this intrinsic feedback is presented to the participant will impact that negotiation.

Participant:content

A second element of interaction is that between participant and content. Although the discourse surrounding e-learning often focuses on collaborative exchanges and community, it must also include the ways in which participants interact with digitally-available content. This is becoming even more critical with the growing focus on reusable content, learning objects, metadata, intellectual property and copyright, as it affects the means by which participants can access and add to that content base (Sims *et al*, 2001). Content relating to learning outcomes may be prescribed through course requirements, generated by participants or accessed from external sources. Engaging with and deriving meaning from that content can only be secured through participants utilizing communication and feedback mechanisms. It is therefore imperative to ensure that the design and dynamics of the feedback do not interfere with the ability of the participants to work with the content.

For example, many content, interface and feedback elements include sounds and animations, which are integrated by designers for aesthetic or interactive reasons, but which may distract from and interfere with the learning process (Sims, 2001b). Content that is provided by the teacher or sourced by the learner should be screened to minimize the chance of interface elements detracting from its contribution to the learning process by masking or disrupting the feedback process.

Participant:participant

Finally, the most critical interaction is that between the course participants. Any communication between learners and/or teachers implies feedback is active, and meaningful interactions will depend on the ways in which that feedback is presented and understood (Schirato and Yell, 1996). While individual participants may establish socially-oriented communication, where the interactions are related to learning, the management of the feedback will determine the success of the educational programme. Issues such as availability, dynamics and timelines will also impact on the success of communication between teacher and learner. While the teacher may act as an equal participant, when necessary his or her role is to provide an informed view of the content domain through both proactive and reactive feedback processes. A typical sequence of participant:participant interaction is shown in Figure 18.3.

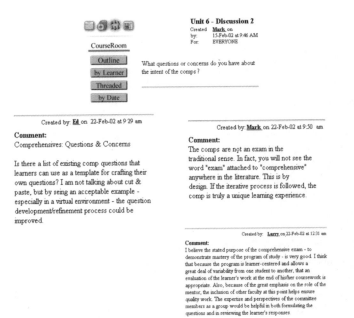

Figure 18.3   *Sequence of proactive and reactive communication and feedback*

Where the interactions are embodied within an accredited course of study, it is critical that learners are also fully aware of the administrative expectations and assessment commitments. In the establishment of relationships between participants, the concept of encounters – the ways in which people meet, interact and communicate within e-learning environments – can be useful, enabling strategies to be implemented that ensure all participants have the skills, experience and confidence to work within that environment (Hedberg and Sims, 2001; Sims, 2001b).

Interactive agents

A new form of what might be termed 'covert' interactivity is also emerging, whereby the system and/or course participants can enable intelligent agents (special software applications) to support the learning environment:

> We see a telelearning system as a society of agents, to use Marvin Minski's term, some of them providing information and explanations, others constructing new information, still others fostering collaboration between agents or providing assistance to the other agents on content, pedagogical process or organization of activities. (Gilbert-Paquette *et al,* 2000, p 6)

These agents support the learner:learner, teacher:teacher and content:content interactions as illustrated in Figure 18.2, and their essential characteristics can be described as:

●   *Learner agents*: supporting research, communications and project management. For example, an agent could be enabled to remind the learner of assessment completion times and to notify them of new Websites with a specific focus on their field of study.
●   *Teacher agents*: supporting searching and communicating, automating routine tasks and research. For example, an agent might inform teachers that all assessment items had been submitted or alert them to recent research outcomes.
●   *Content agents*: supporting search, retrieval and automatic updates; negotiation and monitoring of other interactions. For example, a content agent might maintain the currency of resource materials for a class of study.

Importantly, these agents are able to operate whether or not course participants are online. In this way the feedback takes the form of the content generated by those agents and the meaning for participants will be a function of the accuracy with which those agents perform their tasks and identify materials directly related to the domain of study. The value of these agents will be realized through the extent to which they have appropriate expertise and intelligence to source relevant and reliable material.

Feedback strategies to enhance e-learning

Within the context of these interactive dynamics, the following discussion identifies a set of characteristics of and strategies for feedback that are designed to promote engagement by participants. Within the face-to-face context, the instructor or teacher often plays a dominant role in facilitating and responding to discussion, assessment and activities. With e-learning however, all participants can be empowered and therefore each has to understand the process and value of feedback. Using characteristics of effective feedback as a framework (see Wlodkowski, 1999, pp 245–49), the following strategies elaborate techniques by which feedback can enhance meaning and engagement.

Communities of inquiry

Analysing feedback within e-learning is not only a case of deconstructing the different forms it can take but also ensuring a common understanding of the roles and expectations within the community of learners. Unless there is an agreed set of roles in terms of contributions and format, the feedback, which is ongoing for the duration of the course, will have potentially less meaning. Similarly, the way in which the environment is enabled will also impact on how feedback is viewed and used to construct meaning. Anderson and Garrison (2002) presented three elements for this community of inquiry:

1. *Cognitive presence*: the extent to which the participants in any particular configuration of a community of inquiry are able to construct meaning through sustained communication, using strategies such as exploration and integration.
2. *Social presence*: the ability of learners to project themselves socially and emotionally in a community of inquiry, using affective, interactive and cohesive behaviours.
3. *Teacher presence*: the design, facilitation and direction of cognitive and social processes for the purpose of realizing personally meaningful and educationally worthwhile learning outcomes that can be viewed in terms of the interaction between instructional design, facilitation of discourse and direct instruction.

To illustrate the ways in which some of these dynamics are manifested within e-learning, I will reflect briefly on two scenarios and the impact the facilitation role can take in determining the format and value of the interactions and feedback dynamic.

In the first scenario, learners are presented with a discussion question from the facilitator: 'What is the importance of a Learning Plan?' and the resulting discussion follows a format where individual learners respond to the question and those responses are augmented by feedback from the facilitator. More rarely other students offer reflections to the postings of their colleagues.

While the success of communication between participants in this environment is dependent on their level of motivation, it can also be influenced by the way in which the interface enables discussion and interaction to evolve.

In the second scenario, learners are presented with this activity: 'There is considerable debate on the format of Learning Plans. Compare the two plans provided in the Resource Area and identify what you consider are the benefits of each. Compare your findings with those of other participants and develop a group-summary of the critical elements of a Learning Plan'. In this instance, the activity is focused on achieving a goal rather than finding an answer and demands interactivity between the participants as well as from the facilitator. While the content discipline and learning outcomes can impact on the way such interactions are generated, e-learning is predicated on collaboration and communication and therefore participant:participant interactivity must be established to maximize its benefits.

While the different scenarios will result in different forms of feedback and activity by the participant, their purpose is to illustrate the importance of establishing a community of inquiry where collaboration and contribution become the responsibility of each participant. Once the different elements of *presence* are established, the ongoing contribution by participants will be manifested through feedback and to maintain its effectiveness will require integration of many of the following attributes.

Informative and meaningful

Providing feedback must do more than simply acknowledge the submission: the learner values feedback that relates directly to his or her efforts and the extent to which it is on- or off-task. For example, making a posting that challenges or questions a particular concept requires more feedback than 'Thank you, Rod'. This becomes even more important when dealing with learners and teachers who are considered peers – the feedback needs to both respond as well as augment the original argument.

A more appropriate response might be 'Rod, you have taken Mary's concept of instructional design and added an interesting dimension of influence. How would you relate that to the traditional ADDIE model?' Not only does the feedback acknowledge and praise, but also sets an additional goal for the learner to pursue. This example highlights an increasing requirement for contributors of feedback to understand the environment and develop the necessary skills to create a valuable learning space for all participants.

Granular

Feedback also needs to be provided in manageable *chunks*. In many threaded discussions, all prompts and participant responses can be displayed to enable quick access; however, after a semester's work, the number of responses can be in the thousands. While individual elements of the thread may be appropriately sized, being able to recall a specific response or to identify an appropriate place in the thread to make a new response can be problematic with such high volume. To address this potential limitation, the participants can negotiate the ways in which threads will be titled and responses classified – in other words establish operational standards for that specific set of interactions. Similarly, responses should be relatively concise, with longer elaborations assigned to attachments.

Timely

Being prompt with feedback does not necessarily mean immediate, as there are many instances when a delay in feedback can provide better rewards than incremental conformation (Alessi and Trollip, 2001). For the e-learning environment, it is the timeliness of feedback that is as important as its promptness:

> Many learners report that turnaround time is one of the most important aspects of good feedback. In an open and distance-learning environment, email is a major means of communication. Learners often become anxious when they do not receive a quick response to their concern. The demand for a response can impose an unrealistic burden on the faculty member, especially if it involves reviewing a course paper or project. One simple solution that seems to work well is to send an email indicating that the message or product has been received and a date or time when the learner can expect to hear back from you. Many messages can be responded to on the spot. It is also important to provide meaningful comments. Learners have reported that short, terse comments such as 'good job', 'nicely done' or 'this is an A paper' with no further elaboration often reflect negatively on the faculty member as learners often perceive this response as meaningless and tend to feel the member may not even have read the paper or project. (Rossman, 2002)

The implementation of timely feedback is determined by the design strategies that underpin the learning environment and activities, and the extent to which participants within the programme are familiar with the expectations and protocols of the communication. Certainly within higher education, the critical element is for learners to be informed of the standards for the provision of feedback and the form it is expected to take.

Within discussion groups, individual learners can see immediately that their post has been accepted and the number of responses (feedback) subsequently made to their post. However, rather than responding to each posting, a standard could be set whereby the facilitator (or one of the participants) undertakes to provide a summary of issues raised. How often feedback is provided should therefore be the result of negotiation between course participants. Alternatively, agreement could be reached that the facilitator will respond to postings within 24 hours. While the number of participants and their respective workloads will impact on the negotiation, options such as peer-group assessment and feedback will alleviate the demands on the facilitator to respond to each and every posting.

Individual

One of the important dynamics emerging from implementations of online learning is the need for participants to be acknowledged as individuals, and strategies to address this are common in distance education literature. Within e-learning interactions, developing this shared understanding of roles will enhance individual submissions and assist the establishment of a community based on feedback that is differentiated across participants. This can best be achieved if the person making the feedback has a good knowledge of the person they are responding to and can therefore personalize the exchange. Where numbers of participants are large, it may not be possible for one facilitator to respond to individual contributions. Nevertheless, basic strategies can be implemented to assist this process, such as asking participants what feedback they prefer, establishing their readiness for feedback and ensuring that it has been received and understood.

Another means to individualize the communication and feedback process is to assign roles to participants so they undertake tasks specific to that role. This can be achieved using established forms of activity such as the case study or enabling students to take on a 'virtual persona' whereby they can act out within the learning environment. How this is achieved will depend on the existing community of participants, their familiarity with the e-learning context and the nature of the field of study.

Making it work

These feedback strategies provide insights to enhancing e-learning collaborative environments. However, despite the collaborative nature of the medium, learners are working independently and require models by which to compare their work and construct their own understanding.

Figure 18.4 demonstrates one means by which the environment could be presented to the participant such that all responses to a specific topic are available for viewing in multiple windows and that, if appropriate, the participant could then use these responses to construct further meaning for their own context.

Conclusion

Within this chapter the value of feedback to e-learning environments has been addressed in relation to the essential aspects of communication and interactivity. The ways in which individual participants derive meaning from communication, and subsequently engage with the course content, is dependent on the quality of the feedback created during that interactive process. However, despite the

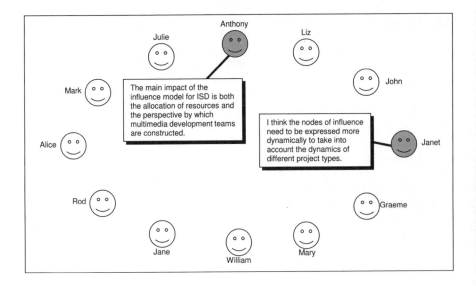

Figure 18.4   *Individual participants extract meaning from community*

proliferation of online learning systems, questions continue to be directed towards the effectiveness of e-learning, especially where it is driven by content rather than communication.

Based on this analysis, it is the way in which e-learning is implemented that is critical, demanding communication, the two-way process where participants, people and resources act upon and have an effect on each other. However, this can only be achieved where feedback is used to provide those individual participants with the means to maintain an ongoing dialogue with their fellow participants. And it is the way this is facilitated that is critical:

> Remember that sometimes the best form of feedback is simply to encourage learners to move forward to the next, more challenging learning opportunity. Too much comment by instructors tends to emphasize our power and can diminish our role as co-learners. (Wlodkowski, 1999, p 249)

It is through this process that engagement and meaning will be generated, and the challenge is to enable participants to achieve *interactive balance* (Sims, 2001b), whereby all actions and inputs are consistent with their mental model, preventing or minimizing any interference with the feedback process.

We know much about sound educational practice, and the provision of feedback is one of the critical elements within that practice. Applying this understanding to the unique environment afforded by e-learning will ensure its ultimate success. What makes good feedback is adherence to accepted principles and ensuring all course participants have a common understanding of the protocols for their learning environment. Equally important is the maintenance of respect for the unique contribution of each and every participant.

References

Aldrich, F, Rogers, Y and Scaife, M (1998) Getting to grips with 'interactivity': helping teachers assess the educational value of CD-ROMs, *British Journal of Educational Technology*, **29** (4), 321–32

Alessi, S M and Trollip, S R (2001) *Multimedia for Learning: Methods and development* (3rd edn), Allyn and Bacon, Boston, MA

Anderson, T and Garrison, D R (1998) New roles for learners at a distance, in *Distance Learning in Higher Education: Institutional responses for quality outcomes,* ed C Gibson, Atwood, Madison, WI

Anderson, T and Garrison, D R (2002) Understanding higher education in a CMC context: current research and a peek at the future. Presented at Deakin University, February

Brennan, R, McFadden, M and Law, E (2001) *Review of Research: All that glitters is not gold: Online delivery of education and training,* NCVER, Leabrook, SA

Collison, G, Elbaum, B, Haavind, S and Tinker, R (2000) *Facilitating Online Learning: Effective strategies for moderators,* Atwood, Madison, WI

Gilbert-Paquette, G, de la Teja, I and Dufresne, A (2000) *Explora: An open virtual campus.* Accessed 3 March 2002, from www.licef.teluq.uquebec.ca/gp/doc/publi/campus/edmediaexplora.doc

Hedberg, J and Sims, R (2001) Speculations on design team interactions, *Journal of Interactive Learning Research,* **12** (2/3), pp 189–204

Laurel, B (1991) *Computers as Theatre,* Addison Wesley, Reading, MA

Laurillard, D (1993) *Rethinking University Teaching: A framework for the effective use of educational technology,* Routledge, London

Palloff, R M and Pratt, K (1999) *Building Learning Communities in Cyberspace,* Jossey-Bass, San Francisco, CA

Plowman, L (1996) Narrative, linearity and interactivity: making sense of interactive multimedia, *British Journal of Educational Technology,* **27** (2), pp 92–105

Rossman, M (2002) Personal email communication received as part of an instructional course run by Capella University

Schirato, T and Yell, S (1996) *Communication and Cultural Literacy: An introduction,* Allen and Unwin, St Leonards, NSW

Sims, R (1999) Interactivity on stage: strategies for learner–designer communication, *Australian Journal of Educational Technology,* **15** (3), pp 257–72

Sims, R (2000) An interactive conundrum: constructs of interactivity and learning theory, *Australian Journal of Educational Technology,* **16** (1), pp 45–57

Sims, R (2001a) The online learning alchemist: preventing gold turning into lead, in *Proceedings of Ed-Media 2001,* eds C Montgomerie and J Viteli, AACE, Tampere, Finland

Sims, R (2001b) Usability and learning in online environments: a case of interactive encounters, in *Proceedings of Ed-Media 2001,* eds C Montgomerie and J Viteli, AACE, Tampere, Finland

Sims, R, Dobbs, G and Hand, T (2001) Proactive evaluation: new perspectives for ensuring quality in online learning applications, in *Meeting at the Crossroads: Proceedings of the 18th Annual Conference of the Australasian Society for Computers in Learning in Tertiary Education,* eds G Kennedy, M Keppell, C McNaught and T Petrovic, Biomedical Multimedia Unit, The University of Melbourne, Melbourne

Wagner, E D (1994) In support of a functional definition of interaction, *The American Journal of Distance Education,* **8** (2), pp 6–29

Wlodkowski, R J (1999) *Enhancing Adult Motivation to Learn* (revised edn), Jossey-Bass, San Francisco, CA

Chapter 19

Fundamentals for structuring feedback in an online learning environment

Christopher K Morgan

Introduction

It is well accepted that active learners benefit from being aware of their learning progress and look to their instructors for feedback. This chapter investigates how the technologies associated with e-learning can be used to leverage the provision of this feedback. In doing so it will examine how such leveraging of feedback might influence student persistence.

In order to structure feedback for optimum gain within an online learning environment, we must first understand what it is about feedback that provides value for the student. Once this is understood, the focus then becomes one of identifying whether there is anything special about the tools of e-learning that, if used astutely, can add further educational value.

Much has been investigated on why some students drop out of courses. Much less has been written about why other students do not drop out. As lack of adequate feedback can be a contributor to student attrition, then one could well presume that the provision of adequate feedback contributes to student retention. But is this too simplistic? The value of feedback lies in its impact on the learner. The instructor needs to think through the development or change that is intended in the learner as a result of providing feedback. How can the tools of an e-learning environment be used to help secure improvements in the learning process?

Learner responses to feedback can vary. It is generally understood that as one progresses through a programme of study the depth of that study will increase and the learning expectations will be of a higher order. Yet despite these rising demands, some students manage to achieve improved grades as they progress through their programme. Why is this so? Could such students have progressively developed their academic skills and learnt how to become more effective learners? If so, how have they achieved this? It is the contention of this chapter that feedback is the key to such a learning improvement and that feedback can be facilitated through astute use of an e-learning environment.

In order to address the issue of using e-learning feedback to improve student persistence, this chapter will initially look briefly at the role of feedback in the learning process and at how this role may relate to student persistence. It will then examine the implications for instructors seeking to capitalize on this while operating in an e-learning environment.

Educational role and impact of feedback

In reflecting on the early work of Lewin (1951), Kolb (1984) conceived the learning process as a four-stage cycle, which is:

> facilitated best by an integrated process that begins with here-and-now experience followed by collection of data and observations about that experience. The data are then analysed and the conclusions of this analysis are fed back to the actors in the experience for their use in the modification of their behaviour and choice of new experiences. (p 21)

This process is illustrated in Figure 19.1.

The important role of feedback is the aspect of Kolb's learning model that is of particular relevance here. The observations and reflections that form the feedback can be derived internally by learners or be communicated to them from external sources. While the internal generation of feedback by learners is important, the concern of this chapter is the feedback provided by the instructor and others as part of the teaching function. The medium for this external provision of feedback to students can be an e-learning environment.

Inadequate feedback processes, Lewin (1951) argues, are likely to result in an imbalance between observation and action, resulting in ineffective learning. Students not achieving learning successes can become demotivated and are more at risk of dropping out (see, for example, Gibson and Graff, 1992). There is a large array of factors that can lead to student attrition (Kember, 1995) and only some

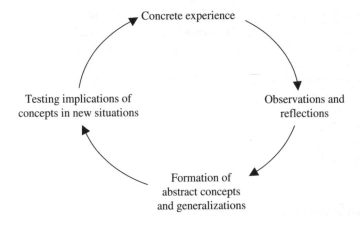

Figure 19.1 *Kolb's learning cycle*

of these are within the influence of instructors. Various writers such as Woodley and Partlett (1983) and Garland (1993) have contributed to categorizing these barriers to participation in four categories of persistence:

1. *Situational* – arise from a student's particular life circumstances, such as changed employment situation, changed marital status or having a baby.
2. *Institutional* – difficulties students experience with the institution, such as admission requirements, course pacing and limited support services.
3. *Dispositional* – personal problems that impact on the students' persistence behaviour, such as their attitudes, confidence, learning styles and motivation.
4. *Epistemological* – impediments caused by discipline content or else the relative perceived difficulty of that content.

A study by Morgan and Tam (1999) revealed that it was common for non-persisting students to encounter many such barriers. Instructors who lift learner morale and motivate through their feedback have a dispositional influence. Similarly, when constructive interaction occurs through feedback it may have an epistemological influence as the student's correct performance is reinforced (or else reoccurrence of incorrect performance is avoided due to the instructional feedback provided when errors are made).

The motivating effect of positive feedback should not be underestimated. There is considerable evidence (for instance in studies reported by Schunk, 1989) to support the contention that superior academic achievement occurs as students develop confidence in their own capabilities. By receiving encouraging information about their progress and learning achievements, the learners build their efficacy beliefs as they succeed and progress. Similarly Tuckman (1999) has reported on a sequence of experiments that confirm a link between obtaining regular perform-ance feedback and the outcome of improved academic success.

There is no less a need for such interaction and feedback in the online environment than in any other. Irrespective of the medium, the processes of interaction and feedback add value that results in improving quality and success. It has been claimed that superior outcomes can be achieved in the online environment. For instance, in writing about asynchronous online interactions and feedback, Garrison (1997) enthused about the disciplined and rigorous form of thinking and communicating that is prompted by means of the reflective and explicit nature of the written word. It is this opportunity for reflection that is seen as a factor in students making connections between ideas and constructing their own knowledge.

Implications for instructors

The e-learning environment is one where otherwise disconnected students can interact with each other, and with their tutor, on an ongoing basis throughout their programme of study. Other strategies, such as weekend or other residential schools and audio and video conferencing, provide only limited opportunities for distance education students to interact in this manner, as they are not available on a continuing basis. Students able to capitalize on the enhanced scope for interactivity through e-learning can gain a sense of community rarely experienced outside the on-campus situation.

There will be qualitative differences between the value to students of real-time verbal feedback in a traditional on-campus tutorial and the asynchronous written interactions of computer conferencing. The reflective and precise nature of the latter is profoundly different from the spontaneous and less structured nature of oral discourse in the former. Similarly the ephemeral nature of oral communication is to its disadvantage while the ability of a written record to be stored and revisited adds further to its value to the learner.

Some fundamentals

Unfortunately many students are reluctant contributors to discussion irrespective of the medium of instruction being employed, and this has implications for the amount and quality of interaction that will occur. In the e-learning environment, posting a message either to their instructor or to their class can be a major step for such students. Instructors generally recognize this and commonly employ an introductory strategy that facilitates each student posting an item on the class electronic bulletin board. While this may serve to familiarize otherwise reluctant or unskilled students with the technology, unless their contribution is positively acknowledged, it is not likely to ease any self-doubts or to build motivation. This suggests that it may be important for messages posted by students to receive a quick and sensitive response.

The question remains, however, as to the feasibility of providing students with the ideal of some positive acknowledgement of all their electronic contributions.

It may be quite unreasonable to expect the instructor to take full responsibility for this. An option may be for the instructor to arrange for the sharing of this responsibility around the student group for acknowledging that each posting has at least been read and noted.

In the face-to-face situation people usually know straightaway whether or not they have been heard. This may be through eye contact or other non-verbal forms such as a smile, nod or shake of the head, and that may be sufficient reassurance. In the online environment, no such feedback subtleties exist and acknowledgement has to be direct and obvious.

Students need to be thought of as fragile and sensitive participants. There can be many factors that contribute to someone's lack of willingness to participate. Reluctance may be due to a fear of being seen as stupid or inadequate, and this may be the reason why some people 'lurk'. While self-doubt can be a factor, so too may be a lack of keyboarding skills or perhaps a time-consuming approach in which they hand write a message before typing it rather than directly entering it onscreen. Some individuals will have a preference for oral over written communication, have a busy life that allows them little time to participate in the online community, perceive little value for them in participation, or any combination of such factors.

Clearly it takes some skill to provide feedback that is sensitive as well as being honest and constructive. In the online environment, where students have never seen their fellow students or their instructor, there may be individuals whose lack of confidence means they are especially tentative in their ventures into a somewhat public forum. Their particular sensitivities may make it difficult for them to deal with feedback given to them, even though it may not be negative. Of course, there can be those at the opposite extreme who readily engage with others online and who may so overdo their contributions that they dominate a forum.

Any response to a message a student posts should help and encourage further participation. Therefore the tone and style of responses are important, and consideration might be given to establishing some rules for all conferencing participants either at the outset or by way of intervention as necessary. The rules could address not only what is to be posted but also the language and tone of interactions. Clearly a personable response rather than a carefully crafted academic but cold one is more likely to contribute to the building of a welcoming community of learners. Palloff and Pratt (1999) press the point that achieving successful online facilitation requires the development of an electronic personality that is recognized as honest, responsive, relevant, respectful, open and empowering.

In any learning interaction there are rules of engagement. While a tutor is likely to encourage students to express themselves, sensitivity and respect for the views and feelings of others are expected. The tutor may point out to all that feedback should be constructive rather than destructive, and while responses will be expressed according to the style of the speaker's personality and may at times be provocative, they are nevertheless not to be offensive and are expected to conform with community standards.

One feature of the online environment is that the creator of the message has the advantage of being able to reflect prior to hitting the send button. This opportunity for reflection before communicating can reduce the likelihood of offensive behaviour occurring and probably makes it even less tolerable when it does. When someone goes outside the acceptable boundaries, then those in the learning community should be prepared to say so. The tutor may need to intervene and spell out some boundaries and limitations.

Automatic, personal, or both?

Feedback is timely when it is provided at an appropriate point in the learning process to highlight students' weaknesses and give guidance on corrective actions. It also enables students to evaluate and monitor their own progress. The timeliness of feedback responses is crucial to the learner. Clearly, if the notion is accepted that, as shown in Figure 19.1, a role of feedback in learning is to inform future actions, there is considerably less value for learners if feedback arrives too late for them to use. For instance, feedback on a way of thinking would likely be seen as having less value if received after a related assessment item had been submitted than if it had been received beforehand.

Few would question the students' preference for immediate and personal feedback by their tutor. With larger groups, however, this might be logistically difficult. Dewar and Whittington (2000) believe it is not feasible to acknowledge every comment made by online students. To overcome this, perhaps feedback could be structured so that responses are automatically generated by the technology in use. This can provide advantages such as giving feedback rapidly even when there are large numbers of students, and when the instructor is not available for example at weekends, evenings or at holiday times.

Some advocate the use of databases for this purpose and see their ongoing improvement as learning resource items are progressively added. When good quality student work is received it can, with the author's permission, be added to the database and made available for reference by future students. Taylor (2001) describes how this can be done:

> (Computer Mediated Communication) provides a rich source of thoughtful interactions, which can be structured, tagged and stored in a database and subsequently exploited for tuition purposes on a recurring basis through the application of automated response systems. It is this judicious use of auto-mated response systems, which has the potential to transform the cost-effectiveness of distance education and thereby to meet the growing demand for access to lifelong learning. (p 5)

The successful conversion of such vision into effective realities would have particular attractions, such as improved institutional responsiveness. It is envisaged that this use of technology could accomplish the ideal of providing a level of affordable, round-the-clock, instant response. This has obvious appeal where individual students may be working independently in different time zones and at different times of the day or night.

The University of Southern Queensland in Australia has developed prototypes of 'intelligent object databases', which can be searched by pre-specified key words. When an electronic query from a student is received, the search engine seeks an appropriate match with a previously asked question. If successful, a response to the current question is triggered. During these early days, the response generated by the system is monitored to check for its appropriateness as a personal response to the student. The goal is to reach a level of development and sophistication at which the system can function without the necessity for human intervention. If that can be achieved, then this system of feedback will be able to provide immediate pedagogical advice to students at any time and at minimal variable cost.

While Taylor (2001) talks of personalized responses, others such as Ryan (2000) fear that responses will cease to be personalized. If effective feedback is personal and individual, then can de-personalized computer responses be truly effective? Ryan talks of how students pore over written responses and comments on their work and the degree to which they value engagement with their instructor whether it is by very personal assignment feedback or through other direct interactions. She sees the linking of automated feedback systems with student assessment as downgrading the teaching/learning process. She equates this to the employment of Skinnerian 'teaching machines', with the result that surface rather than deep learning is achieved.

Nevertheless, it should be recognized that automated feedback is potentially effective as it is based on individual responses to progressive operator decisions. Computerized multiple-choice tests used formatively can be marked automatically and feedback provided instantly. If they are Web-based, for example packages such as PsyCAL (Psychology Computer Assisted Learning), then they may be accessed at any time from any place, whether that be on or off campus, and completed at the student's preferred pace. Once the answers have been submitted the program immediately marks them and generates a feedback page, which refers students to sections in the recommended texts that should be revised. In a study reported by Buchanan (1998, p 73) it was found that the great majority of students were using the program as intended and were purposefully investigating the references to which they were directed. Only a small minority opted for a less pedagogically sound approach and used it as a Skinnerian teaching machine with the consequent achievement of surface learning.

The advantages of this automated feedback approach in formative assessment easily explain its growing popularity and it is not difficult to find other examples of applications. For instance Velan and Kumar (2000) enthuse about their use of proprietary software to furnish their medical students with online formative self-assessments. They point out that feedback is not only instant to students but it also provides academic staff with information about conceptual difficulties encountered by students in particular areas of the course.

Scepticism towards using technology to generate automatic feedback arises from the fear that it may trivialize content knowledge and undermine the attainment of higher order learning outcomes. It is unlikely that supporters of any recognized learning theory could find comfort were this to occur. While assessment approaches such as true/false questions, multiple-choice questions, matching exercises, and 'fill in the blank space' activities may be readily used to provide instant feedback in an e-learning context, they are also prone to be used to obtain regurgitation of received rather than constructed knowledge via low level memorization of facts rather than higher order learning. Those assessment tools seen as most readily adaptable to the provision of automated feedback are less likely to be able to develop, first, conceptual understanding, and second, the ability to apply, evaluate, explain and make new meaning connections.

Additionally, it should not be presumed that instant feedback is optimal. Merrill *et al* (1992) found that when students are dealing with a complex problem, human tutors tend to regulate the timing of their feedback rather than provide immediate feedback at every step. They weigh the relative importance of the error before providing feedback. Research by Farquhar and Regian (1994) on intelligent simulation revealed some contexts where delayed feedback resulted in improved learning outcomes. It may be that instant automated feedback does not allow time for internal reflection by learners as they construct knowledge.

While there are clear advantages associated with automated feedback, it has to be recognized that there are reservations associated with having complete reliance on it. Consider, for instance, an organization with an educational goal of building a mutually supportive learning community to achieve better educational outcomes, including improved student completion rates. Such an organization would be unlikely to rely completely on automated student feedback. Consequently successful virtual campuses, such as the University of Phoenix, De Vry and the Duke Global MBA systems, opt for low student-to-staff ratios to enable their staff to give personal attention to their online students.

Educators in the e-learning environment need to consider whether a mix of feedback strategies should be employed. Each approach can provide different values, and any particular deficiencies of one approach may be offset by the contributions of the other approaches. For example, where classes are large or where there are frequent student submissions there may be value in combining automated feedback with peer feedback to give timely, manageable and personalized feedback to students.

The issues that revolve around utilizing students to provide their peers with personalized feedback in an online environment are fundamentally the same as in any other learning situation. These include the need for instructors to monitor the peer evaluations and to be alerted to students who may be doing poorly and who need intervention.

While the issues may be the same, in an e-learning situation the technology enhances the opportunity to resolve them. Henderson *et al* (1997) cite one such instance in which a database was employed to generate information about peer feedback for monitoring purposes. Here students were expected to link their answers to a selection of exercises to the class Web site that was available for viewing by all other students in the class as well as the instructor. Students were required to comment on a certain number of submissions by other students and to give them a score. Different tools were then used to facilitate the instructor's need to resolve issues of validity and reliability such as detecting large variations in scores on an exercise and detecting exercises with unusually low or high scores. This process was seen to have the potential to improve the collaborative work skills of students as well as contribute to higher levels of understanding.

Leveraging feedback benefits through e-learning

A choice of e-learning feedback approaches is emerging for instructors to utilize as they seek to improve educational outcomes; the following is a short selection.

Distributing selected exemplars

Electronic receipt by course instructors of student work lends itself to storage and ready retrieval of selected pieces of work. This can be a rich educational resource to use with other students through the feedback process. If a student's submission lacks depth or some other component, an appropriate example from the electronic store can be retrieved and sent to the student for guidance. Such examples can provide the necessary scaffolding for other students to follow.

Instructors employing this strategy will need to develop mechanisms for obtaining permission from the authors for their items to be placed in the electronic store and to be used in this way for teaching (a simple electronic pro forma seeking approval should suffice). Additionally, depending on the extent of the collection and the breadth of purpose, instructors will likely need to organize their electronic collection in such a way that they can access the items efficiently for this feedback strategy.

Web-based forms

Web-based forms have been found to be valuable for assessment purposes. These can also be used as diagnostic tools that instructors can employ to alert themselves to the need to intervene and provide timely feedback. The following is an example of one such interchange between instructor and student:

'good job identifying the primary differences (between Piaget and Vygotsky). Your response is right on target. Should this be an exam question, you might want to elaborate a bit on each difference (eg, give an example of each of these differences related to a teaching strategy). Thank you for taking advantage of this opportunity'. The Web-based assessment form creates an iterative process to learning and growing in that the student is then able to provide a new response for further feedback. 'Thanks for the feedback. You suggested that I may need examples of the differences of Vygotsky-vs-Piaget, and I'd like to run some by you to see if I am applying the theory correctly.' (Hazari and Schnorr, 1999, p 34)

Peer feedback as assessment components

One common view is that students need to be given very good reasons to participate in optional activities associated with their courses. Therefore to ask students to give feedback to their peers in an e-learning situation is courting disappointment unless there is some inducement associated with it. One strategy to secure participation is to structure the assessment process in such a way that students will be rewarded for providing quality feedback to their peers. Kinross and Morgan (2001) report on such a situation in which students were asked to respond to set online activities and provide feedback on the postings of their peers. They suggest the following criteria for instructors to use when assessing peer feedback for the online environment:

● commitment to undertaking the activities in a professional manner;
● evidence of a supportive, positive and inquiring attitude to others' comments, whatever their level of experience and expertise;
● adherence to timelines as set;
● engagement with the content in a full and focused manner.

Students can be asked to engage with and comment upon a wide range of activity types. These include issues for debate relevant to the course being studied, challenge exercises and problems to be solved, readings for critique, reviews of linked Web sites, and tasks such as the development of individual student learning contracts. With the latter, students can be allocated to small learning groups and be required to give feedback to their peers as they develop their learning contract for their individual project with the instructor. Matters they can help define and refine include the scope and goals of the project, methodology and timelines, and assessment criteria and weightings. These processes may not be feasible for particular student cohorts other than in the e-learning context.

Conclusions

Some may consider providing feedback in the e-learning environment as being unacceptably time-consuming and burdensome. This is most likely to be the case if the approach is to use technology merely as a vehicle to replicate conventional interactions between instructors and students. However, those prepared to review their teaching paradigm may discover that technology offers new opportunities to facilitate the achievement of learning goals. Palloff and Pratt (1999, p 20) put this saliently:

> The development of community as part of the learning process helps to create a learning experience that is empowering and rich. It is essential to impart the importance of this process to faculty in order to maximize the use of the electronic medium in education. Without it, we are simply recreating our tried

and true educational model and calling it innovative, without fully exploring the potential this medium holds.

The e-learning environment provides instructors with the opportunity to achieve high level learning impact through their astute use of feedback to their students. The tools are sufficiently broad to enable a bewildering array of strategies to be employed to fulfil a spectrum of teaching and learning visions. Learner-centred approaches can involve automated formative assessment systems to provide rapid feedback to help students monitor and evaluate their progress. Other approaches can be more personalized and involve peer as well as instructor feedback. The potential benefits for the teaching/learning process of e-learning feedback strategies are being progressively identified. As further discovery, development and refinement occur, those potential benefits will increasingly be realized.

It was Woodley (1987) who made use of the analogy of cost/benefit analysis when describing students as undergoing a continuous evaluation of their experience by weighing up the negatives and positives involved in continuing with a course. By improving the student's experience by leveraging the provision of feedback through the tools of e-learning, instructors can affect dispositional and epistemological factors associated with student persistence. This influence can be expected to help tip the balance towards the positive side of the student's experience and result in improved retention rates.

References

Buchanan, T (1998) Using the World Wide Web for formative assessment, *Journal of Educational Technology Systems*, **27** (1), pp 71–79

Dewar, T and Whittington, D (2000) Teaching online: a new skill set, in *Working Knowledge: Productive learning at work*, ed C Symes, pp 113–18, University of Technology, Sydney

Farquhar, J and Regian, J (1994) The type and timing of feedback within an intelligent console-operations tutor, *Proceedings of the Annual Meeting of the Human Factors and Ergonomics Society*, **38**, pp 1225–31

Garland, M (1993) Student perceptions of the situational, institutional, dispositional and epistemological barriers to persistence, *Distance Education*, **14** (2), pp 181–98

Garrison, R (1997) Computer conferencing: the post-industrial age of distance education, *Open Learning*, **12** (2), pp 3–11

Gibson, C and Graff, A (1992) Impacts of adults' preferred learning styles and perception of barriers on completion of external baccalaureate degree programs, *Journal of Distance Education*, **7** (1), pp 39–51

Hazari, S and Schnorr, D (1999) Leveraging student feedback to improve teaching in Web-based courses, *THE Journal (Technological Horizons in Education)*, **26** (11), p 30

Henderson, T, Rada, R and Chen, C (1997) Quality management of student-student evaluations, *Journal of Educational Computing Research*, **17** (3), pp 199–215

Kember, D (1995) *Open Learning Courses for Adults: A model of student progress,* Educational Technology Publications, Hillsdale NJ

Kinross, C and Morgan, C (2001) Improving interactivity online for land management distance education students. Paper presented at Ninth Cambridge International Conference on Open and Distance Learning, Cambridge

Kolb, D (1984) *Experiential Learning,* Prentice Hall, New Jersey

Lewin, K (1951) *Field Theory in Social Sciences,* Harper and Row, New York

Merrill, D, Reiser, B, Ranney, M and Trafton, J (1992) Effective tutoring techniques: a comparison of human tutors and intelligent tutoring systems, *The Journal of the Learning Sciences,* **2** (3), 277–305

Morgan, C and Tam, M (1999) Unravelling the complexities of distance education student attrition, *Distance Education,* **20** (1), pp 96–108

Palloff, R and Pratt, K (1999) *Building Learning Communities in Cyberspace,* Jossey-Bass, San Francisco CA

Ryan, Y (2000) Assessment in online learning. Paper presented at the 2000 National Teaching Forum of Australian Universities Teaching Committee, Canberra, Australia

Schunk, D (1989) Self-efficacy and cognitive skill learning, in *Research on Motivation in Education,* eds C Ames and R Ames, pp 13–44, Academic Press, San Diego CA

Taylor, J (2001) *Fifth Generation Distance Education,* Higher Education Series (Rep No 40), Department of Education, Training and Youth Affairs, Canberra

Tuckman, B (1999) A tripartite model of motivation for achievement: attitude, drive, strategy. Paper presented at the annual meeting of the American Psychological Association, August, Boston, MA

Velan, G and Kumar, R (2000) Effectiveness of online assessments as well as criterion-referenced and project-based summative assessments. Paper presented at the 2000 National Teaching Forum of Australian Universities Teaching Committee, Canberra

Woodley, A (1987) Understanding adult student dropout, in *Open Learning for Adults,* eds M Thorpe and D Gudgeon, Longman, Harlow, Essex

Woodley, A and Partlett, M (1983) Student drop-out, *Teaching at a Distance,* **24**, pp 2–23

Commentary

On learning and teaching with technology: principles and practices

Andrew Higgins

The use of information and communication technologies (ICT) for leveraging the learning and teaching experience is becoming endemic among the educational community. In an ideal world, educators and researchers would examine the impact of new developments in teaching and learning with a view to communicating how the innovation might impact educational decision making, both at the teacher and the systemic levels. Learning and teaching do not occur in an artificial environment but within the parameters of society at large. Consequently, teachers adopt innovations without always being able to understand their full learning and teaching implications for them and their students. This is not necessarily a bad thing, because if no one adopted an innovation in practice, there might be nothing to evaluate and little knowledge gained.

This book contains a number of working examples of how ICT is being used to 'leverage' learning and teaching processes. It adds more data for researchers to use in their evaluation of the effectiveness of these technologies. Rapid evolution in technologies offers students and teachers an array of challenges that are being met in schools and tertiary institutions in the western world. It has been suggested that the 'higher education community has a lot to learn regarding how, and in what ways, technology can enhance the teaching and learning process, particularly at a distance' (Phipps *et al,* 1999, p 29).

This book demonstrates how a number of academics and teachers have used ICT to enhance learning, teaching and the assessment of learning outcomes for students. Research needs to be carried out to establish the impact of ICT, including its impacts and implications for learning tasks, learner characteristics, student motivation and teachers' skills and attitudes. The activities reported in this book clearly indicate that learning and teaching issues are foremost in the academics' minds when they implement these technologies. To that extent, this book helps to lift understanding learning and teaching more generally.

Coming through the book very strongly is the central role played by the human factor in education. There are examples here of a shift in the roles of teachers from being the 'sage on the stage' to the 'guide on the side' when fostering independent student learning. Designing student's learning experience involves not only the teacher, but also the learning process, design expert, technology expert, resource management specialists and perhaps project managers. Nowhere does the book suggest that using technology to leverage learning and teaching is a cheap option, or a threat to the teacher. If anything, the contributions in the book suggest that the role of the teacher, although changed, is in fact significantly enhanced.

ICT and distance learning specialists claim that access to learning off-campus is enhanced by the use of computers. Questions need to be asked if the 'quality' of the computer-mediated learning experiences leads to similar outcomes on and off-campus. Implications for this are issues related to access to bandwidth, technical support, affordability of hardware and ability to upgrade software systems.

That technology is having a major impact on the public in general and on students in particular is not in question. Technology is having and will continue to have a deep impact on learning and teaching almost everywhere. Teachers using technology to enhance the flexibility of their work are turning to what was the Cinderella of the academic community: distance learning. However, as this book demonstrates, teachers using information technologies have gone beyond the 'correspondence' version of distance education and moved it to a completely new level. The transition to a new kind of learning and teaching brings with it issues needing to be addressed in novel ways; for example, as access to learning increases, the characteristics of the student population change. As a result, teachers find it appropriate to consider various ways of addressing the circumstances in which students find themselves.

The last decade of the 20th century saw a sea-change in the language and practice of education. Lifelong learning skills and criterion-referenced performance-based student learning outcomes now drive curriculum statements in ways never before imagined, even though the terms are not welcomed by many who teach. Simultaneously, the growing use of ICT provides an opportunity for both curriculum and teaching strategies to be revisited. The philosophy underpinning these changes is also more evident. Concepts such as activity-based learning, teachers as facilitators of learning and collaborative learning are central to the learning and teaching processes. This book demonstrates how some of these principles and processes are translated into practice with the use of ICT.

A feature of these new learning environments is the ease with which students access knowledge and data sources from around the world. Libraries are renamed 'Information Service Centres', partly because they now rely less on books but also because they provide access to electronic information that would otherwise be inaccessible to most. Students, as co-constructors of learning, can make better-informed choices about the validity and reliability of the data they use to learn. The resultant implications of using these sources for intellectual property rights and for copyright law resonate through legal circles.

Receiving responses on the work they do substantially enhances students' learning. Teachers find providing feedback one of their most onerous yet rewarding tasks. The electronic environment provides pathways for students to communicate with each other and with teachers in ways not before envisaged. Sections of this book concerning opportunities for socialization and feedback demonstrate that ICT is capable of providing a very high level and quality of support.

So, what does this book have to say about the teaching and learning transaction? First, it recognizes that subject matter-based teaching is the core of most higher education academic work. It finds that carefully created models designed to engage students in interactive learning are integral to the use of information and communications technologies.

Second, the book reminds readers that although academics aim to produce student-centred and interactive learning, this is sometimes daunting for students because it requires them to manage complex information in open-ended learning environments necessitating additional support strategies to enable them to cope with this challenge.

Third, the book draws on respected educational practitioners to show that students learn a great deal from each other and that students can use computer mediated communication to support one another in their construction of knowledge.

Fourth, the book recognizes that traditional methods of assessment do not readily translate to an online learning environment. This dissonance provides an opportunity to develop criterion-referenced, motivational, affective and cognitive assessment strategies.

Fifth, the authors show that feedback given to students enhances their learning and that workload, type of feedback and form of feedback need to be carefully considered to maximize its impacts.

In summary, this is a book full of carefully collected experiences of practitioners that stand to add significantly to our understanding of technology-enhanced teaching and learning practices.

Reference

Phipps, R, Merisotis, J and O'Brien, C (April 1999) What's the difference? A review of contemporary research on the effectiveness of distance learning in higher education, IHEP. Accessed 5 July 2002 from http://www.ihep.com/Pubs/PDF/Difference.pdf

Index

Page references in *italics* indicate figures or tables.